Ecce Fides
Pillar of Truth
Revised Edition

Fr. John J. Pasquini, Th.D.

An Ecce Fides Publication

Instituti ratione, fides, et cultura

Citations come from the following primary and secondary sources, unless otherwise cited: Greek and Latin translations are from Migne, *Patrologia Graeca,* the *Patrologia Latina* and the *Liber Pontificalis*: Jurgens, William A. ed. and trans. *The Faith of the Early Fathers*. 3 vols. Collegeville: The Liturgical Press, 1970: Quasten, Johannes. *Patrology*. 4 vols. Westminster, Md.: Newman Press, 1962-63: *The Christian Centuries*. 5 vols. Edited by Louis Rogier. New York: Paulist Press, 1978: *The Christian Faith: Doctrinal Documents of the Catholic Church.* Edited by J. Neuner and J. Dupuis. New York: Alba House, 1990: *The Apostolic Fathers: The Loeb Classical Library*. 2 vols. Edited by G.P. Goold and translated by Kirsopp Lake. Cambridge: Harvard University Press, 1998: Chadwick, Henry. *The Early Church: The Story of Emergent Christianity from the Apostolic Age to the Foundation of the Church of Rome*. New York: Penguin Books, 1990.

Bible citations are from the *New American Bible Revised Edition,* unless otherwise cited. Used with permission.

Published with Ecclesiastical Approval

Purchases can be made at Amazon.com

Printed in the United States of America

TABLE OF CONTENTS

Why do we need priests to forgive sins?
What does it mean to be excommunicated?
Why indulgences?
Is there a Sacrament of Holy Orders?
Why celibate priests?
Why "Father"?
Why do Catholics not allow woman priests?
Is there such a thing as the Last Rites?
Prayer and the Doctor?
What about blood transfusions?
Is marriage a sacrament?
What is an annulment?
Why do non-Catholics need an annulment?

INTRODUCTION

Between twenty to eighty percent of Protestant and pseudo-Christian denominations are made up of former Catholics. And sadly, there are too many practicing Catholics who do not believe in the Church's infallibility in the areas of faith and morals.

This book is intended to combat this dangerous trend. *Ecce Fides* is a book intended to reaffirm Catholics in their faith and in the infallibility of their Church. It is intended to bring back home those who have fallen away from their faith, to convince searching Christians of a home in the Catholic Church, and to convert in a gentle manner Protestants and Pseudo-Christians to the fullness of Christianity as found in the Catholic Church.

Ecce Fides is a work dedicated to defending Catholic beliefs through reason, Scripture, and the life of the Holy Spirit.

In the first three hundred years of Christianity, one million Catholics lost their lives as martyrs. Come join the faith that was built on Christ and the blood of his martyrs.

I
HOLY SCRIPTURES
AND TRADITION

Where did the Bible come from?

If you undermine the Catholic Church, you undermine the Bible!
                                                                Anonymous

The Christianity of history is not Protestantism.... To be deep in history is to cease to be a Protestant.
                                John Henry Cardinal Newman, Convert

> *I would not believe in the Gospel, had not the authority of the Catholic Church already moved me.*
> > *Augustine of Hippo*
> > *Contra epistolam Manichaei,* 5, 6: PL 42, 176.

Did the Bible fall from the sky? Certainly not! The Bible is the Word of God, but it is the Word of God because the Holy Spirit guided the Catholic Church in determining it to be such.

In the early Church there was no set Bible. In fact, there were many gospels and writings floating around claiming authenticity. There was the Gospel to the Ebionites (quoted by Epiphanus and Irenaeus), the Gospel to the Egyptians (referenced by Clement of Alexandria), the Gospel to the Hebrews (known by Papias, Hegesippus, and Eusebius, and quoted by Clement of Alexandria, Origen, Cyril and Jerome), the Gospel of the Nazaroeans (known by Hegesippus and Epiphanius, and known and preserved by Origen, Eusebius and Jerome), the Secret Gospel of Mark (quoted by Clement of Alexandria), the Gospel of Truth, the Gospel of Perfection, the Dialogue of the Redeemer, the Gospel of Peter (known by Eusebius), the Gospel of the Twelve Apostles, the Gospel of the Seventy, the Gospel of Philip, the Gospel of Matthias, the Gospel of Jude, the Gospel of Mary, the Gospel of Andrew, the Gospel of Barnabas, the Protoevangelium of James (Justin Martyr and Clement of Alexandria make mention of this source), the Infancy Gospel of Thomas, the Infancy Gospel of James (known by Jerome), the Apocryphon of James, the Apocalypse of Peter, etc. There were the Acts of Andrew, the Acts of John, the Acts of Thomas, and so forth.

It is important to recognize that more than 100 works of writing were being considered as part of what would come to be known as the New Testament.

9

Furthermore, many of the works we accept as part of the New Testament today were not fully accepted into the canon of the Bible until the fourth century—and not without great and fervent debate. For example, Eusebius, the greatest Church historian of his time, writing around the year 324 AD, points out that the epistles of James, Jude, 2 Peter, 2 and 3 John and the epistle to the Hebrews as well as the book of Revelation were still not accepted as part of the Bible. Amphilochius of Iconium (ca. 340-394) explains:

> *Now I am to read the books of the New Testament. Accept only four Evangelists, Matthew, then Mark, to which add Luke. Count John in times as fourth, but first in sublimity of teachings. Son of Thunder, rightly he is called, who loudly announced the Word of God. Accept from Luke a second book also, that of the Catholic Acts of the Apostles. Add to these that Vessel of Election, the Herald of the Gentiles, the Apostle Paul, writing wisely to the churches: One epistle to the Romans, to which must be added two to the Corinthians, and the one to the Galatians, and that to the Ephesians, after which there is one to the Philippians, then those written to the Colossians, to the Thessalonians two, two to Timothy, to Titus and to Philemon, one to each, and to the Hebrews one. Some call that to the Hebrews spurious, but not rightly do they say it; for the gift is genuine. What then is left? Of the Catholic Epistles some say seven need be accepted, others only three: One of James, one of Peter, one of John, or three of John and with them, two of Peter, the seventh that of Jude. The Apocalypse (Revelation) of John is also to be considered.. Some accept, but most will call it spurious (4).*

It was already the fourth century and the structure of the Bible was still being debated.

Things even get more complicated. When we look at the modern day accepted canon of the Bible, particularly the New Testament, we notice something quite interesting. Open up to any good Protestant Bible, such as the RSV or the NRSV, or to any good Catholic Bible such as the NABRE or the NJB and you will notice something that might be shocking to many who overlook the introductions to the various New Testament books. But when we look at them we notice the following: The Gospel of Matthew as we have it today seems, according to the scholars, not to have been written by the disciple of the Lord, but by a Greek speaking convert. The Gospel of

10

John, Revelation and the three epistles of John which make up the Johannine corpus seem to be more the product of a Johannine community than the apostle John. In terms of St. Paul's writings, 2 Thessalonians, Colossians, and Ephesians seem to have been most likely written by another writer. One and 2 Timothy and Titus seem to have been written by a disciple of Paul and not by Paul himself. Hebrews, for a long time attributed to Paul, is now a work whose authorship is completely unknown. One and 2 Peter seem to have questions regarding Peter as the author. Likewise, the same problems occur with James and Jude. (It is no coincidence that most modern scholars, as well as the *Catechism of the Catholic Church*, refer to "sacred authors" when making reference to the authorship of the books of the Scriptures.)

The question must be asked: Why do Protestants not go back and look at the books that the Catholic Church rejected and also look at those books that the Catholic Church accepted into the Bible? This situation in terms of the formation of the canon of the New Testament has to be deeply troubling for a Protestant brother or sister. How can the Protestant know that the New Testament is the Word of God if scholars are capable of proving that the authorship of many of the books of the New Testament is questionable? Furthermore, how can a Protestant know that the Catholic Church did not overlook an authentic work of one of the apostles? Maybe there is a treasure waiting out there to be found? If I were a Protestant, I would be reexamining every book in existence claiming apostolic authenticity. Yet Protestants do not. Protestants accept the Catholic Church's Bible, the entire New Testament, on the authority of the Catholic Church. Given this, the question must be asked: If Protestants accept the Bible as the Catholic Church has produced it--under the power of the Holy Spirit--why do they not accept the authority of the Catholic Church in its interpretation of the Bible?

You may think things are getting out of control at this point. Well, just think about this. We have no original surviving manuscripts of any of the books of the New Testament. They are all copies! Furthermore, the copies we have are not all the same. In fact, no two copies are exactly alike! Some have estimated that there are as much as 200,000 variations within the various biblical texts.

In your free time feel free to examine the following texts and see how different they are from each other: *Codex Vaticanus, Codex Sinaiticus, Codex Alexandrinus, Codex Bezae, Codex Ephraeimi Rescriptus, Codex Washingtonensis, Codex Koridethianus.* Which codex

11

is the perfect text? Which minister is quoting the correct Scripture reference?

The early Church had no set Bible for the first four centuries. In fact, the first letters written in the Church can only be traced to the year 48 AD, some fifteen years after the resurrection. And the Gospel of John can only be traced to approximately the year 110 AD, some 10 years after the death of John.

At this point in the reading of this text, one might be terribly shocked by what you have read, but don't despair! This is where Sacred Tradition (the life of the Holy Spirit within the Church) comes in. It is the apostles and their successors, the bishops, who guided the Church in the ways of the faith. It is only through the guidance of the pope and the bishops in union with him that a Bible started to take shape (This should not be a surprise to us since even during the time of the apostles crucial questions of faith and morals were debated over and decided upon by councils of the Church [Acts 15:1-29]).

A list of what would become the Bible was approved by Pope Damasus I in 382 and reaffirmed by Pope Innocent I in 411. This list of the books of the Bible becomes approved at the Councils of Hippo (393 AD), Carthage III (397 AD) and Carthage IV (419 AD). And it is not till the Council of Trent in 1546 that the canon becomes completely closed.

The formation of the Bible over centuries should not be a source of concern for us since the "Chosen People" of the Old Testament lived without any written Scriptures for centuries. The Hebrew Scriptures were the product of the writing down of Sacred Tradition.

Protestants accept the Catholic New Testament in its entirety. Why? Because of the authority of the Catholic Church!

It is one of the ironies of history that the founder of Protestantism, Martin Luther, had to admit that it was the Catholic Church that gave us the Bible:

We are obliged to yield many things to the Catholics, that they possess the Word of God, which we received from them; furthermore, we would know nothing at all about the Bible if it were not for the Catholics" (Luther, *Commentary on John*).

Even Luther recognized the Bible was not self-authenticating. Luther recognized the authority of the Catholic Church in determining the Word of God.

If Protestants accept this authority in regard to the Bible, why don't they trust its authority in all issues regarding faith and morals? For if the Church was infallible in the fourth century in putting the Bible together, why would it not be infallible throughout the succeeding generations?

Furthermore, does it not make more sense that the Church that put the Bible together in the first place would be the Church with the gift of interpreting it most accurately? How blessed we are to be Catholics!

Would Jesus leave us in confusion?

As we are too well aware of the Bible is interpreted in a variety of ways. Who has the right answer, the right interpretation? Would God leave us in confusion? When we take a look at Bible scholars from the best universities in the world, we see something very puzzling. No matter how well-learned these Bible scholars are they come up with disagreements on religious issues. It is not as if each well-educated scholar is seeing something that the other scholar is not seeing. Top-notch scholars know each other's arguments inside out, yet there is disagreement. Not only is there disagreement, but when we look at the arguments from one denomination of the Christian faith, we find that that denomination's arguments seem quite logical, and when we look at the arguments of another denomination's version of the faith, we find that their arguments seem just as logical. How can this be?

For one thing, the way we approach the Bible affects our interpretation of the Bible. We come to the Bible, as with everything else in life, with a certain predisposition. Our culture, religion, family background, etc. all affect how much weight we place on one argument or another. That is why there are so many disagreements from the best of scholars.

The question still remains, however, "Would God leave us in such confusion?"

Let us take a look at the most basic teachings that most Christians take for granted today. In the early Church, groups argued over whether Jesus was a man, an image, or a phantom; whether he was partially human, partially divine, fully human and/or fully divine. They argued whether there was a Trinity, whether there were three co-equal and co-eternal Persons in one God.

These above issues have all been acknowledged as resolved by mainline Christians. Yet who did the resolving? It is the Catholic Church that fought off all heresies and taught the truth that is so well appreciated by others today. It is the Catholic Church that taught that Jesus was fully human, fully divine, without confusion, division or separation. It is the Catholic Church that taught that the Three Persons of the Trinity are co-equal and co-eternal, without confusion, division or separation. If the Catholic Church was infallible in determining all these truths, why would it not be infallible throughout the succeeding generations?

In the early Church many small groups such as the Docetists, the Gnostics, the Montanists, the Marcionists, and so forth, all fought over

13

the true meaning of the faith. An answer to this confusion had to be found; after all, a faith that is in confusion is not a faith at all.

The theologian Tertullian (ca. 155-240), building upon the great insights of Irenaeus (ca. 130-220) and the early Church, taught that the true faith was to be found in the writings of the apostolic writers (Sacred Scripture) and in the life of their communities (Sacred Tradition, the life of the Holy Spirit within the Church). In others words, the true teachings of Christ were to be found in the communities set up by the apostles and upon their authentic "memoirs," which would eventually be collected into what would become known as the New Testament.

Irenaeus, a disciple of Polycarp, who in turn was a disciple of the apostle John and "a companion of the apostles," and appointed bishop of Smyrna by the apostle John, writes some very pertinent words when he describes in his tract *Against Heresies* (3,4,1) the following:

> *It is necessary to seek among others the truth which is easily obtained from the Church.... If there should be a dispute over some kind of question, ought we not have recourse to the most ancient churches [i.e., communities, dioceses] in which the apostles were familiar, and draw from them what is clear and certain in regard to that question? What if the apostles had not in fact left writings to us? Would it not be necessary to follow the order of Tradition, which was handed down to those to whom they entrusted the churches (The Faith of the Early Fathers, vol. 1, trans. William Jurgens, Collegeville: The Liturgical Press, 1970).*

Tertullian, in *The Demurrer Against Heretics* (21:4; 7) (ca. 200) argued:

> *All doctrine which agrees with the apostolic churches [i.e., communities], those nurseries and original depositories of the Faith, must be regarded as truth, as undoubtedly constituting what the churches received from the apostles, what the apostles received from Christ, and what Christ received from God.... We communicate with the apostolic churches because there is no diversity of doctrine: this is the witness of the truth (Ibid.).*

In section 32:1 we read:

> *Moreover, if there be any [heresies] bold enough to plant themselves in the midst of the apostolic age, so that they might seem to have been handed down by the apostles because they were from the time of the apostles, we can say to them: let them show the origins of their churches, let them unroll the order of their bishops, running down in succession from the beginning, so that their first bishop shall have for author and predecessor some one of the apostles (Ibid.).*

14

It is quite clear that the true faith is to be found in the "memoirs" of the apostles and the Tradition of the Church. Those communities founded upon the apostles and their successors are the places where the true and authentic deposit of the faith can be found.

The Bible flowed from Tradition and Needs Tradition

> *The teaching of the Church has been handed down through an order of succession from the apostles, and remains in the churches even until the present day. That alone is to be believed which is not at variance with the ecclesiastical and apostolic tradition.*
>
> *Origen (ca. 185-253)*

Irenaeus reminds the faithful that the faith was brought into the barbarian lands not by the Bible, but by Tradition: "The Barbarian tribes received the faith without letters."

The need for Tradition along with the Scriptures is unquestionable. The early Church testifies to this. The very reality that the Scriptures flowed out of Tradition points to this reality.

The Bible alone is inadequate! The "Bible only" approach as a rule of faith is nowhere to be found in the Bible. In fact, the "Chosen People" of the Old Testament lived without the Hebrew Scriptures for centuries. The "Bible only" approach was an invention of primarily the 14th century heretic John Wycliffe—a prototype of Protestantism—and the sixteenth century theologian Martin Luther, the first Protestant. It was an invention that was radically contrary to the history and nature of Christianity and Judaism.

God speaks to us in the Bible but also beyond the scope of the Bible. God speaks to us by means of natural revelation (Rom. 1:20; Wis. 13:1-9), by means of Jesus' life and words (Jn. 1:1,14; Lk. 4:44; 5:1), by inspiration (Lk. 3:2-3; Acts 4:31; Heb. 4:12-13), and by the oral preaching of the Gospel (1 Thess. 2:13).

Sacred Tradition is essential. As Papias (ca. 67-130), the bishop of Hierapolis in Asia Minor, "a hearer of St. John" the apostle and a friend of Polycarp--the disciple of St. John—(*Against Heresies*, 5, 33) as well as an "acquaintance" of the other apostles, and a friend to the daughters of the apostle Philip (*Ecclesiastical History*, 3, 39), states in his *Explanations of the Sayings of the Lord*:

> *I shall not hesitate to set before you, along with my own interpretation, everything I carefully learned from the elders and carefully remembered.... It seemed to me that I could profit more from the living voice [of Tradition] than from books.*

The Bible itself points to the need for Tradition: Luke reminds us

15

that his Gospel is the writing down of what had been handed down to him (Lk. 1:1-4). The apostle John reminds us that there are not enough books in the world to describe what Jesus did (Jn. 20:30; 21:25) and that often when he communicated with his own disciples he did not use pen or ink, but spoke face to face (2 Jn. 1:12; 3 Jn. 13). Paul, Timothy, and Jude remind us strongly to hold firm to the traditions that have been handed down by word of mouth and by letter (1 Thess. 2:13; 2 Thess. 2:15; 1 Cor. 11:2; 2 Tim. 1:13; 3:14; Jude 17).

When we as Catholics speak of Sacred Tradition we are not talking about human traditions, such as that which is alluded to in Matthew 15:3; 6-9 or Colossians 2:8, rather what we are pointing to is tradition with a big T; Traditions that were handed down in the Church by Jesus and his apostles (Lk. 1:1-4; 10:16; Jn. 21:25; Acts 2:42; 1 Cor. 15:3, 11; 2 Thess. 2:15; 2 Tim. 2:2).

As Athanasius (360 AD) wrote in *Four Letters to Serapion of Thimius* (1:28):

> *Let us note that the very tradition, teaching, and faith of the Catholic Church from the beginning, which the Lord gave, was preached by the apostles, and was preserved by the Fathers. On this was the Church founded; and if anyone departs from this, he neither is nor any longer ought to be called a Christian....*

Or as Origen (ca. 230) wrote in *Fundamental Doctrines* (1, Preface 2):

> *The teaching of the Church has indeed been handed down through an order of succession from the apostles, and remains in the churches [dioceses] even to the present time. That alone is believed as the truth which is in no way at variance with ecclesiastical and apostolic tradition.*

God has not left us in confusion. He has given us Sacred Tradition and Sacred Scripture. And in the event that confusion should still remain, he left us a teaching office.

A teaching office—what we call the Magisterium—is needed in the Church to determine the true interpretation of the faith, since private interpretation can often lead to heresy. As 2 Peter 3:16 states: There are "certain things hard to understand, which the unlearned and unstable distort, as they do also the other scriptures, to their own destruction" (see also 2 Pet. 1:20). In Acts 8:26-40 we read:

> *Then the angel of the Lord spoke to Philip, "Get up and head south on the road that goes down from Jerusalem to Gaza, the desert route." So he got up and set out. Now there was an Ethiopian eunuch, a court official of the Candace, that is, the queen of the Ethiopians, in charge of her entire treasury, who had come to*

16

Jerusalem to worship, and was returning home. Seated in his chariot, he was reading the prophet Isaiah. The Spirit said to Philip, "Go and join up with that chariot." Philip ran up and heard him reading Isaiah the prophet and said, "Do you understand what you are reading?" He replied, "How can I, unless someone instructs me?" So he invited Philip to get in and sit with him.

This was the scripture passage he was reading: "Like a sheep he was led to the slaughter, and as a lamb before its shearer is silent, so he opened not his mouth. In (his) humiliation justice was denied him. Who will tell of his posterity? For his life is taken from the earth." Then the eunuch said to Philip in reply, "I beg you, about whom is the prophet saying this? About himself, or about someone else?" Then Philip opened his mouth and, beginning with this scripture passage, he proclaimed Jesus to him. As they traveled along the road they came to some water, and the eunuch said, "Look, there is water. What is to prevent my being baptized?" Then he ordered the chariot to stop, and Philip and the eunuch both went down into the water, and he baptized him. When they came out of the water, the Spirit of the Lord snatched Philip away, and the eunuch saw him no more, but continued on his way rejoicing. Philip came to Azotus, and went about proclaiming the good news to all the towns until he reached Caesarea.

Philip the deacon, the representative of the Church, was needed to give the true meaning of the Scriptures to the eunuch.

We see this same pattern in Acts 15 at the Council of Jerusalem. A conflict arose in the early Church (ca. 50 AD) around what to do with Gentile converts. Should they first convert to Judaism through circumcision and then follow the Jewish dietary laws or should they be admitted into the Church without the need to follow these regulations.

Paul was the leader of the opposition who believed that there was no need for circumcision and the dietary laws under the new law of Christ. In 49 AD Paul and some of his associates journeyed to Jerusalem to confer with the apostles, and in particular with the head of the apostles, Peter. After much discussion, Peter and James ruled that Gentile converts would not be required to observe the Jewish regulations.

Again we see the need for a Magisterium. Even Paul recognized the need for seeking the Church's advice and approval for the correct interpretation of the Scriptures and God's will.

Originally the teaching office was made up of the apostles, the first bishops, and Peter, the first pope (Acts 15:1-35). With every succeeding generation the successors of Peter and the other apostles were given charge of protecting the faith from errors—with Peter and his successors having primacy of power (Mt. 16:18f).

We are reminded of the importance of listening to the Church, the Pillar of Truth (1 Tim. 3:14-15; Mt. 18:17-18; Lk. 10:16) in its authority to teach (Mt. 28:20) to interpret the Scriptures (Acts 2:14-36; 2 Pet. 1:20-21; 2:1; 3:15-17) and to bind and loose (Mt. 18:18; Acts 15:28:29).

Sacred Tradition, Sacred Scripture, and the Magisterium are inseparable realities. All three are necessary to assure the proper transmission of the faith.

Vincent of Lerins (ca. 450) in his *Commonitoria* (2,1-3) beautifully illustrates the need for Sacred Tradition, Sacred Scripture, and the teaching office of the Church (the Magisterium) when seeking the authentic word of God.

> *With great zeal and closest attention...I frequently inquired of many men eminent for their holiness and doctrine, how I might, in a concise and, so to speak, general and ordinary way, distinguish the truth of the Catholic faith from the falsehood of heretical depravity. I received almost always the same answer from all of them, that if I or anyone else wanted to expose the frauds and escape the snares of the heretics who rise up, and to remain intact and sound in a sound faith, it would be necessary, with the help of the Lord to fortify that faith in a [pertinent] manner: first, of course, by the authority of the divine law; and then, by the Tradition of the Catholic Church. Here, perhaps, someone may ask: 'If the canon of the Scriptures be perfect, and in itself more than suffices for everything, why is it necessary that the authority of ecclesiastical interpretation be joined to it?' Because, quite plainly, Sacred Scripture, by reason of its own depth, is not accepted by everyone as having one and the same meaning. The same passage is interpreted by others so that it can almost appear as if there are as many opinions as there are men. Novatian explains a passage in one way, Sabellius another, Donatus in another; Arius, Eunomius, Macedonius in another; Photinus, Apollinaris, Priscillian in another; Jovinian, Pelagius, Caelestius in another.... [Without reference to the Tradition as expounded and taught by the apostles and their successors, the bishops, there would be no way of knowing the true meaning of the Scriptures.]* (Jurgens, vol. 3).

The Bible "only" approach to divine revelation is unbiblical and contrary to Sacred Tradition--which we are commanded to hold onto (See 2 Thess. 2:14-15). The Bible "only" approach is a "human" tradition or invention which is contrary to the deposit of the faith (See Matt. 15:3, 6-9; Col. 2:8).

18

We must remember that the Bible tells us that it is the Church and not the Bible that is the "pillar and bulwark of the truth" (1 Tim. 3:15). We must remember what the founder of Protestantism, Martin Luther (1517) had to acknowledge:

> *We are obliged to yield many things to the Papists [Catholics]— that they possess the Word of God which we received from them, otherwise we should have known nothing at all about it (Commentary on St. John, 16).*

What Protestants can't answer!

How can we know with certainty what belongs in the Bible? The Book of Mormon, the Quran, the writings of the Hindus and of the Buddhists, the writings of Mary Eddy Baker, and all the books that Christianity would exclude from the Bible all claim to be self-authenticating! Philosophically speaking and hermeneutically speaking, documents cannot authenticate themselves! An outside source is always needed to authentic a document. So it is with the Bible. An infallible Church, the Catholic Church, founded by Jesus Christ authenticated the books that would make up the Bible. The Bible alone approach is contrary to history and intellectually unsupportable! Again, I repeat the words of Martin Luther:

> *We are obliged to yield many things to the Papists [Catholics]— that they possess the Word of God which we received from them, otherwise we should have known nothing at all about it (Commentary on St. John, 16).*
>
> Martin Luther, Founder of Protestantism

Two forms of Revelation

What many Protestants fail to realize is that there are two forms of God's revelation. One form is often referred to as natural revelation and the other as divine revelation. Natural revelation is divided into two forms, the revealing of God's presence through the material universe (Rom. 1:20; Wis. 13:15) and the revelation of God through the natural and moral law that is embedded in the core of all human beings (Rom. 2:15)—this law becomes perceptible by a clear and informed conscience. Finally, there is divine revelation or the deposit of the faith, as found in Sacred Tradition--the life of the Holy Spirit working through the life of the people of God--and Sacred Scripture--which flowed out of Sacred Tradition. Divine revelation helps to correct the misinterpretations of natural revelation. When we seek truth and God we must seek to grasp the entirety of God's revelation to us!

What about Revelation 22:18-19?

Revelation 22: 18-19 states: *"I warn everyone who hears the words of prophecy of this book: if anyone adds to them, God will add to that person the plagues described in this book; if anyone takes away from the words of the book of this prophecy, God will take away that person's share in the tree of life and in the holy city, which are described in this book."*

Many argue that by resorting to "tradition" one is contradicting Revelation 22. This is not the case. Tradition does not add as much as clarifies the word of God in the Scriptures. The life of the Spirit in the Church (Sacred Tradition) helps us to understand how the Church always understood a particular Scripture passage.

For example, for Catholics, John 6:35-71 testifies to the real presence of Christ in the Eucharist. Yet many do not accept this Catholic and Orthodox understanding of the Eucharist. So as Catholics we look to Sacred Tradition: Ignatius of Antioch, a disciple and friend of the apostles John, Peter, and Paul, wrote in 107, only 7 years after the death of the apostle John, that *"only heretics abstain from the Eucharist...because they do not confess that the Eucharist is the Flesh of our Savior Jesus Christ."* The Church has always maintained the real presence of Christ in the Eucharist. It is only in the 16th century, with the birth of Protestantism, that Protestants began to slowly reject this reality.

Secondly, the Bible is full of additions. The most legendary is the ending of Mark's Gospel. There are three different endings to Mark's Gospel that can be found in ancient manuscripts. For example, Jerome quotes a fourth century manuscript known as the "Freer Logion" (which appears after v. 14). It is usually footnoted in Bibles. But all Bibles contain within the main text a "longer ending" (16: 9-20) and a "shorter ending" (found after v. 8 or v. 20) to the Gospel of Mark.

If you have two different endings in the same text, you clearly have additions. All scholars acknowledge that the "longer ending" is not from Mark and that it was likely written during the second century. Furthermore, the "shorter ending" appears mainly in seventh to ninth century manuscripts of the Bible as well as in an old Latin version of the Bible. Yet both endings are in the Bible and are considered the Word of God, Sacred Scripture. If you check the footnotes in your Bible you will see this explained.

Likewise, when we look at the book of Genesis we notice that Chapter 1 to Chapter 2:1-4 has one account of the creation of the world and Chapter 2:4f has a second account. That is why the Bible has as the heading to Chapter one, "The First Story of Creation," and as a heading to Chapter two, "The Second Story of Creation." If you have two different accounts in the same text, you clearly have additions.

Thirdly, we know that some subtractions have been made since some parts of the Bible are lacking. Let us take just one book of the Old Testament to make our point, the book of Job: Where are the words to Job 24:19-21? Where are the words to Job 28:3-4? Where is verse 30 of Job 34? What happened to Chapter 36, verses 16-20? Clearly, some things have been lost or subtracted or so obscured that they are not represented in the Bible!

What serves to compensate for this? Sacred Tradition! The successors of the apostles, the bishops, express the Spirit in the life of the Church and assure that nothing is lacking in divine revelation.

Fourthly, the book of Revelation itself, like all the books of the Bible, has ambiguities and additions or subtractions in it. For example, the expression "freed us" in Revelation 1:5 is translated in some ancient manuscripts as "washed us"; in 9:13 "four horns" is often found in manuscripts as "horns"; in 11:12 "they" is often found in manuscripts as "I"; in 12:18 "then the dragon took" is often found in manuscripts as "then I stood"; in 13:18 "666" is often found in manuscripts as "616"; in 15:3 "key of the nations" is often found in manuscripts as "king of the ages"; in 15:6 "bright linen" is often found in manuscripts as "stone"; in 18:2 "hateful beast" is often found in manuscripts as "hateful bird"; in 18:3 "for all nations have drunk" is often found in manuscripts as "she has made all nations drink"; in 19:13 "dipped in" is often found in manuscripts as "sprinkled with"; in 22:14 "washed their robes" is often found in manuscripts as "do his commandment"; in 22:21 "the grace of the Lord Jesus be with all the saints" is often found in manuscripts as "the grace of the Lord Jesus be with you." And when you try to find, in some ancient manuscripts, Revelation 13:7, you will not find it.

As was mentioned earlier, the Bible has some 200,000 variations in the manuscript evidence.

If we are to take **Revelation 22:18-19** in such a literalistic view, then how do we explain Deuteronomy 4:2: "You must neither add anything to what I command you nor take away anything from it…" If Deuteronomy 4:2 is taken in such a narrow way, then we as people of God should reject Revelation 22 and the whole New Testament since it came after Deuteronomy 4:2. Obviously this is not what was meant by Deuteronomy or Revelation.

Finally, Protestants violate their own doctrine. In the 16th century they eliminated seven entire books from the Old Testament and parts of two others (Tobit, Judith, 1 and 2 Maccabees, Wisdom, Sirach, Baruch and parts of Daniel and Esther).

The New Testament quotes the Old Testament more than 300 times, and in approximately 86% of those instances the quotation is taken from the Septuagint version of the Old Testament which contains the books that Protestants eliminated. Also, the deuterocanonical books that the Protestants eliminated are quoted in the New Testament not less than 150 times. Protestants violate their own principle.

The meaning of the text is that the Word of God must be accepted authentically and completely. To do so means that one must look to the life of the Holy Spirit within the Church (Sacred Tradition) and the written inspired words of God (Sacred Scripture). And finally, the successors to the apostles in union with the head of the apostles, Peter, the bishops and popes, are entrusted with interpreting this Sacred Scripture and Sacred Tradition.

Is all Scripture to be interpreted in the same way?

As Catholics we seek to understand the Scriptures in the way they were meant to be understood. We allow the Scriptures to say what they want to say (*Exegesis*) as opposed to making them say what we want them to say (*Eisegesis*).

Many people take a particular belief system and then go to the Scriptures and try to find justification for their belief system by forcing a completely foreign interpretation into a particular Scripture passage.

We should never fear the Lord. Let him speak to us the way he intended.

As Catholics we seek to comprehend the *intent* of the inspired authors in their writings. We also try to comprehend the various *senses* in which the Scripture passages were written. Finally, we seek to understand the Scriptures in light of the same *Spirit* in which the inspired writers wrote them.

The Intent

The following provides a helpful guideline regarding author intent:
1) What condition was the author confronting?
2) What was the culture of the area like?
3) What literary genres were common at the time?
4) What modes of feeling, narrating, and speaking were common at the time?

For example, the book of Revelation addresses a Church under persecution by either Nero or Domitian. The sacred author is seeking to encourage the faithful to persevere in Christ amidst great trials and tribulations. "Hold on," "stand fast," victory is at hand for those who remain loyal to God.

The author uses symbolic and allegorical language characteristic of apocalyptic or resistance literature. Apocalyptic literature makes use of visions, animals, numbers, and cosmic catastrophes in a coded language with the express purpose of instructing the faithful in times of difficulty. The very nature of apocalyptic literature--which enjoyed great popularity amongst the Jews and Christians during the first two centuries—was ideal for conveying a secret message to Christians that could not be readily understood by the enemies of Christianity.

The Senses

In terms of the senses of Scripture, the following are important to keep in mind.
1) What is the literal meaning of the text?
2) What is the spiritual sense of the text?
3) What is the allegorical sense?
4) What is the moral sense?
5) What is the anagogical sense?

In the "passion and resurrection narratives" (Mt. 26f; Mk. 14f; Lk. 22f; Jn. 18f) we have the literal reality that Jesus Christ suffered, died, and rose from the dead.

In terms of the spiritual sense of these narratives we recognize that

Christ's death and resurrection was for our salvation—that in Christ we are born to eternal life. We also recognize, amongst other insights, that Christ's death made all suffering redemptive.

In terms of the allegorical sense, Jesus can be seen as the "New Moses." Moses freed the people of God from slavery and brought them to the edge of the "promised land" "flowing with milk and honey." In a much more powerful manner, Jesus, as the new and greater Moses type or figure, freed us from the slavery of sin and brings us into the eternal bliss of heaven. Likewise, the crossing of the Red Sea by Moses is seen as being symbolic of baptism as well as a sign or type of Christ's victory over death.

As for the moral sense that can be acquired through a reading of these narratives, the insights are unending. The moral sense is intended for, as Paul states, "our moral instruction" (1 Cor. 10:11). Jesus reminds us that being moral entails the seeking and fulfilling of the will of the Father (cf. Mt. 26:39).

The anagogical sense of the passion and resurrection narratives focus on realities and events in terms of their eternal significance. The resurrection of Jesus is a sign to us that we too, in him, will likewise rise and be brought into eternal glory after the end of our earthly journey. The anagogical sense is intended to guide us toward eternal life with God in heaven.

The four above senses are beautifully summarized by a medieval couplet that states: "The Letter speaks of deeds; Allegory to faith; The Moral how to act; Anagogy our destiny."

The Spirit

In terms of interpreting the Bible in light of the Spirit in which it was written we pursue the following rules:

1) How is a particular Scripture passage understood within the context of the whole Bible?

2) How is the Bible understood within the Tradition it came out from? If an interpretation of a particular passage makes a person conclude that Jesus was only a phantom or spirit, then one cannot accept this as being an authentic Tradition of the Church. One must reject this interpretation as not being faithful to the life of the Holy Spirit within the Church.

3) How is the passage of the Bible understood in terms of a coherence of truths? All the doctrines of the Church must fit together like a puzzle. You cannot have one belief contradicting another belief. There can only be one coherent truth.

Each Scripture passage is like a piece of a puzzle that depicts a picture. One piece of the puzzle is insufficient for understanding and recognizing what is being portrayed by the whole of the puzzle. One needs all the pieces, or at the very least, the core pieces. The same can be said of the Scriptures. One passage needs to be understood within the context of the whole of the Scriptures for a true interpretation of the Word of God.

This prevents the use of a technique used by many fundamentalists and pseudo-Christians called "proof-text" theology. Let me use an example. In one passage of the Bible Jesus says "Blessed are the peacemakers" (Mt. 5:9), yet in another he says, "I have not come to bring peace, but division" (Lk. 12:51). This may seem a contradiction but it is not. Jesus is pointing out that in the process of being a peacemaker one will inevitably come up against obstacles which could inevitably lead to division. When the one text is understood in terms of the other, both make perfect sense in terms of the Christian way of life. But if one passage is taken without the other passage, confusion can occur regarding Jesus' true teaching.

Another example of the need to interpret a particular Scripture passage within a coherent and historically accurate context within the whole of the Bible is seen in Jesus' words on the cross: "My God, my God, why have you forsaken me" (Mt. 27:46). At first glance this makes Jesus appear as a man on the verge of despair. Yet when this passage is taken within the context of the whole of the Scriptures we see that the contrary is true. Far from being an echo of despair, the words "My God, my God, why have you forsaken me" are an affirmation of Jesus' identity as the Savior and Messiah. "My God, my God, why have you forsaken me" are the first words of Psalm 22 of the Old Testament which foretell of the passion and triumph of the Messiah (While it is true that Jesus suffered the pangs of abandonment, he did not despair; furthermore, the words Jesus proclaimed were far more profound than the pangs of suffering.). If I were to say "Our Father, who art in heaven" everyone would know that I was reciting the first words of the "Our Father"; likewise when Jesus said "My God, my God, why have you forsaken me" the Jewish people would have been fully aware that Jesus was making reference to Psalm 22. He was reminding them that he was the fulfillment of Psalm 22--that he was the Savior and Messiah! (Observe the stunning similarities that exist between Psalm 22 and the passion narratives in the Gospels).

If one took Matthew 27:46 out of context, one could end up with a distorted vision of Jesus' human and divine natures.

Another example comes from the Old Testament vision of God as the "Warrior God." Many people in today's culture find this absolutely abhorrent and refuse to accept what the Scriptures make very clear. These people find the image of a "Warrior God" as abhorrent because they fail to recognize the proper context of the Old Testament image.

In the ancient world, war was part of everyday life. In fact, kings often waited for the good weather of spring to begin new campaigns of war: "the kings go out to war...in the spring of the year" (2 Sm. 11:1). In a world where war is the norm, it does not seem abhorrent to view God as a "Warrior God." For the Jews, God would be there to save them from the attacks of their enemies if they remained faithful to the laws and commandments of Moses, but if they did not, they would be chastised by God by means of defeat. The defeat by the Assyrians and the Babylonians was a mark, according to the Old Testament prophets, of God's chastisement for failing to be faithful to the covenant made between God and his people.

The most egregious abuse of this principle of interpretation today is found amongst fundamentalists who proclaim the "gospel of wealth." This is quite common on fundamentalist Christian television. The argument goes: If you are faithful to God, he will grant you a long life, no suffering, and great wealth. If you are unfaithful you will end up having a short life with great suffering, and you will die a pauper.

This vision of life is strongly emphasized in the early books of the Hebrew Scriptures (the Old Testament), particularly in the wisdom literature, and is often referred to as the "theory of retribution." The key point of this theory is that an ordered and moral society is one that fosters justice and harmony.

Having said this, however, if these Scripture passages were all we had, we would have a distorted image of the Word of God. The sad reality is that so much of modern Christianity focuses on the "theory of retribution" that the Word of God inevitably becomes unrecognizable.

The book of Job is essential for putting a proper perspective on the earlier writings of the Scriptures. The book of Job is a turning point in the Old Testament; it is a key part of the puzzle that puts all into focus.

In the book of Job we are taught that one's finite mind cannot grasp the mysterious plan of God. God's ways are not our ways. Our call is to remain faithful, and in doing so, we help to fulfill God's providential plan for ourselves and the world. This is beautifully illustrated in the words of an unknown civil war soldier:

> *I asked for strength that I might achieve; I was made weak that I might learn humbly to obey. I asked for health that I might do greater things; I was given infirmity that I might do better things. I asked for riches that I might be happy; I was given poverty that I might be wise. I asked for power that I might have the praise of men; I was given weakness that I might feel the need of God. I asked for all things that I might enjoy life; I was given life that I might enjoy all things. I got nothing that I asked for, but everything that I had hoped for. Almost despite myself, my unspoken prayers were answered; I am, among all men, most richly blessed.*

It is for this reason that even the just suffer. We are all aware of the many good people who have died young and poor, and let us never forget that our Savior was poor, young, and suffered death on the cross for us.

The book of Job adds one more piece to the puzzle regarding our understanding of God's mysterious ways!

Seeking to understand the Scriptures the way they were meant to be understood is at the heart of the Catholic Church's approach to the Word of God. We as Catholics seek to understand the intent, the senses, and the spirit of the Scriptures.

Why was the Catholic Church careful in making Bibles available to individual believers?

First, the Church knew that the Bible in the hands of the untrained would lead to disunity and heresies. History has proven this. There are currently some 33,000 Protestant denominations and 150,000 pseudo-Protestant denominations. Without an authoritative teaching office--the bishops in union with the pope--disunity and heresies cannot help but swell in numbers.

Second, the populations of the world prior to modern times were mostly illiterate. So even if people had a Bible in their hands they would not have been able to read it. Preaching and the use of art and stained-glass windows were for the vast majority of people the only means of learning about the Gospel message.

Third, for those people who could read and wanted a Bible, the cost of Bibles was exorbitant. Bibles prior to the invention of the printing press in the 15th century were hand written by monks and took years to produce. This was costly and made the purchase of Bibles impossible for the vast majority.

Finally, the assertion that Catholics never read the Bible is absurd. We wrote it; we put it into a canon; and we developed our theology from it. Any reader of the ancient Catholic writers from the 1st century to the present can see this!

The Bible is at the core of the Church's liturgy. Catholics who go to Mass every day of the week will essentially hear the entire Bible read in two years. For those who attend Mass on Sundays only, they essentially hear the entire Bible read in a three year period. Furthermore, the entire canon of the Mass is Scriptural, from the "Greeting" to the final "Dismissal."

Can many denomination say this?

Why do Catholics have more books in the Old Testament than Protestants or Jews?

During the Protestant Reformation Martin Luther (ca. 1534), after losing a debate against the great Catholic scholar Johann Eck on the topic of purgatory, decided to drop seven books from the Old Testament—many of which Johann Eck made reference to in defense of the Catholic faith--1 and 2 Maccabees, Sirach, Wisdom, Baruch, Tobit, Judith and parts of Daniel and Esther (These books are often referred to as deuterocanonical books). Martin Luther only made this momentous decision some seventeen years after his founding of the Protestant movement. Why did he not make these changes in 1517? What made him change his mind all these years later? The answer is that these books were a problem for his theology and the theology of Protestantism and thus had to be eliminated.

Despite Luther's predicament with Johann Eck, another reason for dropping these books from the canon of the Scriptures by Protestants was because they were written in Greek and found in the Septuagint (Greek) version of the Hebrew Scriptures. It is for this same reason that the Jewish people in the year 90 to 100 AD excluded these books. Many today argue that since these books are not in Hebrew and since the Jewish people today do not have these books in their Hebrew Scriptures, then they do not belong in the Bible.

As Catholics we would respond by taking a closer look at history before coming to such a quick conclusion. The first thing to recognize is that at the time of Jesus these deuterocanonical books were accepted as Scripture. Furthermore, the New Testament quotes the Old Testament more than 300 times, and in approximately 86% of those instances, the quotation is taken from the Greek, not Hebrew, Septuagint version of the Old Testament which contains the books that Protestants and Jews eliminated. Also, the deuterocanonical books that the Protestants and Jews eliminated are quoted in the New Testament not less than 150 times.

It is only after the Jewish Council of Jamnia (ca. 90-100), after the fall of Jerusalem (ca. 70), and after an official break between the Pharisees and Jewish Christians, that a change occurs.

The Pharisees recognized that more and more Christians were coming from the Greek speaking Gentile world, and in order to distinguish themselves from the Christians they sought to remove all traces of Greek from their Scriptures. (Ironically, a lot of the Greek versions of the books they took out have in recent years been found in the original Hebrew).

It is crucial for us as Christians to recognize that the Greek Septuagint (LXX) version of the Scriptures was used by Jews throughout the Greek speaking world and was recognized as inspired prior to the Jewish Council of Jamnia (ca. 90-100).

Another important point is that by the time of the Jewish Council of Jamnia (ca. 90-100) the Christian Church (ca. 33) had already been established as the authoritative determiner on all matters concerning faith and morals, which included the formation of the canon of the Scriptures. Furthermore, the Jewish Council of Jamnia never made a statement regarding the closing of the Canon.

It is important to reiterate that the early Church always accepted the deuterocanonical books as part of the Scriptures. It was often quoted in the early Church (i.e., the *Didache* 4:5 (ca. 70); *Barnabas* 6:7 (ca. 74); *Clement* 27:5 (ca. 80), etc.).

The most important reason why the deuterocanonical books were accepted by the Catholic Church is because the apostles themselves accepted them. The apostles often quoted from the Greek Septuagint version of the Scriptures, thereby affirming its importance and validity. For example, compare Matthew 1:23 with Isaiah 7:14. Matthew is quoting from the Septuagint version of the Scriptures, the same version that holds the deuterocanonicals. Another example can be found in Luke's Gospel. Luke chapter 1:5 to chapter 3 is entirely constructed from the Septuagint version of the Bible.

As you look throughout the New Testament footnotes you will find the abbreviation for the Septuagint, LXX, throughout. There are 340 places where the New Testament quotes the Septuagint and only 33 places where the Hebrew only version of the Bible is quoted.

The point is that if the Greek Septuagint was good enough for the apostles, it is good enough for us Catholics.

Let us look at the following passage from the deuterocanonical book of Wisdom:

Let us lay traps for the upright man, since he annoys us and opposes our way of life, reproaches us for our sins against the Law, and accuses us of sins against our upbringing. He claims to have knowledge of God and calls himself a child of the Lord. We see him as a reproof to our way of thinking, the very sight of him weighs our spirits down; for his kind of life is not like other people's and his ways are quite different. In his opinion we are counterfeit; he avoids our ways as he would filth; he proclaims the final end of the upright as blessed and boasts of having God for his father. Let us see if what he says is true, and test him to see what sort of end he will have. For if the upright man is God's son, God will help him and rescue him from the clutches of his enemies. Let us test him with cruelty and with torture, and thus explore this gentleness of his and put his patience to the test. Let us condemn him to a shameful death since God will rescue him....(Wisdom 2:12-20, NJB).

This passage was written approximately one century before the crucifixion of Christ, yet one cannot but be amazed at the similarity between this passage and the passage describing the Passion of our Lord and Savior. We have here in the book of Wisdom the pre-figuration of the crucifixion of Jesus Christ.

It is not surprising that the Protestant Reformers never completely threw out the deuterocanonical books of the Old Testament. They saw them as worthy of being kept in an appendix. To this very day, these books are found in an appendix to the Old Testament. This very act is a testament to the discomfort that these sixteenth century revolutionaries had and modern day Protestants have in eliminating the deuterocanonical books.

II
THE CHURCH

Who is your founder?

The blessed apostle Paul teaches us that the Church is one, for it has 'one body, one spirit, one hope, one faith, one baptism, and one God.' Furthermore, it is on Peter that Jesus built his Church, and to him he gives the command to feed the sheep; and although he assigns like power to all the apostles, yet he founded a single chair, and he established by his own authority a source and an intrinsic reason for that unity. Indeed, the others were that also which Peter was; but a primacy is given to Peter, whereby it is made clear that there is but one Church and one Chair—the Chair of Peter. So too, all are shepherds, and the flock is shown to be one, fed by all the apostles in single-minded accord. If someone does not hold fast to this unity of Peter, can he imagine that he still holds the faith? If he deserts the chair of Peter upon whom the Church was built, can he still be confident that he is in the Church?

Cyprian of Carthage (ca. 251)
De Catholicae Ecclesiae Unitate, 2-7

If we want to find the true Christian faith--in all its fullness--we need to look at its foundation. Depending on whatever statistics we look at there are anywhere from 33,000 to 150, 000 groups, cults, and denominations each claiming to have the authentic Christian faith.

Who is right? By looking at the founders of these groups we can come up with some key insights. For the purpose of this work, we will look at the founders of the main Christian and pseudo-Christian ecclesiastical communities in the United States and Europe.

All quality historians, from Harvard to Oxford, and all quality history books, whether Catholic or secular, recognize Jesus as founding the Catholic Church (ca. 33 AD). More will be said about this later.

Now let us look at some of the Protestant and pseudo-Christian ecclesiastical communities. Remember, there was no such thing as a Protestant Church until the sixteenth century; Jesus can never be claimed as the founder of any Protestant denomination. Let us look at some of their founders:

Denomination	Founder
Lutherans	Martin Luther (ca. 1517)

Anabaptists	Nicholas Storch/ Thomas Munzer (ca. 1521)
Swiss Reformed	Ulrich Zwingli (ca. 1522)
Hutterites	Jacob Hutter (ca. 1528)
Anglicans	Henry VIII (ca. 1534)
Calvinists	John Calvin (ca. 1536)
Familists	Hendrik Niclaes (ca. 1540)
Unitarians	Michael Servetus (ca. 1553)/ Joseph Priestly (ca. 1785)
Presbyterians	Calvin/ John Knox (ca. 1560)
Arminianism	Jacobus Arminius (ca. 1560-1609
Puritans	T. Cartwright (ca. 1570)
Congregationalists	Robert Brown (ca. 1582)
Baptists	John Smyth (ca. 1609)
Dutch Reformed	Michaelis Jones (ca. 1628)
Quakers	George Fox (ca. 1650)
Mennonites	Menno Simons (ca. 1653)
Cameronians	Richard Cameron (ca. 1681)
Pietism	Philip Jacob Spener (1675)
Amish	Jakob Amman (ca. 1693)
Church of the Brethren	Alexander Mack (ca. 1708)
Moravians	Count Zinzendorf (ca. 1727)
Calvinistic Methodist	Howell Harris (ca. 1735)
American Dutch Reformed	Theodore Frelinghuysen (ca. 1737)
Seceders	Ebenezer Erskine (ca. 1740)
Shakers	Ann Lee (ca. 1741)
Methodists	John Wesley (ca. 1744)
Universalists	John Murray (ca. 1779)
Episcopalians	Samuel Seabury (ca. 1784)
African Methodist Episcopal	Richard Allen (ca. 1787)
Zion Church Unitarians	Joseph Priestley (ca. 1794)
Harmony Society Church	George Rapp (ca. 1803)
Mormons	Joseph Smith (ca. 1829)
Disciples of Christ	Barton W. Stone/ Alexander Campbell (ca. 1832)
Seventh Day Adventist	William Miller (ca. 1844)/ Ellen G. White
Christadelphians	John Thomas (ca. 1848)
Christian Reformed	Gysbert Haan (ca. 1857)
Salvation Army	William Booth (ca. 1865)
Christian Scientists	Mary Baker Eddy (ca. 1879)
Jehovah's Witnesses	Charles Taze Russell (ca. 1884)
Nazarenes	Phineas Bresee (ca. 1895)
Pentecostals	C.F. Parham/ William

Alliance — Albert Benjamin Simpson (ca. 1905); preceded by Seymour/ A.J.Tomlinson (ca.1903/1906)

	Seymour/ A.J.Tomlinson (ca.1903/1906)
Alliance	Albert Benjamin Simpson (ca. 1905)
Church of God in Christ	Charles Mason (ca. 1907)
Foursquare	Aimee Semple McPherson (ca. 1918)
Church of God	Joseph Marsh (ca. 1920)
Worldwide Church of God	Herbert W. Armstrong (ca. 1934)
Confessing Church	Martin Niemoller (ca. 1934)
Evangelical Free	E. A. Halleen (ca. 1950)
Unification Church	Sun Myung Moon (ca. 1954)
Children of God	David Mo Berg (ca. 1969)
Universal Church of the Kingdom of God	Macedo de Bezarra (1977)

Obviously we cannot name all Protestant denominations and their founders, nor the 150,000 plus pseudo-Christian denominations. But I think the point is obvious.

Only one Church was founded upon Christ in the year 33 AD, the Catholic Church. As Ignatius of Antioch, the disciple of John and friend of Peter and Paul, and the one referred to in Mark 9:35, declares in his letter to the *Smyrneans* (8): "[W]herever Jesus Christ is, there is the Catholic Church."

Irenaeus, the disciple of Polycarp, who in turn was the disciple of the apostle John, also makes mention of the Catholic Church as the authentic Church founded by Christ:

The blessed apostles [Peter and Paul] having founded and built up the Church of [Rome], handed over the office of the episcopate to Linus. Paul makes mention of this Linus in the Epistle to Timothy. To him succeeded Anecletus; and after him, in the third place from the apostles, Clement was chosen for the episcopate. He had seen the blessed apostles and was acquainted with them, and had their traditions before his eyes (Against Heresies, 3:3, trans. Jurgens).

History is on the side of the Catholic Church. No one can question with any sense of respectability the founding of the Catholic Church by Christ. Look at any encyclopedia in the world and you will find as the founder of the Catholic Church Jesus Christ.

The Church was founded by Christ and his apostles, and it continues today through, with, and in Christ and the successors of the apostles, the bishops (cf. Eph. 2:20).

- Offshoots of the Lutherans include the Lutheran Brethren, the Evangelical Covenant Church, the Evangelical Free Church,

31

the Evangelical Lutheran Church in America, the Missouri Synod Lutherans, the Wisconsin Synod Lutherans, and the Moravian Church.

- Offshoots of the Anabaptists include the North American Baptist, the Advent Christian Church, the Seventh Day Adventist, the Amish, the Conservative Mennonites, the General Conference of Mennonites, the Old Mennonite Church, the Brethren in Christ, the Hutterite Brethren, the Independent Brethren, and the Mennonite Brethren.
- Offshoots of the Anglican Church include the United Church of Christ, the Free Will Baptist, the Conservative Baptist, the Progressive National Baptist, the American Baptist, the Independent Bible Churches, the Friends United, the Friends General Conference, the United Methodist, the African Methodist, the Episcopal, the Free Methodist, and the many offshoots of the Pentecostal churches.
- Offshoots of Calvinism include the Presbyterian Church in America, the Presbyterian Church in the USA, the Orthodox Presbyterian, the Reformed Presbyterian, the Reformed Church in America, the Christian Reformed, the Churches of Christ, the Disciples of Christ, and the "Christian Churches."

The Catholic Church has many rites, yet one faith that traces itself back to Jesus Christ, the apostles and their successors, the bishops. Their Catholic identity is found in their union to the successor of St. Peter, the pope, in proclaiming the one true faith—in diverse cultural expressions--of Jesus Christ. Whether one is a member of the Roman, Mozarabic, Ambrosian, Byzantine, Chaldean, Syro-Malabarese, Alexandrian, Coptic, Abyssinian, Antiochene, Malankarese, Maronite, or Armenian rite, one is a member of the one Catholic Church founded by Jesus Christ through his apostles.

Was Constantine the founder of the Catholic Church?
Some have tried to make the emperor Constantine the founder of the Catholic Church. No historian from any reputable university accepts this.

Constantine was instrumental in calling together the bishops to meet at the Council of Nicaea (ca. 325). Yet sadly to say, he died denying the very teachings of the council he helped to call together. Instead of receiving baptism from a Catholic bishop, he was baptized by a heretical Arian bishop, Eusebius of Nicomedia. Constantine's death gave rebirth to and strength to Arian Christianity. Constantine's successors would bring Arian Christianity into an even stronger conflict with Catholic Christianity.

It is quite clear that Constantine could never be considered the founder

32

of the Catholic Church, but even if someone were to concede that Constantine was the founder of the Catholic Church (ca. 325) then you would have another problem to deal with. You would have to say that the Bible that all Christians cherish is the result of a Constantinian Church, since the Bible does not get put together until the late fourth century. Instead of a Christian Bible you would have to say we cherish a Constantinian Bible. This is obviously absurd.

The Bible was put together at the Councils of Hippo and Carthage III and IV by the pope and the bishops—the first list of books being initially approved by Pope Damasus in 382 and reaffirmed by Pope Innocent I in 411.

History and historians acknowledge that the Catholic (universal) Church was founded by Christ--the name "catholic" being officially written on paper for the first time in 107 AD by Ignatius of Antioch, a disciple of the apostle John and bishop of Antioch through ordination by the apostles Peter and Paul.

Cyril of Jerusalem (ca. 350) in his *Catechetical Instructions* reminds us why the Catholic Church is the only true Church:

The Church is called Catholic or universal because it has spread throughout the entire world, from one end of the earth to the other. Again, it is called Catholic because it teaches fully and unfailingly all the doctrines which ought to be brought to men's knowledge, whether they are concerned with visible or invisible things, with the realities of heaven or the things of the earth. Another reason for the name Catholic is that the Church brings under religious obedience all classes of men, rulers and subjects, learned and unlettered. Finally, it deserves the title Catholic because it heals and cures unrestrictedly every type of sin that can be committed in soul or in body, and because it possesses within itself every kind of virtue that can be named, whether exercised in actions or in words or in some kind of spiritual charism. (Cf. Cat. 18: 23-25: PG 33, 1043-1047).

Is the Catholic Church the "Whore of Babylon"?

Some fringe or radical Protestants believe that the book of Revelation refers to the Catholic Church in Rome as the "Whore of Babylon" with her seven heads. They often like to cite Revelation 17:1-18.

The seven heads are a reference to the legendary seven hills of Rome upon which the "whore" is found. This cannot be a reference to the Catholic Church or the pope, since no pope has ever been seated on any of the seven hills of Rome. No pope has ever lived on the Capitoline, Palatine, Esquiline, Aventine, or on the three little hills in central Rome which make up the seven hills. The seven hills and in particular the three little hills are where the pagan religions and the Roman governments were situated. When John wrote the book of Revelation, the popes and the Catholics lived in Trastevere, a district across the Tiber River and away from the city. Hence,

33

the Catholic Church could never be associated with the "Whore of Babylon." And even today, the Lateran (the pope's Church) and the Vatican (where the pope lives) could never be associated with the traditional seven hills of Rome.

The sacred author of Revelation was referring to pagan Rome under the leadership of the emperor Nero who persecuted Christians, killing the apostles Peter and Paul. Or for some scholars, it is a reference to the emperor Domitian who brutally persecuted Catholics in imitation of Nero. Some referred to Domitian as the "re-incarnation" of Nero.

Nero and Domitian persecuted the Church from these hills. The Capitoline was the religious and political center of the empire and the Palatine was where the imperial palace was situated.

The historical Babylon persecuted the Jews, the People of God, between 610 and 538 BC. The Babylonians destroyed the temple and sent the Jews into exile. The Romans became the modern day version of the Babylonians by destroying Jerusalem and the temple in 70 AD. To this very day, the temple has not been reconstructed.

Jesus inaugurated the establishment of the new people of God—made up of Jews and Gentiles—in a Church. The Romans were now persecuting the Church, the People of God. Revelation used symbolic language, or apocalyptic language, in order to encourage Christians to persevere through their struggle with the Roman authorities (see also 1 Pet. 5:13). Jews and Christians were quite aware that Babylon was a hidden reference to Rome.

Finally if there is any doubt as to the distinction between the Catholic Church in Rome and the Roman Empire, all you have to do is look to the words of Ignatius of Antioch, the disciple of the apostle John and the friend of Peter and Paul. This is what he thought of the "Catholic" Church in Rome:

> *Ignatius, who is also called Theophorus, to the Church which has found mercy, through the majesty of the Most High Father, and Jesus Christ, His only-begotten Son; the Church that is beloved and enlightened... the Church that presides in the capital of the Romans, worthy of God, worthy of honor, worthy of highest happiness, worthy of praise, worthy of obtaining her every desire, worthy of being deemed holy, the Church that presides in love, named from Christ and from the Father....* (*Address to the Romans*).

Does this sound like the Catholic Church is the "Whore of Babylon"? Does St. Paul's *Letter to the Romans* in the Bible sound like the Church in Rome is a "whore?"

Was there a great apostasy?
Mormons claim that they are part of a "restored Church." They claim that the early Church fell away from the truth of Jesus Christ. They often

34

like to quote Acts 20:29-30, 2 Thessalonians 2:1-3, 2 Peter 2:1 and Matthew 7:15. The only problem with these quotes is that they in no way refer to a total apostasy. In fact, there are no quotes in the Scriptures that point to a complete apostasy in the Church. All the examples of apostasy are examples of individual members or groups committing the sin of apostasy.

To accept the theory of the "great apostasy" is to make Jesus a liar, for he said, "On this rock I will build my Church and the gates of hell shall not prevail against it" (Mt. 16:18). He also reminded us: "Behold, I am with you always, until the end of the age" (Mt. 28:20). To believe in a great apostasy is to believe that Christ would have abandoned us and allowed the gates of hell to prevail against the Church! This cannot be. The Bible tells me so!

It is the Church that is the "Church of the living God, the pillar and foundation of truth" (1 Tim. 3:15). It is the Church that is the pillar and foundation of truth, not the Bible, for the Bible flowed from the Church and is interpreted by the Church. Jesus built his Church on a strong foundation that would never fall (cf. Mt. 7:24-27). And he entrusted his Church with the power of running it according to his will (Mt. 18:15-18). If the Church is the foundation of truth built on a foundation that will never fail, a foundation upon which the gates of hell will not prevail against it, then how in the world could the Church remain true to its mission if there was a great apostasy! It is absurd to think that only with the life of the founder of Mormonism, Joseph Smith, in 1829, that this "great apostasy" would end. It is absurd to think that God would allow his Church to live in apostasy for 19 centuries.

The history of Christianity never, ever makes mention of a so-called "great apostasy." No early Christian writer, non-Christian writer, or hostile opponent of Christianity ever makes mentions of such an apostasy. If an apostasy took place why are there no enemies of the Church pointing to this so-called apostasy in history. And if there was an apostasy, who began it? When did it begin and with whom?

Finally, the same arguments that point to the impossibility of Constantine being the founder of the Catholic Church also apply to those who claim that the early Church experienced a great apostasy. If a great apostasy occurred, then Mormons would be worshiping out of the "Great Apostasy Bible."

- The Bible was put together at the Councils of Hippo and Carthage III and IV by the pope and the bishops—the first list of books being initially approved by Pope Damasus in 382 and reaffirmed by Pope Innocent I in 411.

Who founded the Church in Rome?

In a recent television program the "Roman Church" was attacked as being un-Christian. Anything Roman or associated with Rome, from the point of view of these individuals, is not Christian.

Besides the fact that the apostle Paul was a Roman citizen, history shows us quite the opposite.

> *In this chair in which he himself sat, Peter, in mighty Rome, commanded Linus, the first elected, to sit down. After him, Cletus too accepted the flock of the fold. As his successor, Anacletus was elected by lot. Clement follows him, well-known to apostolic men. After him Evaristus ruled the flock without crime. Alexander, sixth in succession, commends the fold to Sixtus. After his illustrious times were completed, he passed it on to Telesphorus. He was excellent, a faithful martyr. After him, learned in the law and a sure teacher, Hyginus, in the ninth place, now accepted the chair. Then Pius, after him, whose blood-brother was Hermas, an angelic shepherd, because he spoke the words delivered to him; and Anicetus accepted his lot in pious succession.*

> *Tertullian (ca. 193)*
> *Adversus Marcionem libri quinque , 3, 276-285; 293-296*

Some groups like to attack the importance of the Church of Rome by making the claim that Peter could not have been the first pope since there is no evidence of his presence in Rome. This is an absurdity to all historians. The very bones of Peter are found under the altar of St. Peter's Basilica in Rome. It has always been accepted that the apostles Peter and Paul founded the Church in Rome. Virtually all Protestants recognize this reality as well. It is only fringe groups that like to deny this.

The first great historian of Christianity, Eusebius (ca. 324) writes in his *Ecclesiatical History* (3:3, 3:25) the following:

> *It is related that in his time Paul was beheaded in Rome itself, and that Peter likewise was crucified, and the title "Peter and Paul," which is still given to the cemeteries there confirms the story, no less than does a writer of the Church named Caius.... Caius...speaks...of the places where the sacred relics of the apostles in question are deposited: 'But I can point out the trophies of the apostles, for if you will go to the Vatican or to the Ostian Way you will find the trophies of those who founded this Church.'*

It is clear that the Church of Rome was founded by Peter and Paul, with Peter being the first pope. On Vatican Hill, the very place of Peter's death was built St. Peter's Basilica and Vatican City.

- Peter was crucified where the front doors of St. Peter's Basilica now stands. Before the building of the Basilica, an ancient Roman Coliseum for gladiatorial games was present on that site.

36

Peter, the Rock upon which Jesus built his Church!

[Jesus said,] "Who do men say that the Son of man is?"... Simon Peter replied, "You are the Christ, the Son of the living God." And Jesus answered him, "Blessed are you, Simon Bar-Jona! For flesh and blood has not revealed this to you, but my Father who is in heaven. And I tell you, you are Peter, and on this rock I will build my church, and the powers of death [of hell] shall not prevail against it. I will give you the keys of the kingdom of heaven and whatever you bind on earth shall be bound in heaven, and whatever you loose on earth shall be loosed in heaven." (Mt. 16: 13-19, RSV).

There is only one Church that can trace itself back to Peter and thus to Jesus--the Catholic Church. As we saw previously, Peter was the first pope, followed by Linus, Anecletus, Clement, and so forth. This line of succession goes on all the way to our current pope.

The gift of the "keys of the kingdom" to Peter by Jesus is quite significant. It finds its origins in Jewish history and is cited in Isaiah 22:21-22. The keys were given to the chief official within the Kingdom of David. It was a symbol of authority on behalf of the king and was an office that did not end with the death of the official. When the office became vacated another successor took his place. Jesus intended for Peter to have successors, and in fact history proves it!

It is also worth noting that at the time of the writing of Matthew's Gospel (ca. 70 AD) Peter had already been killed by being crucified upside down on Vatican Hill (ca. 67AD). The claim by Jesus that he would build his Church upon Peter, consequently, implies that there would be successors to Peter with the authority of Peter; otherwise, it would have been somewhat odd to place such a text within a Gospel when the person being written about is dead.

It is also interesting to note that the Gospel of Mark is seen by scholars as being at the heart or core of all the other Gospels. This is interesting since Peter dictated this Gospel to Mark!

Another note worth mentioning is that the name Peter, "Rock," had never been used before as a name for someone. It is an odd name to give to anyone. Christ had a purpose for this odd name!

Now let us look at the arguments that Protestants use against this text in order to try to undermine its importance, for if we accept this text, then we have no choice but to recognize the true Church as that founded upon Peter. We have no other option than to recognize the true Church as the Catholic Church.

Many Protestants like to point out the distinction between the Greek *Petros* and *Petra*. They point out that in the Greek text of the Gospel of Matthew, Jesus changes Simon's name to *Petros*, which can at times mean "chip," even though the two Greek words—*Petros and Petra*--are often used interchangeably for the word "rock." They claim that Jesus was referring to Peter as a chip off the block. If he had wanted to name him "Rock" he would have used *Petra*, which has no other interpretation than "Rock."

This argument at first may appear appealing, but it is terribly flawed. First, the reason why Matthew used the Greek word *Petros* as opposed to *Petra* to name Simon Peter is that *Petros* is a masculine proper noun, whereas *Petra* is a feminine proper noun. Matthew would not have Jesus calling Simon Peter a feminine "Rock." Hence, Matthew uses *Petros*, the masculine proper noun.

But all of this is of little significance, since Jesus never spoke Greek. Jesus spoke Aramaic, and so Jesus would not have used either word. It is also worth mentioning that the original text of Matthew, albeit lost to history, was in Aramaic. In any case, Jesus would have used the word *Kepa* which means one and only one thing, "Rock." Therefore, Jesus' exact words to Simon Peter would have been, "You are *Kepa*, and on this *Kepa* I will build my Church." In other words, "Your name is Rock and on this Rock I will build my Church and the gates of hell shall not prevail against it." After 2000 years, the gates of hell have not prevailed against his glorious Church, despite many attacks.

Christ built his Church on *Kepa*. Paul's writings in the New Testament always refer to Peter in the Greek transliteration of the Aramaic *Kepa, Kephas*. Paul, with one exception (Gal. 2:7-8), always refers to Peter as *Kephas*, which means one and only one thing, "Rock."

Saint Leo the Great (ca. 461) succinctly summarizes the reality of Peter as "the Rock" when he paraphrases and develops the implications of the words of Jesus:

> *You are Peter: though I [God] am the inviolable rock, the cornerstone..., the foundation apart from which no one can lay any other, yet you also are a rock, for you are given solidity by my strength, so that which is my very own because of my power is common between us...by participation* (Cf, Sermon 4 de *natali ipsius*, 2-3: PL 54,149-151).

Are the popes antichrists?

Some fundamentalist denominations like to argue that the papacy is the seat of the antichrist. They take the number of the beast, 666, from Revelation 13:18, and use the Latin letters, which also represent numbers, to come up with the number 666 for the pope; that is, by counting up the letters that make up the phrase *Vicar of the Son of God, Vicarius Filii Dei*, they come up with 666.

The only problem with such an assertion is that the pope is never called, nor has he ever been called, by the title *Vicar of the Son of God*. His appropriate title is the *Vicar of Christ, Vicarius Christi*, which in no way adds up to 666.

If you play games such as this, you can almost make anyone turn out to be the antichrist. All you need to do is to make up a title that fits the designation. This was a common practice during the Protestant Reformation; almost everyone, including Luther, was accused of bearing the number of the beast.

Another flaw with this argument is that the book of Revelation was not written in Latin. It was written in Greek, and it was not Latin numerology that was being used, but Hebrew numerology. For example, the Greek form of the name Nero Caesar in Hebrew numerology is *nrwn qsr*, which adds up to 666 (n=50; r=200; w=6; q=100; s=60) (50+200+6+50+100+60+200=666). When we use the Latin form of the name Nero Caesar in Hebrew letters, *nrw qsr*, we end up with 616. This is extremely interesting, since as was mentioned earlier, no two ancient manuscripts of the New Testament are exactly alike. Given this reality, when we look at differing manuscripts, we notice that some of the ancient manuscripts give the number for the antichrist as 666 and others 616--both designating Nero Caesar as the antichrist. This would make a lot of sense since Nero Caesar was known to have begun the first great persecution against the Catholics which resulted in the deaths of Peter and Paul in Rome.

The "whore of Babylon" (17:1-6; 9) symbolizes pagan Rome and the antichrist is the persecuting Nero.

Some scholars place the persecution of the Christians, referred to in the book of Revelation, during the reign of Domitian (81-96) when atrocious persecutions took place. Nero's name would have been used to claim that Domitian was another Nero, another antichrist.

In any event, Revelation was a book written for the encouragement of the faithful in times of persecution. Its relevance for us today is that we as Christians are also persecuted, and we too must fight and persevere against the antichrists of today. Just as in Perganum, where a throne to Satan was erected (Rev. 2:13), many of today's cities and nations have decided to raise thrones to the ways of Satan.

Why is the pope so important?

Had Alexandria triumphed and not Rome, the extravagant and muddled stories [of the Gnostics] would be...perfectly ordinary.
Jorge Luis Borges

Popes have always exercised supreme authority in honor and jurisdiction in Christianity. From Peter to the current pope, the Church has always recognized this reality.

Peter (33-67) arranged for the successor of Judas, Matthias (Acts 1:25f), presided over the first council of the Church in Jerusalem, and admitted Gentiles into the Church (Acts 15). Linus (67-76) developed the clergy in Rome. Anacletus (76-88) was consulted regarding the proper consecration of bishops, and Clement (88-97) was called upon to squash the disobedience of the Corinthians. Alexander I (105-115) issued the decree that unleavened bread was to be used for consecration; Sixtus I (115-125) decreed the praying of the *Sanctus* and Telesphorus (125-136) the praying of the *Gloria*. Pius I (140-155) issued the decree regarding the proper date for the celebration of Easter. Hyginus (136-140) was asked to squash the heresy of Gnosticism, Anicetus (155-166) the heresy of Manichaeism, Soter (166-175) the heresy of Montanism, and Victor I (189-199) the heresy of Adoptionism. Damasus I (366-384) chose which books would be in the Bible and which would not. The popes have led the way for 2000 years.

Whenever the Church sought guidance, it always looked to the successor of Peter, the pope. This pattern continued and continues uninterrupted to this very day! Vatican I would officially affirm this pattern under the doctrine of Papal Infallibility.

The pope is infallible in and by himself in the areas of faith and morals when he speaks *ex cathedra*; that is, when (1) he speaks on faith and morals, (2) on behalf of the universal Church, (3) from the authority or "chair" of Peter, and (4) with a clear affirmation that what he is about to proclaim is to be held infallible. All the above conditions are necessary for an infallible statement.

At the Council of Chalcedon (451) Pope Leo's letter regarding Christ's two natures was read. After Leo's affirmation that Christ was fully human, fully divine, without any confusion, change or division amongst his natures, the bishops sprang to their feet and proclaimed: "Peter has spoken through Leo." The successor of Peter had led the bishops and all the Christian faithful to the truth.

The Holy Father, the pope, is important because he is the successor of the apostle Peter who was entrusted with the keys to the Kingdom and who was entrusted to lead the Church (Mt. 16:18f). In rabbinic terminology the ability to "bind and loose" (cf. Mt. 16:18f) is equated with the authority to decide what is allowed or forbidden by law as well as the authority to include and exclude individuals from a community.

In the naming of the apostles, Peter is always named at the head of the list (Mt. 10:1-4; Mk. 3:16-19; Lk. 6:14-16; Acts 1:13). Of all the apostles Peter is named 195 times in the New Testament, whereas the next most often mentioned apostle, John, is only mentioned 29 times. Peter is also the one who usually spoke as the representative of the apostles (Mt. 18:21; Mk. 8:29; Lk. 9:32; 12:41; Jn. 6:69). (The Bible emphasizes Peter's authority and special role by phrases such as "Simon Peter and the rest of the apostles" or simply "Peter and his companions" (Lk. 9:32; Mk. 16:7; Acts 2:37).) It is to Peter that an angel is sent to announce the resurrection of Jesus (Mk. 16:7). It is to Peter that the risen Christ appears to before appearing to the other apostles (Lk. 24:33-35). It is Peter that leads the apostles in selecting the replacement for Judas with Matthias (Acts 1:15-26). It is Peter who was called upon to strengthen his brothers in the faith (Lk. 22:31-32). Peter is the one who preached to the crowds at Pentecost as the leader of the apostles (Acts 2:14-40) and received the first converts (Acts 2:41). It is Peter who performed the first miracle after the resurrection (Acts 3:6-7) and it is Peter who inflicted the first punishment on the disobedient, on Ananias and Saphira (Acts 5:1-11). It is Peter who excommunicated the first heretic, Simon Magnus (Acts 8:21). It is Peter who led the Church's first council, the Council of Jerusalem, and encouraged the baptism of the Gentiles (Acts 10:46-48). It is Peter who pronounced from the council the first dogmatic decision (Acts 15:17). And it is to Peter that Paul went to make sure his teachings were in line with his (Gal. 1:18). And finally, it is Peter alone who was told before Jesus' Ascension into heaven to nourish the faithful in the faith (Jn. 21:15-17), even though the other apostles were present in their midst.

Because of these realities, the pope is in charge of leading the Church. All are to be obedient to him in faith and morals and in respect. He is infallible in and by himself in the areas of faith and morals when he speaks *ex cathedra*; that is, when he speaks for the universal Church, from the authority of Peter, with the clear indication that what he is to say is to be held infallible. He also speaks infallibly in an "ordinary" manner when he affirms a teaching that has always been held by the Church (i.e., Pope John Paul II reaffirmed two thousand years of Christianity when he stated that the ordination of women is not possible since it is not within the "deposit of the faith.").

Bishops share in this infallibility when they teach in union with the pope.

Let us look at the words of those who walked and talked and learned from the apostles in regards to papal authority.

The fourth pope, Clement of Rome, a convert of the apostle Peter, a friend of Peter and Paul, and the Clement mentioned in Philippians 4:3, makes the following statement (ca. 88-97):

> *The Church of God which sojourns in Rome to the Church of God which sojourns in Corinth....* (*Letter to the Corinthians*, Address, trans. Lake, vol. 1). *Owing to the sudden and repeated misfortunes and calamities which have befallen us, we consider that our attention has been somewhat delayed in turning to the questions disputed among you....* (Ibid., 1).

Clearly the fourth pope is asserting his authority as the successor of Peter. He is addressing, in his letter to the Corinthian community, the abuses to the Gospel that are taking place there.

Why would the bishop of Rome be interfering in the affairs of the Corinthian community? Clearly, he was doing so by authority. The Corinthian community, upon reading the letter, and acknowledging its supreme authority, made it part of their liturgical readings. In fact, this letter would almost take on canonical status, and in fact in some communities it did take on canonical status. It was not until the decisions of the fourth century popes and bishops that this letter would be deemed as not having canonical status. It may not have been Scripture, but it certainly was understood as authoritative in faith and morals.

Let us look at Ignatius of Antioch (ca. 107), the disciple of John, and his understanding of papal authority:

> *Ignatius, who is also called Theophorus, to the Church which has found mercy, through the majesty of the Most High Father, and Jesus Christ, His only-begotten Son; the Church that is beloved and enlightened...the Church that presides in the capital of the Romans, worthy of God, worthy of honor, worthy of the highest happiness, worthy of praise, worthy of obtaining her every desire, worthy of being deemed holy, the Church that presides in love, named from Christ and from the Father....* (Letter to the Romans, trans. Lake).

Irenaeus of Lyon, a disciple of Polycarp, who in turn was a disciple of John, writes in the year 202 AD: "All other churches must bring themselves into line with the Church that resides in Rome, on account of its superior authority." (CCC 834).

If this is not the recognition of papal primacy, what is? The ancient writer Hermas, the man mentioned in Romans 16:14, in "visions" (2) recognized the importance of Rome when he made sure that some key writings were sent to Pope Clement for approval. As he writes:

> *[You] shall write two little books and send one to Clement [the successor of the apostle Peter].... Clement shall then send it to the cities abroad, because that is his duty....*

And in Cyprian of Carthage (ca. 251) we read in *De Ecclesiae Unitate* (cf. 2-7):

> *The blessed apostle Paul teaches us that the Church is one, for it has 'one body, one spirit, one hope, one faith, one baptism, and one God.' Furthermore, it is on Peter that Jesus built his Church, and to him he gives the command to feed the sheep; and although he assigns like power to all the apostles, yet he founded a single chair, and he established by his own authority a source and an intrinsic reason for that unity. Indeed, the others were that also which Peter was; but a primacy is given to Peter, whereby it is made clear that there is but one Church and one Chair—the Chair of Peter. So too, all are shepherds, and the flock is shown to be one, fed by all the apostles in single-minded accord. If someone does not hold fast to this unity of Peter, can he imagine that he still holds the faith? If he*

deserts the chair of Peter upon whom the Church was built, can he still be confident that he is in the Church?

In his *Letter to all his People* [43 (40) 5] written in 251 AD Cyprian reminded his people that the faith of the pope is the faith of the Church:

They who have not peace themselves now offer peace to others. They who have withdrawn from the Church promise to lead back and to recall the lapsed to the Church. There is one God and one Christ, and one Church, and one Chair founded on Peter by the word of the Lord. It is not possible to set up another altar or for there to be another priesthood besides that one altar and that one priesthood. Whoever has gathered elsewhere is scattering.

Obviously, from what we see in these earliest of writings, papal authority was well recognized throughout Christianity.

The first seven centuries of Christianity was divided between Catholic Christianity and Arian Christianity (which denied the Trinity). Catholic Christianity was always supported by the popes, and Arian Christianity almost always found support from the emperors of the East and the bishops seeking the favor of these emperors.

Catholic Christianity would prevail under the influence of the popes. Had it not, Christianity would be radically different than it is today!

- One of the great ironies of history is that Martin Luther, the first Protestant, was a priest in the Augustinian order before his break. His spiritual father in faith, St. Augustine of Hippo, after Rome had spoken regarding the Pelagian heresy, concluded (*Sermons* 131:10): "The matter is at an end." If only Luther would have recognized Rome's authority as much as the founder of his order did, Christianity would be quite different.

Without the popes, the successors of St. Peter, there would be no authentic Christianity!

In 1517, the founder of Protestantism, Martin Luther, had a meeting with the person who would eventually become known as the "father" of English and American Protestantism, the lawyer John Calvin. They met to iron out their theological differences. They could come to no agreement. At one point, in frustration, Luther turned to Calvin and said, "I started all this and you should follow what I started!" Calvin retorted, "Who in the world do you think you are, the pope?" In this ironic retort was a truth that these protestors had not realized--that without an ultimate *decision maker* there could be no consensus on religious belief. President Truman used to say, "The buck stops here!" In other words, the ultimate and final decisions stop with him. So too, the ultimate and final decisions stop with the successor of Peter, the pope. Otherwise, Christianity would simply be an accumulation of confusing beliefs and practices. Truth would be left to personal opinion! And that is a religion doomed to die!

Let us examine the popes of the first five centuries, in particular those Popes that taught doctrines that all mainline Christians take for granted. When we do this we can see that without the popes, Christianity would not exist or would exist as simply an accumulation of confusing beliefs!

The first pope, Peter led the first council of the Church, the Council of Jerusalem, and admitted the Gentiles into the Church. Peter chose his successor: *"After the Holy Apostles Peter and Paul had founded and set up the Church in Rome they gave over the exercise of the office of bishop of Rome to Linus"* (Irenaeus, *Adv. Haereses*, III, iii, 3). The first successor of Peter, the second pope, Linus (67-76), is chosen to lead the Church. He is best known for encouraging the growth of the clergy and the development of parishes to fulfill the spiritual needs of the growing Christian population. The ninth pope, Hyginus (136-140) instituted the use of godparents for infant baptisms. The tenth pope, Pius I (140-155), opposed agnosticism and established the date for Easter as the first Sunday after the March full moon. The eleventh pope, Anicetus (155-166), emphasized the celebration of Easter as the central Christian feast. The twelfth pope, Soter (166-175), affirmed the Sacrament of Matrimony. The twenty-first pope, Cornelius (251-253), opposed the heresy of Novatianism which believed that sins could not be forgiven and that the Church was solely made up of saints. The twenty-second pope, Lucius I (253-254), reiterated the ban on premarital sexual relationships and the living together before marriage. The twenty-sixth pope, Felix I (269-274), affirmed Christ as being God and man, as having two natures in one Person. The thirty-fifth pope, Julius I (337-352), decreed that Christmas should be celebrated on December 25. The thirty-sixth pope, Liberius (352-366), fought against the heresy of Arianism. The thirty seventh pope, Damasus I (366-384), decided which books would make up the Bible and which would not. He then had the Scriptures translated into the vernacular by Jerome. The books he included into the Bible are what all Christians use as their Bible of worship. The books he excluded include the following: The Gospel of Thomas, the Dialogue of the Savior, the Gospel of Mary, the Infancy Gospel of Thomas, the Infancy Gospel of James, the

Gospel of Peter, the Gospel of Bartholomew, the Gospel of Nicodemus, the Gospel of the Nazoreans, the Gospel of the Ebionites, the Gospel of Philip, the Gospel of the Egyptians, and on and on the list goes. He excluded the Apocryphon of James, the Apocryphon of John, the Apocalypse of Paul, the two Apocalypses of James, the Apocalypse of Peter, the Acts of Peter and the Twelve Apostles, the Acts of Andrew, the Acts of John, the Acts of Thomas, etc., etc..

Is it not interesting that no denomination questions the work of Pope Damasus I. In a sense, they are accepting—albeit reluctantly, subliminally, or subconsciously--that when it came to putting the Bible together the pope was infallible.

What other teachings did the popes promote as the norm for Christianity? Remember these beliefs that the popes rejected or accepted were firmly rooted as "competing" versions of Christianity. Yet it is the version of Christianity defined and fought for by the popes that would win the day. It is that version (on the basic doctrines of Christianity) that mainline Christians would accept--even to this day! Why? As Catholics we would say, "Where the pope is there is the faith!"

It is the popes who condemned Docetism and Gnosticism, the beliefs that denied Jesus' humanity. It is the popes who condemned Marcionism, the belief that the Old Testament should be eliminated from the Scriptures. It is the popes who rejected Montanism, Donatism, and Novatianism, the beliefs that held that serious sins could never be forgiven. It is the popes who condemned Modalism, the belief that the Father, Son, and Holy Spirit were modes of one Divine Person—as opposed to three persons in one God. It is the popes who condemned Monarchianism which argued Jesus became divine after his baptism. It is the popes who rejected Subordinationism that viewed the Father and Son as unequal. It is the popes who rejected Sabellianism which denied the distinction between the Father and the Son. It is the popes who rejected Patripassionism which argued that it was the Father that was crucified and not the Son. It is the popes who condemned Manicheaism which held the belief in two competing and equal principles as rulers of the universe, one good, one bad, one matter, one spirit. It is the popes who rejected Arianism which denied Jesus' divinity and the Trinity. It is the popes who condemned Pnematomachism which denied the divinity of the Holy Spirit. It is the popes who condemned Eunomianism which rejected the divinity of Christ and the Holy Spirit. It is the popes who rejected Priscillianism which denied the preexistence

45

of the Son and denied the humanity of Jesus. It is the popes who condemned Monophysitism that claimed that Christ had only one nature. It is the popes who rejected Nestorianism which argued that Jesus was two distinct persons. It is the popes who rejected Pelagianism which denied "original sin" and argued that one could work oneself into heaven without grace. It is the popes who condemned Traducianism which argued that the soul was not created by God but by human beings. It is the popes who rejected Monothelitism which denied that Christ had a human and a divine will. It is the popes who rejected Albigensianism which viewed matter as evil and suicide as a way of freeing oneself from matter, from the body. It is the popes who rejected Cartharianism which renounced baptism and marriage and the holiness of the body. It is the popes who condemned Jansenism which argued that Christ did not die for all. The list goes on and on!

All mainline Christians, today, accept what these Catholic popes taught and fought for. Why do they accept these teachings and yet do not accept all of the popes' teachings? Why the picking and choosing? All the heretics above had the same material to draw upon? Yet they disagreed over what the Scriptures meant and what the Holy Spirit was saying! Why do mainline Christians accept the teachings of the popes if these above groups did not?

Why is apostolic succession so important?

> *The agreement among [Catholics] is astonishing and quite amazing...*
> *Celsus (ca. 170) a renowned anti-Christian philosopher*

The people of God always knew of the importance of spirit-filled successors to their leaders. When Moses' earthly journey was approaching its end, Moses went to Joshua and called the spirit of God upon him by the "laying on of hands" (cf. Ex. 34:1-12). Thus Joshua succeeded Moses in leading the people of God.

In a similar yet more tragic manner, after the death of Judas, the apostles sought out a successor to replace Judas. Two men were proposed to succeed Judas, Barsabbas and Matthias.

The apostles prayed and then cast lots. The lot fell on Matthias. Matthias then became the successor of Judas and took his place alongside the eleven (Acts 1:15-26).

Paul mentions how he "laid the foundation" for others, successors, to build upon (1 Cor. 3:10). Paul mentions Silvanus and Timothy as being ordained to the office of apostle and thus having apostolic authority (cf. 1 Thess. 1:1; 2:6,7; 2 Tim. 1:6). Other examples of passing on the teaching authority of the apostles through apostolic succession and the "laying on of hands" can be seen and implied in Acts 14:23, Acts 20:28, 1 Corinthians 12:27-29, Ephesians 2:20; 4:11, and 1 Timothy 3:1-8; 4:13-14; 5:17-22.

Apostolic succession is that reality that allows the Church of the year 2015 AD to be connected to the faith of the Church of 33 AD. Each Catholic bishop in the world can trace his authority from bishop to bishop all the way down to the apostles themselves.

The apostles did not live in a vacuum. They walked and talked with people and in turn they appointed men to take their place as bishops in guiding their communities, and these bishops were in turn succeeded by other bishops in the same line of succession (cf. Acts 1:15-26; i.e., Matthias succeeded Judas in the office of apostle).

In this way the deposit of the faith would always be protected. The faith of Christ would always be kept pure. Without apostolic succession, Christianity would be a mist of confusion. It is for this reason that Paul instructs Timothy to choose successors with caution (1 Tim. 5:22; 2 Tim. 2:2).

Let us always be faithful to the successors of the apostles, the bishops in union with the pope, the successor of the leader of the apostles.

Irenaeus (ca. 140), as we remember from above, was a pupil of Polycarp (ca. 69-156), and Polycarp was a disciple of the apostle John. This bears repeating because it is a witness to the authority of this man. Irenaeus describes the importance of noting the successors of the churches [i.e., dioceses, communities].

> *The blessed apostles Peter and Paul, having found and built up the Church of Rome, handed over the office of the episcopate to Linus. Paul makes mention of this Linus in the Epistle to Timothy [2 Tim. 4:21]. To him succeeded Anecletus; and after him, in the third place from the apostles, Clement was chosen for the episcopate. He had seen the blessed apostles and was acquainted with them, and had their traditions before his eyes (Against Heresies, 3,3, trans. Jurgens, vol. 1).*

Clement of Rome, Peter's friend and successor, makes it quite clear how important apostolic succession is:

> *Our apostles knew through our Lord Jesus Christ that there would be strife for the title of bishop. For this cause, therefore, since they had received perfect foreknowledge, they appointed those who [were properly chosen], and afterwards added the codicil that if they should fall asleep [that is, die], other approved men should succeed to their ministry (Letter to the Corinthians, 44, trans. Lake).*

Let us always be faithful to the successors of the apostles! And if there is any question about proving such a succession, I have placed in the appendix all the successors of Peter—an affirmation of the primacy of Peter, and an affirmation that the "gates of hell" would never prevail

47

against the Church (Mt. 16:18f).

Cyprian in his *Letter to all his People* [43 (40) 5], written in 251 AD, reminded his people that the faith of the pope is the faith of the Church:

They who have not peace themselves now offer peace to others. They who have withdrawn from the Church promise to lead back and to recall the lapsed to the Church. There is one God and one Christ, and one Church, and one Chair founded on Peter by the word of the Lord. It is not possible to set up another altar or for there to be another priesthood besides that one altar and that one priesthood. Whoever has gathered elsewhere is scattering.

The popes created the West!

The popes can rightly be seen as the founders of the modern Western world. The popes provided for an explosion in the advancement of the sciences and humanities never before seen. When we examine the Catholic clergy only, we see the following:

When examining the history of science between 900 BC and 1800 AD, we are amazed to find that five percent of history's greatest mathematicians are recognized as Jesuit priests—this is particularly impressive when you consider that the Jesuit order did not exist until the fifteenth century. Thirty-five craters on the moon are named after Jesuit scientists.

The popes guided the work of the monks. The monks and their monasteries were responsible for fostering a common language, for protecting, copying, and preserving ancient texts, for developing and elevating astronomy, music, arithmetic, geometry, logic, grammar, and rhetoric to heights never before achieved. They developed a common script with letters, punctuation, spaces, and paragraphs. Through Cathedral Schools they preserved and reproduced for all generations the works of the writers of antiquity. They were the creators and distributers of comprehensive encyclopedias of knowledge.

With over 37,000 monasteries, the monks, known as the *agriculturists of Europe*, saved and perfected the art of agriculture and laid the foundation for industry. They transformed much of Europe, such as modern day Germany, from a forest into a country. The monks introduced crops, developed new production methods (such as complicated irrigation systems), raised better producing bees, developed salmon fisheries, and engineered better fruits and vegetables.

The monks became the great technical advisors to the West, and became rightly so the fathers of what would eventually become the Industrial Revolution. They were the leading iron producers, and the leading miners of salt, lead, iron, and marble. They were among the first to use the byproducts of their iron production as fertilizer for crops.

The popes invented the university system for those who desired an education, whether wealthy or poor. All were offered an education, if they so desired one—inventing the degrees of Bachelor of Arts and Master's. The Catholic Church has founded 1,358 universities! Pope Innocent VII is known as the *father of nascent humanism and the Renaissance.*

Despite the sad Galileo incident, the popes have done more than any organization in the history of the world for the advancement of science. Roger Bacon, a Franciscan, and Bishop Grosseteste are often referred to as the forerunners of the modern scientific method. The priest Georges Joseph Edouard Lemaitre is the originator of the theory of the "Big Bang." He is the first to derive what is known as the Hubble constant. The priest Giambattista Riccioli laid the foundation and principles that would be responsible for all of modern astronomy. The priest Roger Boscovich is often referred to as the father and forerunner of atomic physics, the father of modern atomism. The priest Athanasius Kircher was a master chemist who debunked alchemy and astrology and laid the foundation of Egyptology. Kircher made the interpreting of the Rosetta stone possible. The priest Nicolas Zucchi invented the reflecting telescope. Jean Buridan, the Catholic professor at the Sorbonne, laid the foundation for much of Newton's work, particularly his first law. The priest Nicolaus Steno is acknowledged as a pioneer in modern geology and is considered the father of stratigraphy. The monk Gregor Mendel became the father of genetics and the laws of inheritance. The priest Pierre Telhard de Chardin was part of the team that discovered Peking man.

The popes inspired further revolutions:

Antoine Laurent Lavoisier is associated with the *revolution in chemistry*, Erwin Schrodinger with wave mechanics, Blaise Pascal for his theory of probability and the mechanical adding machine, Enrico Fermi with atomic physics, and Marcello Malpighi with microscopic anatomy.

The Catholic Church as guided by the popes is rightly acknowledged as the *father of modern science*.

The foundations of modern civil law are often attributed to the monk Gratian in his *Concordance of Discordant Canons* (ca. 1140). Western civilization owes its sense of international law and civil law to the Church's legacy. The priest Francisco de Vitoria is often referred to as the father of modern international law. Vitoria would be responsible for laying down what we now call the *law of nations*, laws among nations in peacetime and war. Jacques Maritain's emphasis on the natural law and natural rights would form the core philosophy of the United Nations' Universal Declarations of Human Rights.

Way before Adam Smith, the foundations for modern economic systems or what has become known as *scientific economics* were laid down by the Catholic Church. Abbot Etienne Bonnot de Condillac, the abbot Robert Jacques Turgot, and Francois Quesnay are often referred to as the *founders of the economic sciences*. Nicolas Oresme is considered the founding father of monetary economics; he would lay the foundation for what would evolve into Gershan's law. Cardinal Cajetan would become known as the founder of the *expectation theory* in economics. Pierre de Jean Olivi would become known as the founder of the *value theory of economics*. The abbot Ferdinando Galiani would be instrumental in laying the foundations for the idea that utility and scarcity are determinants to price.

The popes invented the hospital—the modern system where institutions of care are staffed by doctors and nurses. Doctors diagnosed illnesses and prescribed remedies. By the fourth century every major city in Europe had a hospital. One-fourth of healthcare in the world is run by the Catholic Church.

And contrary to popular opinion, the Church and the popes would elevate the status of women to levels unheard of. It is the Church that gave women equal protection and status in marriage—holding men equally responsible and punishable for adultery and fornication. Women became the founders and abbesses of self-governing religious orders and communities. Pope Benedict XIV promoted the first two women professors in Western history to professorships: the physicist Laura Bassi and the mathematician Maria Gaetana Agnesi. Women religious built and ran their own schools, convents, colleges, hospitals, hospices, and orphanages. The American Church, in all its dimensions, is the product of religious women! The Church has produced more famous women than any other institution. The list of canonized women saints alone—at least 5,000--is a mark of this truth.

The Church is made up of humans, not walking gods. The Church has a long legacy of evil. But the fact remains: *No group or institution in world history has done more for the advancement of human beings in the West than Catholic Christianity under its popes!*

The gates of hell shall not prevail against it!

Even though the Church is made up of sinners and saints (Mt. 5:13-16; 7:15-23; 10: 1-4; 13: 1-9, 24-50; 26:69-75; Mk. 3:19; Lk. 22:54-62; Jn. 6:70; 18:2-4) God promised that the gates of hell would never prevail against it (Mt. 16:18f) and he promised that he would keep it from error (Jn. 16:13; 1 Tm. 3:15). God has kept his promise.

He has entrusted the Church with a teaching office—the Magisterium-- which consists of the bishops, the successors of the apostles, in union with the successor of Peter, the pope (Acts 8:30-31; 15:1-35; Eph. 2:20; 3:5; Jn. 14:16f).

The following is a short list of heresies that have attempted to prevail against the Church, but have failed.

Docetism (first century): This heresy denied Jesus' humanity.

Gnosticism (first century): Gnosticism is a mixture of Christianity, the oriental religions, and Greek philosophy. Salvation was only for the elect. All matter was evil; only the spirit was good. Marriage was to be avoided because it produced matter, children.

The Gnosticism of Basilides (second century): The following aspects made up this heresy: 1) Only the few are able to possess the true and secret knowledge (gnosis) that is necessary for salvation; 2) Only the soul is redeemed, the body corrupts; 3) Christians must reject Christ's crucifixion and only emphasize Jesus as the one sent by the Father.

The Gnosticism of Valentinus (second century): According to this heresy, the *aeon* Christ united himself with the man Christ to bring a secret knowledge (gnosis) to the elect, the Gnostics. This secret knowledge was directed at freeing the soul from the body so that the soul could enter into a spiritual realm after death.

The Gnosticism of Ptolemy (second century): The Law of the Old Testament is the product of a demiurge (the world-creator) who is neither the supreme God nor the devil. He is not perfect like the Supreme God nor is he the author of evil like the devil. This demiurge is known as the creator of the universe, the creator of matter which traps the soul in a body.

Marcionism (second century): This heresy denied the Old Testament's validity.

Montanism (second century): Montanism believed in an earthly thousand-year reign (Millenarianism) and taught mortal sins could not be forgiven. Many refused to marry because of a belief in the imminent return of Christ.

Modalism (second century): The Father, Son, and Holy Spirit were simply modes of one divine person.

Monarchianism (second century): Jesus was a human being who, at some point, perhaps at his baptism in the Jordan, received divine power from God.

Subordinationism (second century): Jesus was viewed as not being co-equal with the Father.

Sabellianism (third century): This heresy denied the distinction between the Father and the Son.

Patripassionism (third century): This belief argued that it was the Father, under the guise of the Son, who actually suffered and was crucified.

Novatianism (third century): Serious sinners could not be readmitted into the Church.

Manichaeism (third century): A religious and ethical doctrine which infiltrated much of Christian thought. It held that there were two equal eternal principles, one good, one evil, one spirit, one matter, one light, one darkness.

Arianism (fourth century): This heresy denied Jesus' divinity and the Trinity. This is the greatest heresy the Church has ever fought. Unlike Protestantism, which is still essentially a phenomenon of the Western world, Arianism would affect and infect the entire Church.

Pneumatomachism (fourth century): This belief denied the divinity of the Holy Spirit and therefore of the Trinity.

Eunomianism (fourth century): A radical form of Arianism which denied the divinity of Christ and the Holy Spirit.

Donatism (fourth century): Donatism argued that grave sinners could not be readmitted into the Church, and the sacraments administered by those in mortal sin were to be held as invalid.

Priscillianism (fourth century): As a blend of Manicheanism, Docetism and Modalism, it denied the preexistence of the Son and denied the humanity of the Son.

Monophysitism (fifth century): This heresy claimed that Christ had only one nature.

Nestorianism (fifth century): This belief claimed that Jesus was two distinct persons and therefore denied the title "Theotokos," "God-bearer," "Mother of God."

Pelagianism (fifth century): This heresy denied the existence of "original sin," and believed that one could obtain salvation by works without grace or the Church.

Traducianism (fifth century): This heresy viewed the human soul as not created directly by God but generated by parents in the same way as a body.

Monothelitism (seventh century): Monothelitism denied that Christ had a human will and a divine will.

Paulicianism (seventh century): This heresy rejected the hierarchy of the Church and the sacraments of baptism, Eucharist, and marriage. They denied the Old Testament and parts of the New Testament.

Iconaclasm (eighth and ninth century): This heresy was led by the emperors that argued that icons fostered idolatry.

Albigensianism (eleventh century): This heresy rejected Church authority and the sacraments and denied the power of the civil authority to punish criminals. They viewed matter as evil. Suicide was considered the ultimate way of freeing oneself from one's evil body.

Catharianism (eleventh century): They renounced baptism and marriage. They viewed the body and matter as evil.

Waldensesism (twelfth century): Questioned the number of Church sacraments. They denied the validity of sacraments administered by an unworthy minister; they rejected purgatory and devotion to saints.

Lollardism (fourteenth century): Argued that the Bible should be in the language of the local people. They rejected the doctrine of Transubstantiation in favor of a simply spiritual presence in the Eucharist. They denied the role of the priest as a secondary mediator to the one mediator, Christ.

Hussitism (fifteenth century): Hussitism rejected the Sacrament of Penance, communion under one kind, and condemned the abuse of indulgences.

Protestantism (sixteenth century): Protestantism has taken on so many forms that it is hard to describe its belief system accurately for all. So for the purpose of this section of the book, I will describe the essential beliefs of Protestantism at the time of the Protestant Reformation.

Protestantism can primarily be summarized as follows: 1) Justification is by faith alone, *sola fides*; 2) The Bible alone is the rule of faith, *sola scriptura*; 3) "original sin" perverted human nature as opposed to wounding it; 4) Only baptism and the "Lord's Supper" are sacraments; 5) They rejected transubstantiation for consubstantiation or simple presence or symbol; 6) There is no need for a pope or bishops; 7) Mary's role in the Church is too great; 8) Indulgences should be rejected.

Gallicanism (seventeenth century): Held that a local church was autonomous and not answerable to the pope.

Jansenism (seventeenth century): Argued that one was without free will, that Christ did not die for all, that Christ's humanity was overemphasized, and that only the most holy were to receive the Eucharist.

Febronianism (eighteenth century): The state, guided by the Scriptures and subject to an ecumenical council, was to determine Church affairs. The pope was not to interfere in the affairs of the state.

Americanism (nineteenth century): Argued that there was a unique compatibility between Catholicism and American values. It argued that the United States held a providential role in guiding the universal Church into the modern age and particularly into the sphere of contemporary social issues.

Modernism (twentieth century): In its extreme form, it denied Christ's divinity, the sacredness of the Bible, the sacredness of the Church, and it believed that doctrines should change with the times; thereby denying infallible teachings.

Secular Christianity (twentieth/ twenty-first century): Secular Christianity is related to Modernism and is an outgrowth of Modernism. As opposed to molding and changing cultural values through the power of Christianity, this heresy seeks to mold and change Christianity according to modern cultural and secular values.

The Promise

The Church deals with heresies continuously, yet the promise of Jesus that he would be with the Church always (Mt. 28:20) and that the gates of hell would not prevail against it (Mt. 16:18f) has been kept.

Heresies have existed in the past and will continue into the future. In fact, heresies tend to transform themselves with every succeeding generation. Much of the "new age" movement can find its roots in many of these heresies. To accept any of these heresies is to say that God did not preserve his promise of keeping the Church from error (Mt. 16:17-19; Jn. 16:13; 1 Tim. 3:15). How can that be?

Let us ponder once more the words of Ignatius of Antioch, the friend of the apostles John, Peter and Paul:

> *For as many as belong to God and Jesus Christ these are with the bishop. [A]s many as repent and come to the unity of the Church, these...shall be of God, to be living according to Jesus Christ. Be not deceived, my brethren, if any one follow a maker of schism, he does not inherit the Kingdom of God; if any man walk in strange doctrine he has no part in the Passion* (*Philadelphians*, 3, trans. Lake).

Jesus told Peter, *Kepa*, that he was the Rock, the *Kepa*, upon which he would build his Church: He promised that the gates of hell would not prevail against it (Mt. 16:18f). There was no such thing as Protestantism for 1500 years. The very word Protestant comes from the "protesting" of Catholicism. If we accept the Protestant claim that the Catholic Church went wrong during these 1500 years, then Jesus becomes a liar. Once more, Jesus

54

said that he would build his Church on the Rock, on Peter, and the gates of hell would not prevail against it (Mt. 16:18f; 28:20). If Catholicism was wrong during any period during these 1500 years in its infallible teachings, or since those 1500 years, then the gates of hell would have had to prevail against the Church. Would Christ have allowed souls to be misled for 1500 years? Impossible! He has always been with his Church and will always be with her for all eternity (Mt. 28:20).

The major councils of the Church and the assurance of the true faith!
The councils of the Church that were approved and guided by the popes have protected the Church throughout the ages. For every series of heresies, God protected his Church through the successors of the apostles, the bishops, and the successor of the head of the apostles, Peter, the pope.

Council of Jerusalem (ca. 50): The apostles affirm the role of Gentiles in the Church.

Council of Nicaea (325): The council condemned the heresy of Arianism and affirmed that the Son was consubstantial (one with) the Father. The heresy of Arianism argued that the Son was created and not co-eternal with the Father. Arianism therefore denied the reality of the Trinity.

Constantinople I (381): The council condemned the heresy of Macedonianism which argued for a hierarchy in the Trinity instead of an equality. The council declared that the Holy Spirit was consubstantial (one with) the Father and the Son.

Councils of Hippo (393), Carthage III (397), and Carthage IV (419): A list of books are compiled that will become known as the Bible.

Council of Ephesus (431): Condemned Nestorianism and Pelagianism. The Heresy of Nestorianism denied the title "Mother of God" thus separating Christ's human nature from his divine nature; thereby making Christ essentially two distinct Persons. Pelagianism held essentially five key heretical points: 1) Adam would have died whether he sinned or not. 2) The sin of Adam injured only himself and was not passed on to further generations. 3) Newborn children are not affected or wounded by "original sin." 4) Christ's salvific event was not absolutely necessary for salvation, since sinless people existed prior to Christ. 5) One could work oneself into heaven by means of one's human efforts alone.
In response, the council affirmed the reality that the Son of God was the second Person of the Trinity and that he had two natures, one human, one

divine—without change, confusion, separation or division between the natures. It thus affirmed the title of Mary as the "theotokos" "God-bearer," the "Mother of God." Against Pelagianism the Church affirmed the necessity of Christ's life, death, and resurrection for our salvation and the wiping away of "original sin." It affirmed that grace was necessary for salvation and that one could not earn or work oneself into heaven without the aid of grace. It affirmed that "original sin" is passed down to the entire human race and is cleansed in baptism.

Council of Chalcedon (451): The council condemned Monophysitism. Monophysitism denied Christ's two natures (divine and human) and argued for a composite nature. The council reaffirmed the teaching that the Son of God was one Person with two natures, without change, separation, confusion, or division between the natures. Jesus was fully human, fully divine. He was God and man.

Constantinople II (553): The council re-condemned the Nestorian heresy.

Constantinople III (680): The council condemned Monothelitism which argued that Christ had only one will. Constantinople affirmed that Jesus had two wills, a human will and a divine will. His human will was in perfect conformity with his divine will.

Nicaea II (787): The council condemned Iconoclasm which forbade the use of images as prayer aids. Nicaea affirmed the use of images for inspiring prayer. The incarnation, an icon of God, made images of the invisible God visible.

Lateran I (1123): It issued decrees banning simony (the buying and selling of something spiritual, such as religious offices) and lay investiture (the appointing of bishops by lay persons, as opposed to by the Church). It also affirmed the gift of celibacy in the priesthood.

Lateran II (1139): It ended the papal schism between Innocent II and Anacletus II. Anacletus was declared an anti-pope. Clerical celibacy was also reaffirmed and usury—the taking of interest for a loan--was prohibited.

Lateran III (1179): It condemned the Cathari who renounced baptism and marriage.

Lateran IV (1215): It condemned the Albigenses and Waldenses. Albigensianism rejected the sacraments and Church authority. The Waldenses rejected the sacraments, purgatory, the communion of saints and Church authority. The council reaffirmed its always held beliefs in these teachings.

Lyons I (1245) deposed Frederick II and planned a crusade to free the Holy Land.

Lyons II (1274) reunited the Church with the Orthodox churches and enacted reforms in discipline regarding the clergy.

Vienne (311-1312) enacted reforms in the Church and abolished the Knights Templars.

Constance (1414-1418) ended the papal schism and condemned the theology of John Huss.

Basle, Ferrara, Florence (1431-1445) reunited the Church with the Orthodox churches and again enacted disciplinary reforms.

Lateran V (1512-1517) dealt with the neo-Aristotelian influences in the Church and also enacted disciplinary reforms for the clergy.

The Council of Trent (1545-1563) affirmed what Protestantism denied. It reminded the Protestants of the beliefs that were always held from the beginning of the Church. It affirmed that the deposit of faith was found in Sacred Scripture and Sacred Tradition. It affirmed the reality of the seven sacraments. The doctrine of Transubstantiation was reiterated; that is, that bread and wine, once consecrated, become the body, blood, soul, and divinity of the resurrected Christ. It declared that justification is by faith, but not by faith alone: works are necessary. It rejected the negative view held by Protestants regarding human nature. Protestants believed that "original sin" destroyed human nature; The Catholic Church would reassert the faith and declare that "original sin" "wounded" but did not destroy human nature. The Catholic Church would reassert the reality of free will and the reality of providence--early Protestantism believed in absolute predestination and the lack of free will; that is, some people are predestined to heaven and some to hell.

<u>Vatican I (1869-1870)</u> clarified and reaffirmed the always held teaching of papal primacy in honor, jurisdiction, and infallibility.

<u>Vatican II (1962-1965)</u> was a pastoral council that sought "renewal, modernization, and ecumenism." Vatican II also reasserted the faith of 2000 years of Catholicism.

Christ has always been with his Church and will always be with her for all eternity (Mt. 28:20). "You are Peter and upon you I will build my Church and the gates of hell shall not prevail against it" (Mt. 16:18f).

Why is there so much confusion in belief among Protestants?

Confusion in belief is the necessary consequence of having no apostolic successors--that is, authentic bishops--to resort to in determining questions of faith and morals. When we examine the main Protestant denominations we see that within each denomination, whether we are dealing with Baptists, Methodists, Presbyterians, etc., there are divergent beliefs, often radically divergent beliefs. This has led, unavoidably, to fundamentalism, the strict literal interpretation of the Scriptures.

Since the Scriptures can be interpreted in so many different ways, and since Protestantism does not have an infallible teaching office to determine correct interpretations, one is left with resorting to a narrow, literalistic interpretation of the Scriptures. This is the only way to assure a clear interpretation of the Gospel message, so it seems. But in reality, even among the strictest of fundamentalist, divergent beliefs abound.

Protestantism, although not conscious of it at the time of the Reformation, was doomed to failure from the start when it rejected the authority of the successors of the apostles.

Luther, the first Protestant, during a moment of depression, recognized the damage that he had begun when he saw denominations popping up in every place. During a moment of self-reflection, he wrote:

> *Who called you to do things such as no man ever before? You are not called.... Are you infallible?.... See how much evil arises from your doctrine.... Are you alone wise and are all others mistaken? Is it likely that so many centuries are wrong?.... It will not be well with you when you die. Go back, go back; submit, submit* (Grisar Hartman, *Luther*, St. Louis: Herder Book Co., 1914, II, 79; V, 319ff).

III
SACRAMENTS

Are sacraments just symbols?

For the Catholic sacraments are efficacious. That is, they produce what they signify. A sacrament imparts grace to the individual (Acts 2:38; 8:17; 19:4-7; 1 Pet. 3:19-22).

The seven sacraments of the Church are foreshadowed in a powerful manner in the Hebrew Scriptures, in the Old Testament signs and symbols of the covenant--circumcision, anointing, consecration, the laying on of hands, sacrifice, Passover. These signs of the Old Covenant foreshadow the signs of the New Covenant—Baptism, Confirmation, Holy Orders, Eucharist, Penance, Anointing of the Sick and Matrimony. Each of the sacraments of the "new covenant," of the New Testament, can find similarities in the Old Covenant, Old Testament, in signs and symbols--baptism replacing circumcision, anointing of the sick replacing the ancient anointings, consecrating or ordaining priests by the laying on of hands replacing the consecration of kings and Levitical priests, the institution of the Eucharist as presence and sacrifice replacing the Old Testament sacrifices of lambs and the Passover experience.

What do Catholics mean by being "born again" (Jn. 3:3-5) and why do they baptize children?

> *Baptism is God's most beautiful and magnificent gift.... We call it gift, grace, anointing, enlightenment, garment of immortality, bath of rebirth, seal, and most precious gift. It is called gift because it is conferred on those who bring nothing of their own; grace since it is given even to the guilty; Baptism because sin is buried in the water; anointing for it is priestly and royal as are those who are anointed; enlightenment because it radiates light; clothing since it veils our shame; bath because it washes; and seal as it is our guard and the sign of God's Lordship.*
>
> Augustine of Hippo, Letter to Jerome
> (*Oratio* 40, 3-4: PG 36, 361C)

In the Old Testament, the reality of baptism is beautifully prefigured in Ezekiel 36:25-27:

> *I will sprinkle clean water upon you to cleanse you from all your impurities, and from all your idols I will cleanse you. I will give you a new heart and place a new spirit within you, taking from your bodies your stony hearts. I will put my spirit within you and make you live by my statutes, careful to observe my decrees.*

59

In 1 Peter 3:20-21 we read:

[Eight persons, in the account of Noah's flood] were saved through water. This prefigured baptism, which saves you now.

Jesus taught Nicodemus that one must be born again by *water* and the *Spirit* (Jn. 3:5), not by the Spirit *only*, but by *water* and the *Spirit*.

Most fundamentalists view baptism as merely a symbol which signifies something that has already taken place. That is, one becomes "born-again" by accepting Jesus as one's Lord and Savior (Jn. 3:16), and then one is baptized to symbolically affirm what has already taken place. Baptism, for evangelicals, therefore implies the use of reason. Consequently, children under the age of reason cannot make such a reasoned decision. Children should not be baptized according to their view.

Besides the idea of infant baptism being contrary to their theology, fundamentalists argue that there is no proof of infant baptism in the Bible and since there is no proof of infant baptism in the Bible, it is not a Christian practice.

For the Catholic to be baptized is what it means to be "born again." Baptism is a sacrament with real power and it is a sacrament which is necessary for salvation, for it is by baptism that we are "born again" of water and the Spirit (Jn. 3:5; Mk. 16:16). God "saved us through the bath of rebirth and renewal by the holy Spirit, whom he richly poured out on us through Jesus Christ our Savior, that we might be justified by his grace and become heirs in hope of eternal life" (Titus 3:5-7). In baptism one enters into Christ's death and resurrection (cf. Rom. 6:3-4). One has put on Christ in baptism (Gal. 3:27). Baptism cleanses one from "original sin," personal sin, and the punishment for sin (Mk.16:16; Jn. 3:5; Acts 2:38f; 22:16; Rom. 6:3-6; Gal. 3:7; 1 Cor. 6:11; Eph. 5:26; Col. 2:12-14; Heb. 10:22).

Psalm 51:7 states: "In guilt was I born, and in sin my mother conceived me." One becomes a new creation in Christ and a partaker in the divine nature (2 Pet. 1:4). One becomes a member of the Church as an adopted child of God (cf. 1 Cor. 12-13; 27). One becomes a Temple of the Holy Spirit (Acts 2:38; 19:5f) with an indelible mark or character on the soul which enables one to share in the priesthood of Christ and in his passion (Mk. 10:38f; Lk. 12:50).

Because of this reality, infants are encouraged to be baptized. As Irenaeus explains in *Against Heresies* (cf. 2, 22, 4) (ca. 180): "Jesus came to save all for all are reborn through him in baptism—infants, children, youths, and old men." To deny a child baptism is to deny a child the precious gifts of baptism. How contrary to God's will (Mt: 19:14; Lk. 18:15-17): Let the children come to me, sayeth the Lord." As Augustine of Hippo (ca. 415) so poignantly states in his *Letter to Jerome* (166, 7, 21):

Anyone who would say that even infants who pass from this life

without the participation in the Sacrament [whether by a baptism
of desire, blood, or water] shall be made alive in Christ truly goes
counter to the preaching of the apostles and condemns the whole
Church, where there is great haste in baptizing infants because it
is believed without doubt that there is no other way at all in which
they can be made alive in Christ.

St. Hippolytus of Rome (ca. 215) argues: "Baptize first the children; and if they can speak for themselves, let them do so. Otherwise, let their parents or other relatives speak for them" (*Apostolic Tradition*, 21). The ecclesiastical writer Origen in 244 AD wrote: "The Church received from the apostles the tradition of giving baptism to infants" (*Commentary on Romans*, 5:9).

In terms of Bible quotations with reference to infants in particular, I would refer you to the following quotes: Acts 16:15, 33 and 1 Corinthians. 1:16. In these quotations we see that whole families were baptized. Given the culture of the ancient world, this most likely implied the baptism of infants. How can whole households not have any infants, any children?

In the Acts 2:38-39 we read a direct account of where Peter baptized adults and children: "Peter said to them, 'Repent, and be baptized every one of you in the name of Jesus Christ for the forgiveness of your sins; and you shall receive the gift of the Holy Spirit. For the promise is to you and to your ***children*** and to all that are far off, every one whom the Lord our God calls to him…. (RSV)."

Many argue that one must be old enough to accept the faith: No one, not even your parents, can stand in for you. This might sound appealing but it is contrary to the Scriptures. God often bestowed spiritual gifts on peoples because of the faith of others. The centurion's faith brought about the healing of his servant (Mt. 8:5-13); the Canaanite's woman's faith brought about the healing of her daughter (Mt. 15:21-28); and in Luke 5:17-26 a crippled man is healed by the persistent faith of his friends. A parent's faith bestows the gifts of baptism upon their children.

Furthermore, Paul in Colossians 2:11-12 reminds us that baptism replaces circumcision for the Christian. In the Old Covenant, the Old Testament, one became a member of the people of God through circumcision on the eighth day. Now in the New Covenant, the New Testament, one becomes a member of the people of God through baptism as early as possible! For the Christian baptism is a replacement for circumcision (Col. 2:11-12). If Jewish parents would covenant with God on behalf of their eight-day old children through the command to circumcise their children, then Christian parents covenant with God on behalf of their children through the command to baptize. How could people deny children entrance into the covenant, into the people of God? As Jesus said: "Let the children come to me for the Kingdom of God belongs to such as these" (cf. Mk. 10:14; Lk. 18:15).

And as alluded to above, the fact that "whole households" were baptized in the New Covenant makes absolute sense since "whole households" were circumcised in the Old Covenant (Gen. 17:12-14), including house-born slaves and "foreigners acquired with money." Children were circumcised under the Old Covenant, and under the New Covenant they were baptized.

In Judaism a child had no say as to whether he was circumcised or not! On the eighth day he became a part of the people of God by virtue of the will of his parents and the act of circumcision. The same applies with the baptism of children! And just as in the Old Testament, when one reached the age of reason and could reject the gift received as an infant, one could likewise, in New Testament times, reject the gift of baptism. The gift is given to be affirmed or rejected, to be nourished or to be allowed to die.

The following quotes are also worth noting when understood within the context of all the previous quotes from this section on infant baptism (Mt. 18:14; 19:13f; Mk. 10:13-16; Lk. 18:15; 17). To deny infant baptism is to thwart Jesus' call to the children when he said, "Let the children come to me. The Kingdom of God is for such as these" (Mt. 19:14).

Hermas, often referred to as the man named by Paul in Romans 16:14, writes in *The Shepherd, Parable 9*: "One cannot enter the kingdom of God without coming up through the water of baptism so that one may attain life.... The person goes down into the water dead, and then comes up alive." In the *Epistle of Barnabas* (11; 16) (ca. 96), the Barnabas often referred to as the companion of the apostle Paul by men such as Clement of Alexandria, Eusebius, and Jerome, we read: "In baptism we receive the forgiveness of our sins, and trusting in the name of the Lord, we become a new creation.... God truly dwells in our house, in us."

Given these early teachings and the teachings of the Bible, why do so many reject the efficaciousness of baptism and the baptism of infants?

In the ancient *Jerusalem Catechesis* we find a precious synthesis on the beauty of baptism:

> *As our Savior spent three days and three nights in the depths of the earth, so your first rising from the water represented the first day and your first immersion represented the first night. At night a man cannot see but in the day he walks in the light. So when you were immersed in the water it was like night for you and you could not see, but when you rose again it was like coming into broad daylight. In the same instant you died and were born again; the saving water was both your tomb and your mother.... Let no one imagine that baptism consists only in the forgiveness of sins and in the grace of adoption. Our baptism is not like the baptism of John, which conferred only the forgiveness of sins. We know perfectly well that baptism, besides washing away our sins and bringing us the gift of the Holy Spirit, is...[an entrance into] the sufferings of Christ. That is why Paul exclaims: 'Do you not know that when we were baptized into Christ Jesus we were, by that very action, sharing in his death?' By baptism we went with him into the tomb (Cat. 21,*

Mystagogica 3, 1-3: PG 33, 1087-1091 quoted from *The Liturgy of the Hours*).

- The Anabaptists, the forerunners of the Baptist, denied infant baptism in the sixteenth century. It is significant that in an unusual moment of unity among the Protestant denominations the Anabaptists were condemned as denying a long held practice of Christianity.

Baptism by blood and desire for adults and infants
The scriptures and the tradition of the Church refer to three forms of baptism for salvation. One is the one that we are all familiar with where Jesus sends all his disciples throughout the world to baptize in the name of the Father, and of the Son, and of the Holy Spirit (Mt. 28:19-20).

The other two forms are referred to as baptism by blood and baptism by desire. The Church has always maintained that those who suffer death for the sake of the faith before having been baptized are baptized by their blood, by their death in, for, and with Christ. The fruits of the sacrament of baptism are given to the person even though they did not receive the sacrament. Similarly, those who die before being baptized and yet desired baptism in their lifetime likewise receive the fruits of the sacrament without receiving the sacrament itself.   Those who are moved by graced and may not be explicit Christians are equally considered as having a baptism by desire. And children who die before baptism are baptized by the desire of the parents or the mystical body, the Church.

The Scriptures point to the salvation of the Holy Innocents by Herod (cf. Mt. 2:16-18): The infants that were massacred died for Christ and therefore can be considered to have been baptized by their blood. On the cross of Calvary, the good thief, Dismas, called for mercy and received God's forgiveness and salvation. He certainly could not come down off the cross to be saved in a water baptism. He was saved and baptized by his desire (Lk. 23:42-43).

(For a more detail understanding of the baptism of desire and the baptism of blood and its relationship to grace, go to the section referring to the salvation of 'non-explicit Christians.'').

Does baptism require immersion?
From ancient times baptism took place by a triple immersion in water with the use of the Trinitarian formula (i.e., I baptize you in the name of the Father, and of the Son, and of the Holy Spirit). But the early Church also recognized as valid the pouring of water over the head of a person with the same use of the Trinitarian formula. The *Didache* (ca. 65), often attributed to the apostles, states:

Regarding baptism, baptize this way: Baptize in the name of the

Father, and of the Son, and of the Holy Spirit in running water. But if you have no running water, baptize in any other. [In that case] pour [water] three times on the head in the name of the Father, and of the Son, and of the Holy Spirit (*Didache*, 7, trans. Francis Glimm in *The Fathers of the Church: A New Translation*, Washington: The Catholic University Press, 1962).

The early Church theologians such as Justin Martyr (ca. 148-155), Tertullian (ca. 206), and Hippolytus (ca. 215) emphasized that baptism could be done by immersion, infusion, or aspersion.

- The *Didache* is one of the oldest existing Christian documents, predating many of the New Testament writings. It is believed to have been written by the twelve apostles as a guide for Gentile Christians in terms of Church law and order. Some scholars, however, like to place the writing of the *Didache* shortly after the death of the last apostle John (ca. 100) at around 120 AD. In either case, the *Didache* was considered by men like Hermas, Irenaeus, Origen, Clement of Alexandria, Eusebius, Cyprian, Lactantius, and many others as part of Sacred Scripture. The *Jerusalem Codex* of the New Testament contains the *Didache* within it. Again, it is the pope and the bishops in union with him that excluded the *Didache* from the final canon in the fourth century.

Baptism of the dead?
Mormons like to quote 1 Corinthians 15:29 to affirm the practice of baptizing the unbaptized dead. This is a practice that is approximately 150 years old and is the invention of the founder of Mormonism, Joseph Smith. It is not mentioned in the writings of the early Church--not even once. And the Scriptural reference to Corinthians is never affirmed by the apostles in the Scriptures or anywhere else. Ironically, even the *Book of Mormon*, which supposedly contains the fullness of the Gospel, does not mention it!

The baptism of the dead has never been practiced by informed and orthodox Christians. Mormons are the first to make it a practice. The Scriptures are clear that one acquires one's salvation or ends up being condemned during this lifetime, not in the afterlife.

But how do we explain 1 Corinthians 15:29? Paul was making what is philosophically called an *Ad Hominem* argument for the resurrection of the body.

Just north of Corinth there was a city named Eleusis. Pagans in that city adopted the practice of baptizing themselves for the dead. Homer, a Greek pagan, alludes to this practice in his *Hymn to Demeter*. In other pagan cities people practiced the baptism of corpses. Being a large bustling port city, it would not be unthinkable that some Corinthian Christians would have incorporated into their practice—erroneously--the Eleusian observance of baptizing themselves for the dead.

Influenced by Greek culture, the Corinthians viewed the soul as somehow trapped within the body. The materialism of the world was somewhat unappealing to Greek sentiments. The Corinthian Christians therefore found the resurrection of the body as somewhat unattractive or unbelievable. The logic was flawed: They baptized themselves for the dead, yet did not believe in the resurrection of the body!

Paul takes advantage of this pagan practice of baptizing oneself for the dead—which was adopted by this group of Corinthian Christians--by arguing for the resurrection of the body. Paul basically argues that it is absurd to baptize oneself for the dead if one does not believe in the bodily resurrection.

Paul's whole theology of baptism makes it quite clear that Paul would never have approved of this practice. Paul was simply using this practice to his advantage.

Baptism is necessary for salvation, and so one can see why the Mormons would want to baptize the dead. However, salvation or condemnation takes place in this earthly journey, not in the afterlife. Hell is eternal (Mt. 25:41; 2 Thess. 1:6-9) as is heaven (Mt. 5:8; 25, 33-40; Rom. 8:17; Phil. 4:3; Heb. 12:23; Rev. 3:5; Mt. 5:12; Jn. 12:26; 14:3; 17:24; 1 Cor. 13:12, etc.). Why then would one baptize the dead? For what reason?

Even the book of Mormon, ironically, seems to contradict the belief in the baptism of the dead (i.e., Alma 34:31-35; 5:28, 31; 2 Nephi 9:38; Mosiah 16:5, 11; 26:25-27). Only in this life can one gain or lose one's salvation!

Because one can interpret the Scriptures in a legion of ways, one is subject to error. That is why there are over 33,000 mainline Protestant denominations and 150,000 pseudo-Christian denominations. That is why the Church that put the Bible together is the only one that can interpret it properly and infallibly--and who put the Bible together? The Catholic Church!

Where do we find the Sacrament of Confirmation?

> *After coming from the place of baptism we are thoroughly anointed with a blessed unction. After this, the hand is imposed for a blessing, invoking and inviting the Holy Spirit. The unction runs on the body and profits us spiritually, in the same way that baptism is itself a corporal act by which we are plunged into water, while its effect is spiritual, in that we are freed from sins....*
>
> *Tertullian (ca. 200)*
> *Baptism (7, 1, 2, 5; 8, 1)*

Confirmation perfects baptismal grace. Notice that in Acts 19:5-7

Paul "lays his hands" on the recently baptized invoking the Holy Spirit, thereby confirming them. Likewise, in Acts 8:14-17 Peter and John "lay their hands" on the converts of Samaria, for as the Bible says: "the Spirit had not come upon any of them; they had only been baptized in the name of the Lord Jesus" (Acts 8:16). Peter and John were confirming, perfecting, what had begun at baptism in the converts of Samaria.

Once confirmed we are strengthened by the Holy Spirit to be powerful witnesses of Christ's self-communicating love to the world. We become strengthened members in the mission of the Church, the proclamation of the Gospel. Like baptism, a sacred mark or seal is imprinted on the soul, forever changing it (cf. 2 Cor. 1:21-22; Eph. 1:13). In Acts 1:6-8 we see how, despite being baptized previously, the apostles received the gift of the Holy Spirit to be witnesses to the world.

In receiving this sacrament by a bishop or a delegated priest, one is making a commitment to profess the faith and to serve the world in word and deed as a disciple of Christ (Acts 19:5-6; 8:16-17; Heb. 6:1-2; 2 Cor. 1:21-22; Eph. 1:13).

Cyril of Jerusalem (350 AD) beautifully summarizes the power and the necessity of the Sacrament of Confirmation:

And to you in like manner, after you had come up from the pool of the sacred streams, there was given chrism, and this is the Holy Spirit (21 [3] 1). But beware of supposing that this is ordinary ointment. For just as the bread of the Eucharist after the invocation of the Holy Spirit is no longer simple bread, but the Body of Christ, so also this holy ointment is no longer plain ointment, nor, so to speak, common, after the invocation. Rather, it is the gracious gift of Christ; and it is made fit for the imparting of his godhead by the coming of the Holy Spirit. This ointment is applied to your forehead and to your other senses; and while your body is anointed with the visible ointment, your soul is sanctified by the Holy and life-creating Spirit (21 [3] 3). Just as Christ, after his baptism and the coming upon him of the Holy Spirit went forth and defeated the adversary, so also with you; after holy baptism and the mystical chrism of the [Sacrament of Confirmation] and the putting on of the panoply of the Holy Spirit, you are able to withstand the power of the adversary and defeat him by saying, 'I am able to do all things in Christ who strengthens me (21 [3] 4) (Mystagogic).

Why do Catholics believe the Eucharist is the Body and Blood of Jesus?

If the words of Elijah had power even to bring down fire from heaven, will not the words of Christ have power to change the

66

natures of the elements [of bread and wine into the body and blood of Jesus]?

...The Lord Jesus himself declares: This is my body. Before the blessing contained in these words a different thing is named [bread]; after the consecration a body is indicated. He himself speaks of his blood. Before the consecration something else is spoken of [wine]; after the consecration blood is designated.

Ambrose (397d), On the Mysteries
(Cf. Nm. 52-54, 58: SC 25 bis, 186-188. 190)

Jesus came to us in Bethlehem, which means "house of bread," and was placed in a "manger" which is an eating vessel. Today Jesus is present in the tabernacle, those houses where the bread of eternal life, the body, blood, soul and divinity of Christ is present throughout the world. He is given to us in a manger, an eating vessel, the chalice and the paten at every Mass. From the very moment of his incarnation, his entrance into the world, the Son of God was pointing to his wonderful gift of the Eucharist!

Belief in the Eucharist as the Body and Blood of Christ has declined in recent years. This is the sad consequence of the growth of secularism, modernism, and fundamentalism.

Despite this, the Scriptures and Tradition affirm the Catholic position on the Eucharist. Let us examine a powerful passage from the Bible that supports the Catholic view:

The Jews...disputed among themselves, saying, "How can this man give us his flesh to eat?" So Jesus said to them, "Truly, truly, I say to you, unless you eat the flesh of the Son of man and drink his blood, you have no life in you; he who eats my flesh and drinks my blood has eternal life, and I will raise him up at the last day. For my flesh is food indeed and my blood is drink indeed. He who eats my flesh and drinks my blood abides in me, and I in him. As the living Father sent me, and I live because of the Father, so he who eats me will live because of me. This is the bread that came down from heaven, not such as the fathers ate and died; he who eats this bread will live forever.... Many of his disciples, when they heard it, said, "This is a hard saying; who can listen to it?" ...After this many of his disciples drew back and no longer went about with him (Jn. 6:52-58; 60; 66, RSV; also make reference to the following passages: Mt. 26:26-28; Mk. 14:22-24; Lk. 22:19f; 1 Cor. 10:16; 11:24f; 27; 29).

How can anyone deny the Real Presence? John's Gospel emphasizes not just the "body," but the "flesh" of Christ that one is called to partake in. Furthermore, when one looks at the word that John uses for "eat," the word that John uses is not the classical Greek word for eat, rather it is--during this particular time in history--a vulgar term used to describe animals eating. The best translation today would probably be "munch" or "gnaw." Obviously John is emphasizing the reality of the Body and Blood of Christ.

Some like to emphasize the fact that Jesus called himself a door (Jn. 10:9), a vine (Jn. 15:1), a lamb (Jn. 1:29), a light (Jn. 8:12), living water (Jn. 4:14), etc. They would claim that Jesus was clearly being symbolic here. They would argue consequently that Jesus in referring to the Eucharist as his Body and Blood was doing no different than calling himself living water.

While it is true there is a symbolic dimension to calling Jesus the Bread of Life, the early Christians, however, understood that Jesus was referring to that which transcended the simply symbolic. Jesus was talking about his Real Presence in the Eucharist, his real Body and Blood.

When we look to history, we recognize that Christians were often sent to their deaths by the Romans under the accusation of being cannibals—as testified to by the 1st century pagan historian Tacitus in his *Annals*. Where would they get such a thought unless the Real Presence was not obviously and fervently believed? (What Tacitus did not realize is that Catholics eat the Risen Christ! Cannibals eat dead flesh).

No one went to his or her death for proclaiming Jesus as a door, a vine, a lamb, or symbolic bread. No one went to his or her death in the amphitheater for worshiping a door or living water. The early Church always distinguished that which was symbolic from that which was to be taken literally. Acts 10:39 describes Jesus as being hung on a tree; all Christians knew he had been crucified on a cross; all Christians knew that Paul was using symbolic language.

It is also interesting to read that after Jesus' discourse on the Bread of Life, many of the disciples abandoned him. *Why would they abandon him if all they thought was that Jesus was using symbolic language?* Why run away if all that is being talked about is a symbol?

The disciples knew that Jesus was not simply talking symbolically. That is why they ran away! Genesis 9:3-4 and Leviticus 17:14 strongly forbade the eating or drinking of blood. The disciples abandoned Jesus because they knew of these quotes from the Old Testament and they knew that Jesus was talking literally.

The disciples never abandoned Jesus for being the "door," the "vine," the "lamb," or "the Son of God." They never abandoned Jesus when he said he was the way, the truth, and the life, and that no one goes to God the Father except through him (Jn. 14:6). Nor did they abandon him for forgiving sins, which only God can do! But they certainly ran away when they heard Jesus describe his Real Presence in the Eucharist.

Whenever in the Scriptures there was confusion among his disciples, Jesus corrected the misunderstanding and explained to them the true meaning of what he meant (see Jn. 3:3-5; Jn. 11:11-14; Mt. 19:24-26; Jn. 8:21-23; Jn. 8:31-36; Jn. 6:32-35). And when Jesus wanted his words to be taken literally he repeated and reaffirmed what he said (see Mt. 9:2-6; Jn.

8:56-59; Jn. 6:41-51).

Jesus, in this Eucharistic passage, not only does not explain away what he says, he re-enforces the literal meaning of what he is saying by repeating it over and over again. In fact, Jesus repeats six times in six verses the same literal truth (Jn. 6:53-58). Jesus wants to make the point perfectly clear. Notice, that Jesus does not run after the departing disciples and say, "Wait a minute, you misunderstood what I said! I was only talking symbolically!" Rather, he turned to the remaining disciples and said, "Are you going to leave me too" (Jn. 6:67)?

Now some like to point to verse 64 where we read, "It is the spirit that gives life, while the flesh is of no avail." They claim this proves that Jesus was only talking symbolically since flesh is worthless.

This argument makes no philosophical sense. What do they make Jesus out to be? Would Jesus at one moment be saying "eat my flesh" and then in the next moment be saying, "but my flesh is no good?" That would simply be absurd!

John 6:64 must be understood as John 3:6 is understood; that is, only by a gift of God can one truly comprehend and believe in what Jesus has said. Only by a gift from above, the gift of the Spirit, can one believe in the Real Presence of Christ in the Eucharist, for "no one can come to [Jesus] unless it is granted him by my Father" (Jn. 6:65).

Now one may argue, "How can Jesus be present in different ways?" That should be easy to answer for all Christians. Christ is present in the individual, in the congregation, in the minister, in the proclamation of the Word and so on. So too, Christ is sacramentally present in the Eucharist.

Let us examine one more powerful passage:

[A]nyone who eats the bread and drinks the cup of the Lord unworthily is answerable for the body and blood of the Lord. Everyone is to examine himself and only then eat of the bread or drink from the cup, because a person who eats and drinks without recognizing the body is eating and drinking his own condemnation (1 Cor.11:27-29, NJB).

Can a symbol bring one's own condemnation? Paul gets right to the point. We are dealing with the Real Presence of Christ in the Eucharist under the appearance, or what is technically called the "species," of bread and wine.

Let us now look at one who walked and talked and learned from the apostles themselves. What did he believe about the Eucharist? Would you believe the word of a person who lived in the sixteenth century who had no personal contact with an apostle or would you prefer the word of one who was taught by an apostle? I suspect that we would all prefer the testimony of a person that learned his Christianity from one of the apostles.

Ignatius of Antioch (ca. 107), the disciple of John and friend of

Peter and Paul, writing only seven years after the death of the apostle John, reprimands the Docetists in his letter to the *Smyrneans* (6:7) for failing to believe in Christ's Real Presence in the Eucharist:

> *For let nobody be under any delusion; there is judgment in store for the hosts of heaven, even the very angels in glory, the visible and invisible powers themselves, if they have no faith in the blood of Christ. Let him who can, absorb this truth.... But look at the men who have those perverted notions about the grace of Jesus Christ which has come down to us, and see how contrary to the mind of God they are. They even absent themselves from the Eucharist and from prayer because they do not confess that the Eucharist is the flesh of our Savior Jesus Christ....*

In another passage, Ignatius reminds us that there is only one authentic Eucharist:

> *Be careful...to use one Eucharist, for there is one flesh of our Lord Jesus Christ, and one cup for union with his blood, one altar, as there is one bishop with the presbytery [priesthood] and the deacons my fellow servants, in order that whatever you do you may do it according to God* (*Philadelphia*, 4, trans. Lake).

In another passage to the Romans, Ignatius writes:

> *I have no taste for corruptible food nor for the pleasure of this life. I desire the Bread of God, which is the Flesh of Jesus Christ, who was of the seed of David; and for drink I desire His Blood, which is love incorruptible (Romans, 7:3, Jurgens).*

Ignatius of Antioch is a giant in Christendom. His words were recognized as truth, for they came from the mouth of a disciple of the apostles John, Peter, and Paul.

Irenaeus, the friend of Polycarp, who in turn was the friend of the apostle John wrote:

> *Jesus declared the cup, a part of creation, to be His own Blood, from which He causes our blood to flow; and the bread, a part of creation, He has established as His own Body, from which He gives increase to our bodies (Against Heresies 5, 2, 2).*

Justin Martyr, well-known by the disciples of the apostle John, wrote:

> *We call this food Eucharist...since Jesus Christ our Savior was made incarnate by the word of God and had both flesh and blood for our salvation, so too, as we have been taught, the food which*

70

*has been made into the Eucharist by the Eucharistic prayer set
down by Him, and by the change of which our blood and flesh is
nourished, is both the flesh and the blood of that incarnated Jesus.*

Justin further goes on to say:

*None is allowed to share in the Eucharist unless he believes the
things which we teach are true...for we do not receive the
Eucharist as ordinary bread and ordinary wine, but as Jesus
Christ our Savior.*

Cyril of Jerusalem, another man acquainted with the disciples of
John, wrote:

*[Jesus] himself...having declared and said of the Bread, "This is
My Body," who will dare any longer to doubt? And when He
Himself has affirmed and said, "This is my Blood," who can ever
hesitate and say it is not His Blood" (Catechetical Lectures 22,
Mystagogic 4).*

*Do not, therefore, regard the bread and wine as simply that, for
they are, according to the Master's declaration, the Body and
Blood of Christ. Even though the senses suggest to you the other,
let faith make you firm. Do not judge in this matter by taste, but be
fully assured by faith, not doubting that you have been deemed
worthy of the Body and Blood of Christ (Ibid.).*

The Real Presence of Christ in the Eucharist has always been held.
No one seriously or significantly questioned the Real Presence of Christ
until the eleventh century with the writings of Berengarius of Tours.
Would God allow eleven centuries to go by with a false belief? If he
said he would be with the Church for all eternity (Mt. 16:18; 28:20),
then he would not lead it into error.

How sad it must be for those who do not receive the real Eucharist
for it is, as Ignatius says in *Ephesians* 20, "the medicine of immortality,
the antidote that we shall not die, but live forever in Jesus Christ."

Before we move on to the nature of the Mass whereby bread and
wine become the Body and Blood of Christ under the appearance or
"species" of bread and wine, I would like to leave you with a reflection
on a very significant passage from the Scriptures, Luke 24:13-35. After
the resurrection, Jesus in his glorified body joins two discouraged
disciples on the way to Emmaus. Because of Jesus' glorified body, the
disciples do not recognize Jesus until significantly "the breaking of the
bread." Notice the similarity between Jesus' words at the Last Supper
(Lk. 22:19) and his words in Luke 24:30-31: "[W]hile he was with them
at table, he took bread, said a blessing [this implies a change], broke it,

and gave it to them. With that their eyes were opened and they recognized him, but he vanished from their sight." Jesus vanished from their sight, but his presence was recognized in the "breaking of the bread." To the disciples, Jesus was "made known in the breaking of the bread" (Lk. 24:35).

Today, in every Catholic Church, Jesus is made known to us in the "breaking of the bread," in his body and blood, in his Real Presence under the "species" of bread and wine. And let us not take this gift lightly. For as Origen (ca. 185-253) states in his homily on Exodus:

> *You are accustomed to take part in the divine mysteries, so you know how, when you have received the Body of the Lord, you reverently exercise every care lest a particle of it fall, and lest anything of the consecrated gift perish. You account yourself guilty, and rightly so, if any of it be lost through negligence (13, 3).*

By the Word of God Jesus became "flesh and blood" in the Incarnation. Likewise, by the Word of God—Jesus--bread and wine become "flesh and blood."

It is ironic that those who say they accept the Bible literally do not do so in the discourses on the Eucharist! Why? Because they know, consciously or subconsciously, that without apostolic succession they have no power to do what Christ wanted them to do!

But why do we still call the Body and Blood of Christ "bread" and "wine"? The answer is simple: After the consecration the appearances or accidents of bread and wine remain, but the reality, the substance, is the sacramental Body, Blood, Soul, and Divinity of the resurrected Christ. Also, the "bread" of Christ reminds us of his presence in other ways (i.e., in the Scriptures, the will of God, the minister, the person, the sacraments, etc.).

Let us finish with the words of the founder of Protestantism, Martin Luther (1517 AD). Even the founder of Protestantism had to admit to the historical truths of the Catholic Church's belief:

> *[Of] all the fathers, as many as you can name, **not one** has ever spoken about the sacrament as these fanatic [Protestants] do. None of the [early Christian writers] use such an expression as, 'It is simply bread and wine,' or 'Christ's body and blood are not present.' Yet [the subject of the Eucharist] is so frequently discussed by [the early Christian writers], it is impossible that they should not at some time have let slip such an expression as 'It is simply bread,' or 'Not that the body of Christ is physically present,' or the like, since they are greatly concerned not to mislead the people; actually, they simply proceed to speak as if no one doubted that Christ's body and blood are present. Certainly among so many fathers and so many writings a negative argument should have turned up at least once, as happens in other articles [of the faith];*

but actually they all stand uniformly and consistently on the affirmative side' (Luther's Works, St. Louis: Concordia Publishing, 1961, vol. 37, 54).

Even Luther could not deny history!

It would have been wise for the Protestants to have taken the advice of the former Protestant, John Cardinal Henry Newman: "The Christianity of history is not Protestantism.... To be deep in history is to cease to be a Protestant."

Why do Catholics have a Mass?

Catholics have a Mass because Jesus instituted the Mass and the early Church always had a Mass. Let us look at an example from Luke's Gospel:

When the hour came, he took his place at table with the apostles. He said to them, "I have eagerly desired to eat this Passover with you before I suffer, for, I tell you, I shall not eat it [again] until there is fulfillment in the kingdom of God." Then he took a cup, gave thanks and said, "Take this and share it among yourselves; for I tell you [that] from this time on I shall not drink of the fruit of the vine until the kingdom of God comes." Then he took the bread, said the blessing, broke it, and gave it to them, saying, "This is my body, which will be given for you; do this in memory of me." And likewise the cup is the new covenant in my blood, which will be shed for you (Lk. 22:14-20).

When we look at history, the Mass is a well-established reality for Christians. At first Christians celebrated Mass in their homes and with time they moved into public worship spaces, but the fundamental structure always remained the same.

It is astonishing to see in the year 150 AD, just 50 years after the death of the last apostle John, the existence in the Church of a set Mass structure that had to have been in place from the time of the apostles.

Justin Martyr, known by the friends of the apostles, wrote to the emperor Antononinus Pius in 150 about the long-standing practice of Christian worship in order to calm the anger and fear of the emperor in regard to the practices of the Christians.

Let us look at his description of the Mass in his letter:

On the day we call the day of the sun, all who dwell in the city or country gather in the same place, for it is on this day that the Savior Jesus Christ rose from the dead [In the early Church, according to Pliny, the Roman Governor of Pontus, in his Letters to the Emperor Trajan (ca. 111-113 AD,) the Christian faithful would often sing a "hymn to Christ as God" as they began their celebration of the

"Lord's Supper."]

The memoirs of the apostles and the writings of the prophets are read, as much as time permits.

When the reader has finished, he who presides over those gathered admonishes and challenges them to imitate these beautiful things.

Then we all rise together and offer prayers* for ourselves...and for all others, wherever they may be, so that we may be found righteous by our life and actions, and faithful to the commandments, so as to obtain eternal salvation.

When the prayers are concluded we exchange the kiss.

The faithful, if they wish, may make a contribution and they themselves decide the amount. The collection is placed in the custody of the one who presides over the celebration to be used for the orphans, widows, and for any who are in need or distress.

Then someone brings bread and a cup of water and wine mixed together to him who presides over the brethren.

He takes them and offers praise and glory to the Father of the universe, through the name of the Son and of the Holy Spirit and for a considerable time he gives thanks (in Greek: eucharistian) that we have been judged worthy of these gifts.

When he has concluded the prayers and thanksgiving, all present give voice to an acclamation by saying: "Amen."

When he who presides has given thanks and the people have responded, those whom we call deacons give to those present the "eucharisted" bread, wine, and water and take them to those who are absent (Apol. 1, 65-67; PG 6, 428-429).

In explaining the mystery indicated by the word "eucharisted," Justin states in his *First Apology* (65):

We call this food Eucharist...since Jesus Christ our Savior was made incarnate by the word of God and had both flesh and blood for our salvation, so too, as we have been taught, the food which has been made into the Eucharist by the Eucharistic prayer set down by Him, and by the change of which our blood and flesh is nourished, is both the flesh and the blood of that incarnated Jesus.

Justin further goes on to say:

None is allowed to share in the Eucharist unless he believes the things which we teach are true...for we do not receive the Eucharist as ordinary bread and ordinary wine, but as Jesus Christ our Savior.

It is a wonder to me how anyone could be anything but Catholic! What you would have experienced in the year 150 and earlier is exactly what you experience today in any Catholic Church!

Is the Mass a true sacrifice?

> *For I received from the Lord what I also handed on to you, that the Lord Jesus, on the night he was handed over, took bread, and, after he had given thanks, broke it and said, "This is my body that is for you. Do this in remembrance of me." In the same way he took the cup, and after supper, said, "This cup is the new covenant in my blood. Do this, as often as you drink it, in remembrance of me." For as often as you eat this bread and drink this cup, **you proclaim the death of the Lord** until he comes (1 Cor. 11:23-26).*

The expressions "This is my body, this is my blood" are taken from the Jewish language and theology of Temple sacrifice. For Jesus, these expressions designate himself as the *true and ultimate sacrifice.*

In the Old Testament, the Hebrew Scriptures, sacrifices of lambs, bulls, goats, and other animals were offered in the temple for the forgiveness of sins. Today, this sacrifice takes place in the mystery of the Mass, the bloodless sacrifice of the Lamb of God, Jesus Christ, at the altar of every Church, the New Temple of God. (It is no coincidence that John's Gospel has Jesus die at the exact time that the Jewish Temple sacrifices are taking place. It is Jesus who is the true Lamb, the true sacrifice. Jesus is the true Lamb who takes away the sins of the people).

The bloodless sacrifice of the Mass has traditionally been seen to have been prefigured in Genesis 14:18; 22:13, foretold in Malachi 1:10f, and attested to in 1 Corinthians 10:16, 18-21; 11:23-26 and Hebrews 13:10.

When the Jews were preparing for the Passover into the Promised Land, they offered up a paschal lamb and afterwards consumed the lamb, the victim, for strength for the journey (Ex. 12:1-20). This prefigures the Eucharistic sacrifice where Jesus, the Lamb of God, is offered up for our sins and then eaten sacramentally for the spiritual nourishment necessary for the journey into the Promised Land of Heaven.

The Mass is a *re-presenting*, or making present of what took place once and for all at Calvary (Heb. 7:27; 9:12, 25-28; 10:10-14). Just as the Passover meal made present to those who participated in it the Exodus events, the Mass in a fuller way makes present what happened at Calvary. As Gregory of Nyssa (ca. 383) in his Sermon on the Resurrection (4) explains:

> *Jesus offered himself for us, Victim and Sacrifice, and Priest as well, and 'Lamb of God, who takes away the sin of the world.' When did he do this? When he made his own Body food and his own*

Blood drink for his disciples; for this much is clear enough to anyone, that a sheep cannot be eaten by a man unless its being eaten be preceded by its being slaughtered. This giving of his own Body to his disciples for eating clearly indicates that the sacrifice of the Lamb has now been completed.

At every Mass Calvary is made present to us. Mass is a participation in that one and only sacrifice of Jesus on the cross at Calvary (cf. Heb. 7:27).

Our sin will not be small if we eject from the episcopate those who blamelessly...offered its Sacrifices (Clement, 4, trans. Jurgens). *.[W]e ought to do in order all things which the Master commanded us to perform at appointed times. He commanded us to celebrate sacrifices and services....at fixed times and hours* (Ibid., 40, trans. Lake).

Clement of Rome (ca. 80)

The Council of Trent would affirm, in opposition to the Protestant Reformation, the belief of the early Church regarding the sacrificial nature of the Mass.

*[Christ] our Lord and God, was once and for all to offer himself to God the Father by his death on the altar of the cross, to accomplish for them an everlasting redemption. But, because his priesthood was not to end with his death (cf. Heb. 7:24, 27) , at the Last Supper, "on the night when he was betrayed" (1 Cor. 11:23), in order to leave to his beloved Spouse the Church a visible sacrifice (as the nature of man demands)"by which the bloody sacrifice which he was once and for all to accomplish on the cross would be re-presented, its memory perpetuated until the end of the world and its salutary power applied for the forgiveness of the sin which we daily commit"; declaring himself constituted "a priest for ever after the order of Melchizedek" (Ps. 110(109)4), He offered his body and blood under the species of bread and wine to God the Father, and, under the same signs...gave them to partake of to the disciples (whom he then established as priests of the New Covenant), and ordered them and their successors in the priesthood to offer, saying: "Do this as a memorial of Me," etc., (Lk. 22:19; 1 Cor. 11:24), as the Catholic Church has always understood and taught.
[After Christ] celebrated the old Pasch, which the multitude of the children of Israel offered...to celebrate the memory of the departure from Egypt (cf. Ex. 12:1f), Christ instituted a new Pasch, namely himself to be offered by the Church through her priests under visible signs in order to celebrate the memory of his passage*

from this world to the Father when by the shedding of his blood he redeemed us, "delivered us from the dominion of darkness and transferred us to His Kingdom" (cf. Col. 1:13).

This is the clean oblation which cannot be defiled by any unworthiness or malice on the part of those who offer it, and which the Lord foretold through Malachi would be offered in all places as a clean oblation to his name (cf. Mal. 1:11). The apostle Paul also refers clearly to it when, writing to the Corinthians, he says that those who have been defiled by partaking of the table of devils cannot be partakers of the table of the Lord. By "table" he understands "altar" in both cases (cf. 1 Cor. 10:21). Finally, this is the oblation which was prefigured by various types of sacrifices under the regime of nature and of the law (cf. Gen. 4:4; 8:20; 12:8; Ex. passim). For it includes all the good that was signified by those former sacrifices; it is their fulfillment and perfection.... (J. Neuner and J. Dupuis, eds. The Christian Faith: Doctrinal Documents of the Catholic Church, New York: Alba House, 1990), ND 1546-1547).

It is no coincidence that the Eucharist as the Body and Blood of Christ as well as Jesus' sacrifice and death on the cross were considered foolishness to many and a stumbling block to others (cf. Jn. 6:60; 1 Cor. 1:23). To believe in the Eucharist and in the death and resurrection of Jesus can only occur through a gift from God (cf. Jn. 6:65).

- The Greek for "Do this in memory of me" (Luke 22:19), *Touto poieite tan eman anamnasin*, can also be translated as "Offer this as a memorial offering." The *Didache* often applies the Greek word *thusia*, or sacrifice when referring to the Eucharist.

Why do we celebrate the Lord's Day on a Sunday?

The Seventh Day Adventists are the ones who most often condemn Catholics and Protestants of various denominations for celebrating the Sabbath on Sunday. They argue that this is a violation of Exodus 20:8-11 where the Sabbath is designated as Saturday. They also point out that Christ went to worship on the Sabbath on Saturday (Lk. 4:16; Lk. 23:56). Hence, if Christ worshiped on the Sabbath, on Saturday, we are called to do the same.

As Catholics we respond by reminding them that the Sabbath, the "Lord's Day," was eventually moved in the early Church by the apostle Peter to Sunday because Jesus Christ rose on a Sunday (Rev. 1:10; Acts 20:7).

In the *Didache*, also known as *The Teachings of the Twelve Apostles*, (9) we read:

On Sunday, the Lord's Day, break bread and give your Eucharistic thanks....

The Bible also commands the obligatory sacrifice of animals (Gn. 4:4; Lv. 1:14), the following of dietary Kosher practices (cf. Deut. 12:15-28; 14:3-21) and circumcision (Gn. 17:10; Lk. 2:21). Jesus was circumcised and he offered sacrifices in the Temple. Yet I don't see Seventh Day Adventists sacrificing animals, or for that matter, following all the Levitical laws that Jesus would have observed!

Jesus is the "Lord of the Sabbath" (Mt. 12:8) and he entrusted his authority over the Sabbath and other things to his Church, his Body (cf. Mt. 10:40; 16:19; 18:18-20; Lk. 10:16). Furthermore, Jesus reminds us that the Spirit will guide us on how and when to pray (cf. Rom. 8:26-27).

Just as Peter was empowered to change the dietary laws (cf. Acts 10:9-33), and just as Peter, James and the rest of the apostles were empowered to eliminate the demand for circumcision for converts (cf. Acts 15:1-35) the Church, the Body and Bride of Christ (1 Cor. 12:12f; 2 Cor. 11:2; Rom. 12:5; Eph. 1:22f; 5:25; Rev. 19:7), was empowered to change the day for the Sabbath.

The early Church recognized that the true Sabbath was now to be celebrated in Christ and it was to be held on Sunday, the Lord's Resurrection Day. Sunday came to be understood as the *first* day and the *eighth* day, the eighth day signifying perfection.

Why do we need priests to forgive serious sins?

Father, I have sinned against heaven and against you (Lk. 15:21).

You are to confess your sins in the Church. This is the way of life.
                                        Didache 4, 12, 14 (ca. 65)

Serious sin, or what we call mortal/ deadly sin (1 Jn. 5:17) requires the authority of the priest as an authoritative, power-filled representative of God and of the community. When we look at the Scriptures (Mt. 18:18; 16:19; Jn. 20:21-23) it becomes obvious that God entrusted his apostles with the gift of forgiving sins. In the words of the apostle John:

Jesus said to [the apostles], "Peace be with you. As the Father has sent me, even so I send you." And when he had said this, he breathed on them, and said to them, "Receive the Holy Spirit. If you forgive the sins of any, they are forgiven; if you retain the sins of any, they are retained (Jn. 20:21-23, RSV).

Notice that Jesus didn't say "Now go out into the world and tell people to confess their sins directly to God and he will forgive everyone's sins." Rather he said, "If **you** forgive the sins of any, they are forgiven; if **you** retain the sins of any, they are retained." Jesus empowered the apostles to forgive sins in his name! (Notice Jesus "breathed" on the apostles. Throughout the Scriptures the breath of God is associated with new life and God's creative work. The breathing on the apostles made them priests, the first bishops, and made them able to forgive sins *in persona Christi capitas*. And by forgiving sins they were making those forgiven into "new creations" in Christ.)

Pacian of Barcelona (392 AD) notes the necessity of priests for the forgiveness of sins in his *Sermon on Penance*:

> *Certainly God never threatens the repentant; rather, he pardons the penitent. You will say that it is God alone who can do this. True enough; but it is likewise true that he does it though his priests, who exercise his power. What else can it mean when he says to his apostles: 'Whatever you shall bind on earth shall be bound in heaven; and whatever you shall loose on earth shall be loosed in heaven?' Why should he say this if he were not permitting men to bind and loose? And he clearly was not permitting this to the apostles alone? Were that the case, he would likewise be permitting them alone to baptize, them alone to confer the Holy Spirit in confirmation, them alone to cleanse the pagans of their sins; for all of these things are commissioned not to others but to the apostles. But if the loosing of bonds and the power of the Sacrament is given to anyone in that place, either the whole is passed on to us priests from the form and power of the apostles, or nothing of it can be imparted to us priests by whatever decrees. If, then, the power both of baptism and confirmation, greater by far than charisms, is passed on to bishops and priests by apostolic succession, so too is the right of binding and loosing (1, 6).*

Jesus has an important reason for giving us the Sacrament of Penance. When we sin we harm our relationship with God, the community, and we do damage to ourselves (cf. Lk. 15:21). That is because when we sin we break the commandments that God placed side by side, the love of God and the love of neighbor as ourselves (Mt. 22:37-40). For example, if one steals one dulls one's conscience, hurts the person whose property was stolen, and breaks God's seventh commandment.

Since sin damages our relationship with God, our relationship with ourselves, and our relationship with others, it needs to be healed in all three dimensions.

The priest—as a member of the human race--therefore is a representative of God and of the community and he brings Christ's healing and the community's healing, as the Body of Christ, to the sinner. That is why God chose the apostles, the first bishops, the first priests, to forgive sins.

When Jesus said to Peter, "Whoever sins you bind shall be bound, and whoever sins you loose shall be loosed" (cf. Mt. 16:18f), he was saying-- within the Judaic and Hebrew understanding of the terms "bound" and "loose"--whoever you exclude from your communion will be excluded from communion with God and whoever you receive into your communion God will welcome back into his. Reconciliation with God is inseparable from reconciliation with the Church (cf. 1 Cor. 12:12f; Rom. 12:5; Eph. 1:22f; 1 Cor. 3:9, 10, 16; 1 Thess. 1:4; 1 Tim. 3:5, 15) (CCC 1445).

Christ forgives sins by means of priests in the Sacrament of Penance because God gave that authority to the apostles and their successors (Mt. 18:18; 16:19; Jn. 20:21-23). Paul reminds the faithful that he has been entrusted with the "ministry of reconciliation" (2 Cor. 5:18-20); James reminds us, within the context of the Sacrament of Anointing, that the presbyter, the priest, administers Christ's forgiveness (Jms. 5:14-16).

God knew that a human person acting in the Person of Christ the Head, *in persona Christi capitas*, or as Another Christ, *alter Christus* (cf. Mt. 10:40; Lk. 10:16; Lk. 25:47), could bring the only true healing that people need to have. People need to hear from someone they are forgiven. I don't know how many times a person has broken down crying after having his or her sins forgiven after a priest has given the gift of Christ's absolution. The sense of being created anew is miraculous for that person.

Studies in the past, when Catholics practiced going to Confession on a weekly or monthly basis, noted that Catholics had the lowest rate of psychological disorders in America. It is interesting to cite that in this modern era where Catholics have abandoned the frequent use of the Sacrament of Penance the rate of psychological disorders by American Catholics has increased to match that of the rest of the American population.

Ignatius of Antioch (ca. 107), the disciple of the apostle John, recognized the importance and absolute necessity of confession to a priest when he said: "The Lord...forgives all who repent, if their repentance leads to the unity of God and the council of the bishop" (*Philadelphia*, 8, trans. Lake). In Cyprian of Carthage's *Letter to the Clergy* (ca. 250) [cf. 16 (9), 2] he writes: "Sinners may come to confession and, through the imposition of hands by the bishop and priests, may receive re-admittance into the life of the Church." And in his letter to *The Lapsed* (ca. 351) (28) Cyprian writes: "I beseech you, brethren, let everyone who has sinned confess his sin while he is still in this world, while his confession is still admissible, while satisfaction and remission made through the priests are pleasing before the Lord."

The Sacrament of Penance is a healing sacrament. Why do we confess to priests our mortal sins? Because Christ commanded it!

The spiritual effects of the Sacrament of Penance are beautifully summarized in the *Catechism of the Catholic Church* (1496):

-reconciliation with God by which the penitent recovers grace;

-reconciliation with the Church;
-remission of the eternal punishment incurred by mortal sins;
-remission, at least in part, of temporal punishments resulting from
sin;
-peace and serenity of conscience, and spiritual consolation;
-an increase of spiritual strength for the Christian battle.

Theodore of Mopsuestia (ca. 428) reminds us of the above. He reminds us that the priest is a father (as in 1 Cor. 4:14-15; 1 Tim. 1:2; Tit. 1:4; Philem. 10; 1 Thess. 2:1) who takes care of his children, a spiritual doctor who brings healing to souls:

If we commit a great sin against the commandments we must first induce our conscience with all our power to make haste and repent of our sins as is proper, and not permit ourselves any other medicine. This is the medicine for sins, established by God and delivered to the priests of the Church, who make diligent use of it in healing the affliction of men. You are aware of these things, as also of the fact that God, because he greatly cares for us, gave us penitence and showed us the medicine of repentance; and he established some men, those who are priests, as physicians of sins. If in this world we receive through them healing and forgiveness of sins, we shall be delivered from the judgment that is to come. It behooves us, therefore, to draw near to the priests in great confidence and to reveal to them our sins; and those priests, with all diligence, solicitude, and love, and in accord with the regulations mentioned above, will grant healing to sinners. The priests will not disclose the things that ought not to be disclosed; rather, they will be silent about the things that have happened, as befits true and loving fathers who are bound to guard the shame of their children while striving to heal their bodies... (Catechetical Homilies, 16).

The Church has always, from the beginning of its existence, had confession of sins to priests.

- The priest acts in the Person of Christ the Head, in the second person of the Trinity, in the place of God, for only God can forgive sins (cf. Mk. 2:7). It is Christ, God, forgiving sins through the priest.

What does it mean to be excommunicated?

The Catholic Catechism describes excommunication in the following manner in section 1463:

Certain particularly grave sins incur excommunication, the most severe ecclesiastical penalty, which impedes the reception of the sacraments and the exercise of certain ecclesiastical acts, and for which absolution consequently cannot be granted, according to canon law [canon 1331], except by the pope, the bishop of the place or priests authorized from them.

One can be excommunicated by means of an ecclesiastical trial or proceeding. One can also--due to the extreme severity of an offense--be excommunicated automatically. The procurement of an abortion is such an example of where an automatic excommunication takes place at the moment of the action.

From first appearances, the idea of being excommunicated may seem quite frightening, and it should. But the real purpose of excommunicating an individual or an individual excommunicating himself or herself is to call that person to repentance. Excommunication is a call to come back home into the fold of Christ and his Body, the Church. Excommunication is the Church's way of warning people about their eternal destiny. It is a way of warning people of the consequences of their actions.

When one recognizes one's wrongful act or acts, and repents, one may have his or her sentence of excommunication lifted by a pope, a bishop, or a priest with the proper authorization.

Examples of excommunication in the Scriptures can be found in 1 Corinthians 5:3-5, 9-13, in 2 Thessalonians 3:6,14, in 1 Timothy 1:20 and in Titus 3:10f. Protecting the souls of the faithful is at the heart of excommunication. Paul reminds the Corinthians to "purge the evil from [their] midst" (5:13) and to "deliver [the unrepentant evil] to Satan for the destruction of [their] flesh" (5:5). In his second letter to the Thessalonians the community is reminded to "shun any brother who conducts himself in a disorderly way and not according to the tradition they received from us" (3:6), and "if anyone does not obey our word...take note of this person so as not to associate with him" (3:14). In 1 Timothy we read how Hymenaeus and Alexander have been "handed over to Satan to be taught not to blaspheme" (20). And in Titus 3:10f we read: "After a first and second warning, break off contact with a heretic, realizing that such a person is perverted and sinful and stands self-condemned" (11).

Excommunication is the Church's way of warning people about their eternal destiny. It is a way of warning people of the consequences of their actions.

Why Indulgences?

The *Catholic Encyclopedia* describes indulgences in the following manner:

> *Remission of the temporal punishments for sins, and therefore the giving of satisfaction owed God for one's sin. Indulgences are granted either after the sacrament of Penance or by perfect contrition. Indulgences are either plenary (when all punishments are remitted) or partial (when only part of that punishment is remitted). Plenary indulgences demand that one be free of all venial sin, but partial indulgences do not require this.*
>
> *Partial indulgences remit that amount of temporal punishment that would be remitted in the ancient Church by performances for the designated period of time. Indulgences can only be gained for oneself or for those in purgatory, but not for other living human beings. Indulgences are derived from the treasure of merits of the saints, from Christ Himself or from His Mother (Catholic Encyclopedia, ed. Peter M. J. Stravinskas, Huntington: Our Sunday Visitor, Inc., 1991, 509).*

The problem with indulgences, prior to the Protestant Reformation, was not so much a problem dealing with the belief as much as a problem dealing with the abuse of the use of indulgences. Sinners often paid professional penitents to expiate their temporal punishments; some priests sold indulgences without pointing out the requirements that were associated with indulgences; and some priests sold indulgences to raise money to build churches. The right motives and the right understanding of the role of indulgences were not present in these abuses.

When Pius V refused to grant any indulgences that had to do with any form of monetary transactions, the abuses eventually disappeared.

Today indulgences have returned to the intended purpose, a gift from the "Treasury of the Church."

As members of the Church we make up the Body of Christ, with Christ as the Head. Because of this reality we share in the life of the whole Church, the Church on earth, in purgatory, and in heaven. As one Body we profit from the prayer and good works of others. As Paul mentions in Romans 12:4-8:

> *Just as each of us has various parts in one body, and the parts do not all have the same function: in the same way, all of us, though there are so many of, make up one body in Christ, and as different parts we are all joined to one another. Then since the gifts that we have differ according to the grace that was given to each of us: if it is a gift of prophecy, we should prophesy as much as our faith tells us; if it is a gift of practical service, let us devote ourselves to serving; if it is teaching, to teaching; if it is encouraging, to encouraging (NJB).*

This sense of interconnectedness in prayer, works, and gifts is also described beautifully by Ambrose (ca. 340) in his *Treatise on Cain*:

You are told to pray especially for the people, that is, for the whole body, for all its members, the family of your mother the Church; the badge of membership in this body is love for each other. If you pray only for yourself, you pray for yourself alone. If each one prays for himself, he receives less from God's goodness than the one who prays on behalf of others. But as it is, because each prays for all, all are in fact praying for each one. To conclude, if you pray only for yourself, you will be praying, as we said, for yourself alone. But if you pray for all, all will pray for you, for you are included in all. In this way there is a great recompense; through the prayers of each individual, the intercession of the whole people is gained for each individual. There is here no pride, but an increase in humility and a richer harvest from prayer (Cf. *Lib.* 1, 9, 34, 38-39: CSEL 32, 369. 371-372).

We are all indispensable to one another in our prayers and gifts. What one is lacking another has an extra amount of, and vice versa.

Now let us look at Colossians 1:24 where Paul states,

I rejoice in my sufferings for your sake, and in my flesh I am filling up what is lacking in the afflictions of Christ on behalf of his body, which is the church....

Paul is suffering for the Body, the Church. This is an allusion to how the debt for sin can be made up by another.

And when we look to the above citations with reference to 1 John 2:2 (where Jesus expiates sins) we recognize, by the merits of Christ, the Church, his Body, his Bride (cf. Mk. 2:19; Lk. 5:34), we have an inexhaustible fund for the payment or satisfaction of sins.

Likewise, all the saints, and particularly the greatest saint of all, Mary, by their prayers and works and sufferings have built up a reservoir of prayers and works for others, a reservoir of satisfaction. Again as Paul reminds us: *"I rejoice in my sufferings for your sake, and in my flesh I am filling up what is lacking in the afflictions of Christ on behalf of his body, which is the church..."* (Colossians 1:24). Christians have been blessed by their savior in sharing in his redemptive work!

When we take these Scriptural principles together we come up with the Church's understanding of indulgences, and why the Church has always recognized the reality of indulgences.

Jesus expiates sins (1 Jn. 2:2) and therefore his body, the Church, which is inseparable from it head, also expiates sins (Rom. 12:4-8)--for one cannot decapitate the head from the body. When we put these two quotes together with Paul's insight in Colossians 1:24 that states that we make up in our sufferings "what is lacking in the afflictions of Christ on behalf of the body, which is his Church," then we can see how the Church can possess a spiritual reservoir of satisfaction for the good of others. For nothing spiritual is ever wasted; It always finds a home!

Christ forgives sins. When one's sins are forgiven the guilt is completely washed away, completely forgiven and forgotten. Yet divine justice demands that the injury that results from sin be repaired. If one has murdered a person and repents and seeks God's forgiveness, God shall bring that forgiveness, in this particular case, through the Sacrament of Penance.

While Christ thus forgives the person of all his or her guilt, the world is injured by the loss of a person whose contributions to the world have been lost. I think in particular of an account told by a woman regarding the confession of the sin of abortion to Padre Pio, the great Stigmatist and saint. Padre Pio conferred God's forgiveness upon her, but he reminded her that the world had lost in that aborted child a future pope. The sin is forgiven, but the damage from the sin lingers on.

It is this lingering damage that needs to be paid off. The greater the damage, the greater the payment. In the Sacrament of Penance the eternal punishment for grave sin is forgiven, but the temporal punishment still awaits payment—sometimes the penance imposed by the priest suffices at other times more is required.

In the case of very holy people, the penance expiates or pays off the temporal punishment, the lingering damage. In the case of less holy individuals, the penance pays part of the payment for the lingering damage. Again, the sin is forgiven, heaven is guaranteed, but if one has not paid the whole debt off in this life, one pays it off in purgatory.

For he is purged as if by certain works of the whole people, and is washed in the tears of the multitude; by the prayers and tears of the multitude he is redeemed from sin, and is cleansed in the inner man. For Christ granted to His Church that one should be redeemed through all, just as His Church was found worthy of the coming of the Lord Jesus so that all might be redeemed through one (1, 15, 80).

Ambrose of Milan (ca. 333)

This sense of temporal or lingering punishment that needs to be cleansed, even after God's forgiveness, is seen in 2 Samuel 12:14f. David is completely forgiven by God, but still pays a price for his sin. Nathan said, "The Lord on his part has forgiven your sin.... But since you have utterly spurned the Lord by this deed, the child born to you must surely die." This is an extreme case of temporal punishment, but it is one that makes the point.

Let us recognize the giftedness of our prayers, works, and sufferings for the good of ourselves or those loved ones in purgatory. The next time we have a difficult day at work, or feel ill, let us offer it up for the good of our soul and/or the good of the souls in purgatory.

Is there a Sacrament of Holy Orders?

Let the bishop be ordained after he has been chosen. When someone pleasing to all has been named, let the people assemble on the Lord's Day with the presbyters and with such bishops as may be present. All giving assent, the bishops shall impose hands on him, and the presbytery shall stand in silence (2). When the presbyter is to be ordained, the bishop shall impose his hand upon his head while the presbyters touch the one to be ordained....(8). When a deacon is to be ordained the bishop alone shall lay his hands upon him (9).

Hippolytus of Rome (ca. 200)

The Sacrament of Holy Orders is an indispensable part of the Church. Without it the Church could not trace itself back to apostolic times, and therefore back to Christ.

As in Old Testament times (cf. Ex. 19:6; Num. 18:1-7), the Church makes a distinction between the common priesthood of all the faithful (1 Pet. 2:9) and the ordained priesthood. The Levitical priesthood would be replaced by Jesus by his own priesthood and his own priests. Through the providential mystery of God the ancient temple where sacrifices were performed by the Levitical priests was destroyed in 70 AD by the Romans, never to be rebuilt! Thus the new priests would be the priests of the New Covenant, the priests according to the order of Melchizedek, priests who act in the person of Jesus Christ himself.

All Christians are called to be a priestly people, a healing, loving, forgiving people, but some of the faithful were specifically set aside by Jesus and the apostles for unique ministerial roles.

The priesthood conferred by the Sacrament of Holy Orders is one that is specifically designated for teaching, leading worship, and meeting the pastoral needs of the people. Holy Orders confer an indelible spiritual mark on the soul.

The most important of the Holy Orders is that of the bishop because he serves as the visible head of the local or particular church (cf. 1 Tim. 3:1-7; Titus 1:7). Every bishop in the world can trace himself from one bishop to another bishop to another bishop all the way back in time to an apostle. Consequently, they have the fullness of the priesthood and are crucial in protecting the true faith. The greatest of the bishops is of course the pope, since he is the successor of the leader of the apostles, Peter.

The next order is the order of presbyter or what we commonly call the priest (cf. 1 Timothy 5:17f). He is a "prudent-coworker" and extension of the bishop. He receives his authority from the bishop, and teaches in power because of his tie to the tree of apostolic succession.

The final order is that of the deacon who likewise is attached to the bishop, but who is entrusted primarily with works of charity (cf. Acts 6:1-7; 1 Timothy 3:8-13).

Holy Orders were instituted by Christ (Lk. 22:19; Jn. 20:22f), conferred by the imposition of hands by an apostle or his successor (Acts 6:6; 13:3; 14:23), and give grace (1 Tim. 4:14; 2 Tim.1:6-7).

Clement of Rome, the friend of the apostle Peter, eloquently teaches us about the gift of the priesthood.

> *The apostles preached to us the Gospel received from Jesus Christ, and Jesus Christ was God's Ambassador. Christ, in other words, comes with a message from God, and the apostles with a message from Christ. Both these orderly arrangements, therefore, originate from the will of God. And so, after receiving their instructions and being fully assured through the Resurrection of our Lord Jesus Christ, as well as confirmed in faith by the word of God, they went forth, equipped with the fullness of the Holy Spirit, to preach the good news that the Kingdom of God was close at hand. From land to land, accordingly, and from city to city they preached, and from among their earliest converts appointed men whom they had tested by the Spirit to act as bishops and deacons for future believers. And this was no innovation, for, a long time before the Scriptures had spoken about bishops and deacons, for somewhere it says: I will establish overseers in observance of the law and their ministers in fidelity* (Clement of Rome, *Epistle to the Corinthians*, 42, quoted in *The Companion to the Catechism*, San Francisco: Ignatius Press, 376).

In chapter 44 we read:

> *Our apostles, too, were given to understand by our Lord Jesus Christ that the office of the bishop would give rise to intrigues. For this reason, equipped as they were with perfect foreknowledge, they appointed the men mentioned before, and afterwards laid down a rule once for all to this effect: when these men die, other approved men shall succeed to their sacred ministry.... Happy the presbyters [priests] who have before now completed life's journey and taken their departure in mature age and laden with fruit* (*Epistle to the Corinthians*, 44, quoted in *Companion*, 377)!

In chapter 40 of Clement's letter we see the distinction between the priesthood of all believers and the ordained priesthood:

...[T]o the priests a proper place is appointed, and...[the] layman is bound by the ordinances of the laity (*Epistle to the Corinthians*, 40, trans. Jurgens).

This is likewise seen in the second century *Dascalia Apostolorum*:

In your holy churches, your assemblies, arrange places for the brethren carefully and with all sobriety. Let a place be reserved for the presbyters [priests] in the midst of the eastern part of the house, and let the throne of the bishop be placed among them; let the presbyters [priests] sit with him; but also at the other eastern side of the house let the laymen sit; for thus it is required that the presbyters [priests] should sit at the eastern side of the house with the bishops, and afterwards the laymen, and then the women. When we pray the bishop and presbyters should stand first, followed by the laymen and women (2;8;9).

Ignatius of Antioch, the disciple of the apostle John, reaffirms Clement and the *Dascalia* with the following statement:

Every man who belongs to God and Jesus Christ stands by his bishop.... (Philadelphia, 3, trans. Jurgens). Follow your bishop, every one of you, as obediently as Jesus Christ followed the Father. Obey your clergy [priests] too, as you would the apostles; give your deacons the same reverence that you would to a command from God. Make sure that no step affecting the church is ever taken by anyone without the bishop's sanction. The sole Eucharist you should consider valid is one that is celebrated by the bishop himself, or by some person [presbyter/priest] authorized by him. Where the bishop is to be seen, there let all his people be; just as wherever Jesus Christ is present, we have the catholic Church.... This is the way to make certain of the soundness and validity of anything you do.... (Smyrnaeans, 8). Let the bishop preside in the place of God, and his clergy [presbyters/priests] in the place of the apostolic conclave, and let my special friends the deacons be entrusted with the service of Jesus Christ.... (Magnesians, 6). Without these three orders no church has any right to the name (Trallians, 3).

The gift of the priesthood is exactly that, a magnificent gift of God's love for his people.

St. Francis of Assisi once gave an account of what he would do if he was approached by an angel on one side and the most evil priest to have ever existed on the other. He asked his confreres which one would they give respect to, the angel or the evil priest? They all responded by saying, *"Obviously the angel. We would want nothing to do with the evil priest!"* Francis responded by saying that he would give respect to the most evil priest first, for the priest could do what the angel could not. The priest can bring Jesus to him in the Eucharist, Jesus' Body, Blood, Soul, and Divinity. The priest can make Calvary present! The angels cannot. The priest can forgive his sins, the angels cannot! The disciples of Francis now understood the great gift of the priesthood.

Why celibate priests?

Often people argue that it is unfair that priests cannot marry. Some even go so far as to say that an unmarried priesthood is evil and contrary to God's will, for Genesis reminds us to "be fruitful and multiply."

Why do Catholics of the Roman rite have unmarried priests?

God's providence has for many reasons shown the beauty and dignity of a celibate priesthood. From a practical point of view (a view we often want to overlook for various reasons, including discomfort) if we had married priests we would as a community have to provide support for the homes and the families of these married priests. That means health insurance and a pension plan for the wife and kids. It means college tuition for the children when they grow up. If the individual parish communities had to pay for all priests that were married, the Church would suffer greatly from a financial point of view. In fact it would be disastrous. How many poor people would go without food? How many people that are served by all aspects of Catholic charitable organizations would suffer because of money being directed toward the families of priests as opposed to others? Given this, you can just imagine the strain the Church would be placed in—particularly when you take into account the fact that Catholics are notorious for not tithing.

A second reason that points to the impracticality of a married priesthood can be found in those members of other denominations that have converted to the Catholic faith and have received permission from Rome to become priests in the Roman Church while keeping their families together. Many such wives of these married priests mention that they can see how much time is taken away from the parish community by their husbands' family responsibilities. After all, a husband has an obligation to his wife and children. That is his primary vocation (cf. 1 Cor. 7:32-35).

An unmarried priest is freed from such an obligation and therefore is free to serve the people at all times, including at three o'clock in the morning when an emergency call comes in.

A fourth point is that the priest is, in the words of Pope St. John Paul II, a "sign of contradiction" in a world drenched in promiscuity. It reminds the faithful that the gift of sex is precious. It is a gift to be experienced in a bonding, unitive way, with an openness to life, and with a respect to the natural order.

Finally, the most important reason for a celibate priesthood comes from

Christ himself. Let us remember that Jesus was not married, and that a priest acts in "the person of Christ the Head," as "another Christ" (cf. Mt. 18:18-19; 2 Cor. 5:18-20).

Jesus sees celibacy as a gift for the sake of the kingdom of God (Mt. 19:12): *"Some are incapable of marriage because they were born so; some, because they were made so by others; some, because they have renounced marriage for the sake of the kingdom of heaven. Whoever can accept this ought to accept it."*

We see the gift of celibacy and the blessedness of celibacy in Paul's writings in the Scriptures as well. Paul himself was celibate (cf. 1 Cor. 7:8). Let us reflect on 1 Corinthians 7:32-35:

I should like you to be free of anxieties. An unmarried man is anxious about the things of the Lord, how he may please the Lord. But a married man is anxious about the things of the world, how he may please his wife, and he is divided.

Virginity and celibacy are also commended in 1 Corinthians 7:8-9, 36-40, and 1 Timothy 5:9-12. In Revelation 14:3-4 the 144,000 saved (a symbolic number) are described as virgins. And in Matthew 22:30-32 and Mark 12: 25-27 we are reminded that those in "heaven neither marry nor are given in marriage." The priest, as a sign of contradiction, is a reminder of what our ultimate future in heaven will be like.

Given what has been said, the Church does recognize that celibacy is a discipline and not a doctrine of the faith. That is why many Catholics from the Eastern rites of the Church are married—the marriage taking place prior to ordination.

The Roman rite has chosen to keep the practice of celibacy. While it is true that many of the early popes and bishops were married, and in fact most of the apostles were married, with the exception of Paul and John, the Church has always seen two currents of priestly life, one which incorporated celibacy into the priesthood, and one which incorporated marriage into the priestly life. Both are currents that have existed from the beginning, and both are precious to the Church. Ignatius of Antioch (ca. 107) reminds his clergy in his letter to Polycarp (5): "If anyone can live in a celibate state for the honor of the Lord's flesh, let him do so without ever boasting." Tertullian (ca. 200) in *The Demurrer Against the Heretics* (40, 5) states that the Lord has "virgins and celibates" in his service.

Why "Father"?

Why do we call priests "Fathers"? The Bible says that we are to call no man "Father" (Mt. 23:9). Are Catholics being disobedient to God by calling their priests "Father" and are priests promoting this disobedience by allowing themselves to be called "Father"?

A priest is referred to as "Father" because the early apostles referred to themselves as "Fathers." When we look at Paul's First Letter to the

90

Corinthians (1 Cor. 4:15-17) and John's Epistle (1 Jn. 2:12f) we see that these two apostles perceive and name themselves as "Fathers." Right in the Bible we have two apostles referring to themselves as "Fathers." As the apostle Paul states: "I became your father in Christ Jesus through the gospel" (1 Cor. 4:15). And in 1 Corinthians 17 the apostle Paul refers to his friend Timothy as his "beloved and faithful son in the Lord."

Paul never shied away from referring to others and himself as a father. In Acts 22:1 Paul addresses the Jerusalem Jews as "brothers and fathers." In Romans 4:16-17 Paul calls Abraham "the father of us all." In 1 Thessalonians 2:11 Paul reminds the Thessalonians that he has "treated each one as a father treats his children," and in 1 Timothy 1:2 and Titus 1:4 he calls Timothy, "my true child in faith and Titus "my true child in our common faith." In Paul's letter to Philemon 1:10 he encourages the community to accept Onesimus when he states: "I urge you on behalf of my child Onesimus, whose father I have become in my imprisonment, who was once useless to you and me but is now useful to both you and me."

In Acts 6:14 and 7:2 Stephen, the first martyr of the Church, calls the Jewish leaders "fathers." And in Hebrews 12:7-9 we are reminded that we have earthly "fathers" to discipline us.

Are we dealing with a contradiction? No. Jesus in Matthew 23:9 is pointing out that we have one ultimate Father, one ultimate source of being and teaching. God is the ultimate Father. He is also pointing out that the title "Father" can be abused when the person who bears the title does not bear it worthily.

Paul and John are not pointing to the same understanding of "Father" as is seen in Matthew's Gospel. They are primarily pointing to a spiritual fatherhood in the sense of spiritual guides who proclaim the Gospel by their lives and works.

Christ placed Paul, John and all the apostles as spiritual guides to the ultimate Father, God. In turn, all those with authentic authority may bear the name of 'Father" as understood by Paul and John. Thus, priests, by means of the gift of Holy Orders, serve as spiritual guides for their communities. They serve as spiritual "Fathers."

Jesus himself uses the term "father" in Matthew (15:4-5; 19:5, 19, 29; 21:31), John (8:56) and several other places. Jesus actually has Lazarus using the address "father Abraham" twice (Lk. 16:24, 30). In Acts 7:38-39, Acts 7:44-45, and Acts 7:51-53 "father Abraham"—as mentioned before--is attested to as our father in faith.

Ironically, Matthew 23:9 also mentions that we are not to call anyone "teacher." Yet ministers often call themselves "doctor" which is Latin for "teacher."

Anti-Catholics, in an effort to avoid the name "father," will often address priests by the title "Sir." This is ironic since Jesus is never referred to as "father" but many times as "Sir."

91

Why do Catholics not allow women priests?

The issue of women priests is not really a matter of allowing or not allowing women to be admitted to the priesthood as much as it is a call to be obedient to the deposit of faith. Christ, his apostles, and all their successors, never ordained women to the priesthood. Two thousand years of Sacred Tradition cannot be wrong.

Some may argue that Jesus and his apostles were living in a paternalistic society and therefore were caught up in the culture of their time which viewed women less than kindly.

The reality is, however, that although Christ was influenced by his culture as a man, he was not bound nor controlled by his culture. After all, Jesus was and is the Son of God. He walked the earth as God and man, as fully divine, fully human—knowing all that was necessary for our salvation in faith and morals. Such a mystery cannot be bound to culture.

Jesus' very life illustrates this. He associated with sinners and had a great many faithful women followers. In one of the Gospels the resurrected Jesus appears to the women first! Furthermore, with the exception of John, it was the women who stood at the foot of the cross; the other apostles fled.

The ordination of women is an issue of faith, and as mentioned above, Jesus, despite growing in wisdom and understanding (cf. Lk. 2:52), knew all that was necessary for our salvation (CCC 474; cf. Mk. 8:31; 9:31; 10:33f; 14:18-20, 26-30), and priests are necessary for our salvation (cf. Acts 6:6; 13:3; 14:22; 20:28; Lk. 22:19; 1 Tim. 4:14; 2 Tim. 1:6; Tit. 1:5). Therefore, a belief must have, either in an implicit or explicit manner, indications of existence in the deposit of the faith. Yet, neither the Scriptures nor Sacred Tradition affirm implicitly or explicitly the right to ordain women to the priesthood.

Jesus never chose any women to be apostles or their successors. (There are no lines of women successions.) In many ways he chose the least qualified to be his apostles. If qualifications were important, he would have chosen the greatest creature of all time, the Blessed Mother, to serve as an apostle. Yet he didn't choose her to be an apostle.

Women have been granted many gifts. The Church could not go on without them. In virtually all Catholic parishes and Catholic schools, the vast majority of the staff is made up of women. The vast majority of ministries are led by women. The Catholic hospitals and Catholic schools were built on the hard labor and sacrifice of thousands of religious nuns. The greatest Catholic television network, EWTN, is produced and operated by religious sisters. There are over 5,000 canonized women saints! Catholicism in this country and in all countries owes a great deal to the response of women to the gifts of the Spirit.

Yet in God's divine plan, just as men have not been given the gift of childbirth, so women have not been given the gift of Holy Orders. Just as some men are given the gift of living a married life, some men are given a gift of living a priestly life. We could go on and on. The point is that we all have a part to play in God's divine plan, in Christ's Body, the Church.

Some women may argue that they feel "called" to the priesthood by God. The feeling of being called does not mean that one is authentically called. I "felt" called to the priesthood, but it was not until that call was confirmed as authentic by the "laying on of the hands" by a bishop that I knew for certain that in God's providential will I was to serve his people as a priest.

The priest is a man of the Church. The priest is, as what has been previously mentioned, "another Christ" or a person who "acts in the Person of Christ the Head" (cf. Mt. 18:18-19; 2 Cor. 5:18-20). Jesus was a man, and so to best fulfill this imagery of acting in his place he chose men.

Men and woman are equal, yet God has chosen them to serve his Church in different and indispensable ways. The following quotes from the Scriptures might be helpful in determining the Church's constant Tradition and understanding regarding the beauty and role of women and the Church's position on the ordination of women: Genesis 2:22; 12:4; Song of Songs 1:8; 4:1-5; 7:2-10; Proverbs 19:14; Sirach 7:19; 26:14f; 36:22-24; Matthew 19:4; Mark 10:7f; 1 Corinthians 11:7; 14: 34f, 37; 1 Timothy 2:11f.

The ordination of women is not in the "deposit of the faith." No matter how politically correct or appealing something may be, if it is not in the deposit of the faith, the Church cannot do anything to change that which is in this deposit! In the *Catechism of the Catholic Church*, which was approved by the universal Church, the bishops in union with the Holy Father—and therefore arguably infallible by means of the ordinary magisterium of the Church in this particular teaching—states: *"The Church recognizes herself bound by this choice made by the Lord himself. For this reason the ordination of women is not possible"* (CCC 1577).

Is there such a thing as the Last Rites?

In the Bible, in James' letter, chapter 5 verses 13-15, we read:

Is anyone among you sick? He should summon the presbyters [priests] of the church, and they should pray over him and anoint [him] with oil in the name of the Lord, and the prayer of faith will save the sick person, and the Lord will raise him up. If he has committed any sins, he will be forgiven.

This is the Sacrament of the Anointing of the Sick or what was often called the "Last Rites." Origen writing in 244 AD affirms this biblical teaching when he wrote:

Let the priests impose their hands on the sick and anoint them with oil and the sacrament will heal the sick persons and forgive them their sins.

Homilies on Leviticus, 2, 7, 8, trans. Jurgens

The Sacrament of Anointing confers a special grace on those suffering from illness or old age. It is a sacrament that can only be administered by a bishop or a priest.

Its power is in the unifying of a person's sufferings with the Passion of Christ. It brings God's healing and loving presence upon the person.

At times the healing is spiritual, at times it is emotional or physical, but God brings about in the person whatever is best for a person's eternal destiny, his or her salvation (cf. Jms. 5:13f).

If a person is unable to receive the Sacrament of Penance—for example, due to incapacitation from an approaching death—the sacrament forgives the sins of the person (Mk. 6:12-13; Jms. 5:13-15) and the temporal punishment associated with the sins. If a person recovers, however, he or she is bound to the Sacrament of Penance.

Prayer and the Doctor?

A small number of groups feel that if one's faith is strong enough God will heal them of any disease. Many television faith healers are so successful it is a wonder that anyone with faith should ever become ill, or for that matter, ever die.

We as Catholics believe that God does in fact heal people, but we also believe that God has given us the gift of doctors whom God has blessed to help people in their ailments.

Prayer is a must, but so is a good doctor and good medicine. In fact, many miracles happen in cooperation with a doctor's medical attention.

Let us never forget Paul's advice to Timothy: "Stop drinking only water, but have a little wine for the sake of your stomach and your frequent illnesses" (1 Tim. 5:23). In other words, take something for your stomach ailments and illnesses.

What about blood transfusions?

Because the "eating" or "drinking" of blood is forbidden by God in Deuteronomy 12:23-25, many Jehovah's Witnesses prohibit the medical practice of blood transfusions (see also Gen. 9:3-4; Lev. 17:14; Acts 15:29).

How do we answer the Jehovah's Witnesses?

First of all, the prohibition is against the "eating" and "drinking" of blood, not of transfusing blood into one's veins.

Secondly, the prohibition against the "eating" and "drinking" of blood was primarily meant to provide a manner of separation between the beliefs of the people of God and the pagans. It was also meant to keep the people of God healthy.

By the time of Jesus, these realities would forever change: Peter is reminded that God has made all things clean (Acts 10:9-16) and Jesus

94

reminds us that "unless you eat the flesh of the Son of Man and drink his blood, you do not have life within you. Whoever eats my flesh and drinks my blood has eternal life, and I will raise him on the last day. For my flesh is true food, and my blood is true drink. Whoever eats my flesh and drinks my blood remains in me and I in him" (Jn. 6:53-56).

The transfusion of blood is in no way associated with paganism nor dietary contamination. For that matter, it is not even biblical.

Is marriage a sacrament?

> *How can I ever express the happiness of a marriage joined by the Church, strengthened by an offering, sealed by a blessing, announced by angels, and ratified by the Father? How wonderful the bond between two believers, now one in hope, one in desire, one in discipline, one in the same service! They are both children of one Father and servants of the same Master, undivided in spirit and flesh, truly two in one flesh. Where the flesh is one, one also is the spirit.*
>
> Tertullian (ca. 155-240)
Ad uxorem, 2, 8, 6-7: PL 1, 1412-1413

Jesus infused his very presence into the wedding feast at Cana (Jn. 2:1f) and forever changed the mystery of marriage.

In Matthew 19:5-6 we read: "A man shall leave his father and mother and be joined to his wife, and the two shall become one flesh. They are no longer two, but one flesh. What God has joined together, no human being must separate." Just as Christ's union with his Body, the Church, cannot be separated (Eph. 5:22-32), likewise the union between husband and wife, a union which mirrors the relationship between Christ and his Church (ibid.), cannot be separated.

Christ elevated marriage to the level of a sacrament by the gift of grace, the gift of his very self. The reality of a man who gives himself completely, without doubt, without reservation, fully to his wife, and a wife who gives herself completely, without doubt, and fully to her husband can only come about by the supernatural gift of grace. It is only in this way that two can really become one (Mt. 19:3-6; Mk. 10:6-9).

Because of this unity to which God calls a couple, marriage must be holy, indissoluble, open to life, and according to the natural order (Mt. 19:5; Mk. 10:7f; Eph. 5:22-32; 1 Thess. 4:4; 1 Tim. 2:15; Gn. 38:9-10; Lv. 20:13). Marriage must mirror Christ's love for his own Bride, the Church (Eph. 5:25, 31-32). It must mirror God's covenant with his people (cf. Song of Songs).

Because of the above reality, marriage is that which must be blessed by the Church. As Ignatius of Antioch (ca. 107), the disciple of the apostle John, states:

It is right for men and woman who marry to be united with the bishop's approval. In that way their marriage will follow God's will (Letter to Polycarp, 5).

Marriage is that precious gift where spouses are called to aid each other on the journey towards holiness. Marriage is a vocation directed toward the salvation of spouses and the perpetuation of the mystery of Christ and his Church to the world.

What is an annulment or declaration of nullity (in regards to two baptized persons)?

People often refer to annulments as the Catholic version of divorce. Nothing could be remoter from the truth!

A Catholic annulment does not deny that a civil, worldly or paper marriage existed. But what an annulment does assert is that this civil union was not a sacramental union, a marriage elevated by God's blessing. In other words, it was a civil marriage between two baptized persons that was never elevated to the level of a sacramental marriage.

How can this be? The answer lies in what makes a sacramental marriage: The key to a valid sacramental marriage is based on the consent between two baptized people. Two people must enter into marriage freely and without any natural (i.e., pathological or psychological) or ecclesiastical hindrance (i.e., outside the proper form required by the Church).

It is important to recognize that a marriage under its proper form is always presumed to be sacramental, no matter what pathological or psychological factors may be present in the marriage. If a couple remains together, grace is keeping it together in all likelihood. However, if at one point the marriage breaks up, then the Church can investigate, upon the request of a spouse or spouses, whether the consent at the time of the wedding was possibly invalid, whether a couple or one of the spouses lacked the capacity for making a true and valid consent.

The determination of the validity of the consent between spouses at the time of their wedding is left to professionals in various fields, including canon lawyers and judges.

One might ask: "How do we justify an annulment in terms of Scripture?" After all, doesn't the Bible say, "A man shall leave his father and mother, and he shall cling to his wife, and the two shall become one" (Eph. 5:31); "they are no longer two but one flesh" (Mk. 10:8); and "what God has joined no man must separate" (Mk. 10:9; cf. 16:18; 1 Cor. 7:10-11).

If there are marriages that God has joined together, there must necessarily be some marriages or unions which God has not joined together. Likewise, the reality of two becoming one in marriage implies that one must in fact have the free will and capacity to live this reality of oneness! Hence, from a purely philosophical point of view, some marriages are not sacramental marriages, that is, marriages elevated to the level of a sacrament since they are not joined by God's blessing nor are they blessed with the ability of two people becoming one.

Scripture supports these philosophical conclusions when it refers to "unlawful marriages," marriages prohibited by God (cf. Acts 15:20; 15:29; Mt. 19:5-9; cf. Lev. 18).

It is in part for this reason that John the Baptist was beheaded. John condemned the unlawful, invalid relationship between King Herod and Herodias, the wife of Herod's brother Philip (Mt. 14:3-12).

An annulment is a recognition of a non-binding, non-sacramental union. It is based on Scripture and the natural philosophical conclusions that flow from the Scriptures.

Why do non-Catholics need annulments (a declaration of nullity)?

A marriage by two properly baptized Protestants is presumed to be a sacrament by the Catholic Church. Those who divorce civilly and would like to marry in the Catholic Church would thus require a declaration of nullity.

Natural marriages (non-sacramental marriages) are between two unbaptized persons or between a baptized person and a non-baptized person. Those who divorce civilly and would like to marry in the Catholic Church would require a declaration of nullity. Natural marriages are seen "as a covenant in which a man and a woman establish between themselves a partnership for the whole of life...which is ordered by its nature to the good of spouses [their complementarity] and the procreation and education of offspring" (cf. can. 1055). An annulment recognizes in what is referred to as natural marriages that one or both spouses lacked the proper consent in regards to this covenant.

IV
THE TRINITY AND THE COMMUNION OF SAINTS

Is there a Trinity? Who is Christ? Who is the Holy Spirit?

*Christians are brought to future life by one thing...that they
recognize that there is a oneness, a unity, a communion between the
Son and the Father, and that there is a oneness, a unity, a
communion, albeit a distinction, between the Spirit, the Son, and the
Father.*

Justin Martyr (ca. 148 AD), Legat. Pro Christ

In Genesis 1:26 we read in the story of creation: "Then God said: 'Let
us make man in *our* image, after *our* likeness." In Genesis 3:22 we read:
"Then the Lord God said, 'See, the man has become like one of *us*...'" Who
is this *us*? Who is this *our*?

In Genesis 18:1-3 many of the early Fathers of the Church saw the
foreshadowing of the Trinity. Abraham meets three mysterious men
(understood to be three divine persons or guests) whom he addressed by the
singular as opposed to the plural phrase "My Lord" (a title most often
reserved by the Jews for God). When studying the shifting back and forth
between the three divine guests and Yahweh, we find something of great
interest. At times Yahweh represents the three, at times Yahweh is one of
the three, at times all the three refer to a single divine being. When taken as
a whole, we can see why the Church Fathers often saw the foreshadowing of
the Trinity in this passage.

In the Hebrew Scriptures, the Old Testament, God is referred to as
Yahweh or Elohim, Elohim being translated as God and Yahweh being
translated as Lord. What is of particular interest is that Elohim is a plural
noun for God. The name Elohim indicates a oneness and a plurality.
Therefore, Elohim indicates a oneness and a plurality in God. For the
Christian, there is one God in three persons or modes of expression; there is
a "oneness," yet a "plurality." The Hebrew Scripture's, the Old Testament's,
name for God attests to the plurality of persons in the one God!

At the baptism of Jesus in the Jordan we hear: "When Jesus had been
baptized he at once came up from the water, and suddenly the heavens
opened and he saw the Spirit descending like a dove and coming down on
him. And suddenly there was a voice from heaven, 'This is my Son, the
Beloved; my favor rests on him'" (Mt. 3:16f). Right at his baptism the
Trinity was manifested to the world: The voice is the Father, Jesus is the
Son, and the image of the dove is the Holy Spirit.

At the Transfiguration Jesus is manifested in the midst of a cloud
casting a shadow: "A bright cloud covered [Moses, Jesus, and Elijah] with a
shadow, and from the cloud came the voice which said, 'This is my beloved

Son in whom I am well pleased. Listen to him" (Mt. 17:5). The voice is that of the Father, the beloved one is Jesus, and the cloud covering Jesus with a shadow is the Holy Spirit (Note that throughout the Hebrew Scriptures, particularly in Exodus, Numbers, and Deuteronomy, a cloud or a shadow represents God's presence).

Before Christ's ascension he reminded his apostles to go throughout the world and baptize in the "name of the Father, and of the Son, and of the Holy Spirit" (Mt. 28:10). Notice Jesus says to baptize in the "name" (singular) and not the "names" (plural) "of the Father, and of the Son, and of the Holy Spirit. There is one God, yet three Persons within that one God.

In the Gospel of Luke and the Acts of the Apostles, the sacred writer emphasizes the theme that in the Hebrew Scriptures the Father was most apparent, in the Christian Scriptures, the New Testament, Jesus became the center of attention, and in the acts of the early Church, the presence of the Holy Spirit was the main character. Obviously all three persons of the Trinity are present in each, yet the revelation of the Trinity took place through the process of revelation.

The word "Trinity" is first recorded in the writings of Theophiles, the bishop of Antioch, to describe the mystery of One God in Three Persons, Father, Son, and Holy Spirit. And according to the ecclesiastical writer Tertullian, by the year 211, the signing of oneself with the sign of the cross, with the sign of the Trinity, had become a well-established custom of the Christian faithful.

"Yahweh is the true God and there is no other" (Dt. 4:35). God is One and has One nature (cf. Is. 40:25-28; 43:10-13; 44:6-8; 1 Chron. 17:20; Mk. 12:29; 1 Cor. 8:4-6). There are Three Persons in One God, the Father, the Son, and the Holy Spirit. There is no confusion, change, division, nor separation between the Persons of the Trinity.

The Three Persons are distinct in their relations of origin: The Father generates, the Son is eternally begotten (Jn. 1:1-4f) and the Holy Spirit eternally proceeds from the Father and the Son (cf. Jn. 15:26).

Let us examine the following Scripture citations: John 1:1; 5:18; 10:30; 14:1; 15:26; 16:14; 17:10; 20:28; Acts 5:3f; 13:2; 13:21; 20:22; 20:25; Romans 9:5; Philippians 2:5f; 3:3; 1 Corinthians 2:10; Galatians 5:18; Ephesians 6:18. When we look at and study the following Bible quotes in relation to each other, we come to the incontrovertible conclusion that we have a Triune God.

The Son

> *I will redeem you with an outstretched arm and with mighty acts of judgment.*
>
> *God (Exodus 6:6)*

At Jesus' birth the prophet Isaiah is quoted (Mt. 1:23: Is. 7:14): "'Behold a virgin shall be with child and bear a son, and they shall name him

Emmanuel," which means God is with us.'" Jesus is "God [who] is with us." "In Christ the fullness of deity resides in bodily form" (Col. 2:9). He is the "I AM" of the burning bush (Ex. 3:14) as attested to by the apostle John (Jesus makes use of the words "I AM" in reference to his divinity at least 11 times in John's Gospel alone). Jesus is, as Thomas proclaims, "my Lord and my God" (Jn. 20:28). In the Hebrew Scriptures the title "Lord" refers to Yahweh, to Adonai, to God. In the New Testament, the name "Lord" refers to only one reality, God! In John 20:16 Mary Magdalene calls the risen Christ by the title "Rabbuni" which was often a title used to address God. Likewise, the phrase "to him be glory for ever," which is often used to address Jesus (2 Tim. 4:18; 2 Pet. 3:18; Rev. 1:6; Heb. 13:20-21), is a phrase that was usually reserved to God alone (cf. 1 Chron. 16:38; 29:11; Ps. 103:31; 28:2). And in Titus 3:5 Jesus is referred to as "God our savior." The Old Testament God is likewise referred to as savior: "It is I the Lord; there is no savior but me." The Old Testament "savior" and the New Testament "savior" are one and the same, since there is "no savior but [God]" (Is. 43:11). Can anyone doubt that Jesus is Lord and God? Can anyone doubt that whoever has seen Jesus has seen the Father (Jn. 14:9)?

The Son of God that existed from all eternity became incarnate some 2000 years ago. He assumed a human nature (Mt. 1:21; Lk. 2:7; Jn. 19:25). The Son is one Person, the second Person of the Trinity, with two natures, a human nature (like us in all things but sin) and a divine nature. He is fully human, fully divine, and there is no confusion, change, division, nor separation between the two natures (cf. Mt. 3:17; 9:6; Mk. 1:1; 8:31; Lk. 1:32; 19:10; Jn. 1:34; 3:13-14; 8:46; Rm. 1:3; 2 Cor. 5:21; Heb. 4:15; 1 Pet. 2:22).

The reality that Christ is both human and divine, the God-man, is attested to by Ignatius of Antioch (ca. 107), the convert of the apostle John, and the friend of Peter and Paul when he says that Christ is "both flesh and spirit, born and unborn, God in man, true life in death,…first subject to suffering and then beyond it."

The Governor of Pontus, Pliny, in his *Letters to the Emperor Trajan* (ca. 111-113) makes reference to the common practice of Christians "singing hymns to Christ as God." Likewise, the Jewish Council of Jamnia (ca. 95) expelled Christians from the synagogues in part because of their belief that Christ was God as well as a man. For the early Christians, Jesus was fully human, fully divine, the God-man.

Jesus had a divine will and a human will. His human will was in complete conformity to his divine will (Mt. 11:25; Mk: 36; Lk. 2:49; Jn. 4:34; Phil. 2:8).

Jesus assumed a human, rational soul (Phil. 2:7f). In his human nature Jesus grew in "wisdom and stature" (Lk. 2:52). In his human nature Jesus had the "fullness of understanding of the eternal plan he had come to reveal" (Mt. 13:32).

Jesus is the Creator of all things (Jn. 1:3; Col. 1:16f; Heb. 1:2), the

Lord of Glory (1 Cor. 2:8), the King of kings (Rev. 17:14; 19:16), the Alpha and Omega (Rv.1:7f). He preached the Kingdom (Mt. 3:2; Mk. 1:15; Acts 2:38). He was immune from sin (Jn. 8:46; 2 Cor. 5:21; Heb. 4:15). He died for all (Jn. 3:16f; Heb. 4:15) and rose from the dead (Mt. 12:39f; Acts 1:22; Rom. 4:24; 1 Cor. 14:4) and will come again to judge the living and the dead—a uniquely divine prerogative according to Hebrew theology (Mt. 19:28; 25:31; Jn. 5:22; Acts 10:42). (For a deeper understanding of Jesus in his human and divine natures, review chapter V on Mary, for the "school of Mary" teaches us about the mystery we call Jesus).

The Holy Spirit

"Peter said, 'Ananas, why has Satan filled your heart so that you lied to the Holy Spirit....You have not lied to human beings, but to God'" (Acts 5:3-4).

The Holy Spirit is the Third Person of the Trinity and is the source of Holy works. His divinity and consubstantiality or oneness with the Father and the Son is attested to throughout the New Testament (i.e., Jn. 14:16-18; 14:23; Acts 5:3f; 28:25f; 1 Cor. 2:10f; 3:16; 6:11, 19f; 1 Pet. 1:1-3; Ep. 4:4-6). As the Third Person of the Trinity, he proceeds from the Father and the Son: "When the Advocate comes whom I will send you from the Father, the Spirit of Truth that proceeds from the Father, He will testify to me" (Jn. 15:26).

Through the operation of the Holy Spirit we are made aware of the Incarnation (Mt. 1:28, 20; Lk. 1:35), the mysteries of the Church (1 Cor. 2:10), the forgiveness of sins (Jn. 20:22-23), the justification and sanctification of souls (1 Cor. 6:11; Rom. 15:16), and the charity of God (Rm. 5:5).

The Holy Spirit is the Spirit of truth (Jn. 14:16-17; 15:26). The Spirit strengthens our faith (Acts 6:5), dwells within us (Rom. 8:9-11; 1 Cor. 3:16; 6:19) and guides our works (Acts 8:29). The Spirit gives us a supernatural life (2 Cor. 3:8) with supernatural gifts (1 Cor. 12:11).

The gifts of the Spirit are wisdom, understanding, counsel, fortitude, knowledge, piety, and fear of the Lord (wonder and awe) (cf. Isa. 11:1-2). The fruits of the Spirit are love, joy, peace, patience, kindness, generosity, faithfulness, gentleness, and self-control (Gal. 5:22-23).

Many attempts have been made to understand the mystery of the Trinity. Some attempts to describe the Trinity include that of a married man and father. The man is himself, a husband, and a father. Another analogy is that of the three states of water—water as liquid, as gas, as solid. St. Patrick used the example of the clover by pointing out that there is only one clover, yet three petals. St. Hildegard of Bingen used the example of fire—the flame being made up of a brilliant light, red power, and fiery heat. St. Ignatius of Antioch (ca. 107) used the example of three notes making one musical sound. St. Gregory Nazianzen (*Orat.* 31:31-32), St. Cyril of Alexandria (*Thesaurus Assert.*, 33), and St. John Damascene (*Fid. Orth.* 1:13) used the image of the sun, the ray, and the light as well as the source, the spring, and

the stream. Mathematicians are familiar with the principle that infinity
+ infinity +infinity=infinity.

Despite the fact that the above analogies all fall short of explaining the great mystery of the Trinity, they still help us in striving to grasp that which is beyond our grasp. As Marius Victorinus wrote in *The Generation of the Divine* word in 356 AD:

> *Because no name worthy of God can be found, we give a name to him from those things which we do know, while bearing in mind that we cannot give to God a name or appellation that is proper to him. That is how we say, 'God lives,' or 'God understands.' Hence, from our own actions, we give a name to the actions of God, considering them as being his in a super eminent way; not such as he really is, but as an approach to what he really is. It is likewise in this way that we impose substance, existence, and other such concepts, upon God. And we speak in a certain way of his ousia or essence, in hinting at what really pertains to him and at what his being really is, by the consideration of created substance (28).*

God is mystery. Yet in many ways, this very mystery is what makes the reality of the Trinity all the more true.

We as human beings are attracted to mystery. Thus, since the Trinity is a mystery, we are attracted to it. Even in heaven, while experiencing the beatific vision, there will still be mystery. For as St. Thomas Aquinas states, the very mystery of God in heaven will keep us eternally attracted to him.

"May the grace of the Lord Jesus Christ and the love of God [the Father] and the fellowship of the Holy Spirit be with all of you" (2 Cor. 13:13).

• The earliest picture of the Crucifixion is found scribbled in an army officer's quarters on the Palatine Hill in Rome in the early 200's. The captions reads: "Alexamenos worships his God."

Do Catholics worship saints?

Catholics do not worship saints. We honor them or what we as Catholics like to say is that we venerate them. We give a lower form of veneration, called *dulia*, to saints and angels and to Mary we use the term *hyperdulia* to indicate a higher form of veneration. But God alone receives worship or adoration, *latria*.

We as Catholics venerate or honor the saints, but we do not worship the saints. Only God is worthy of worship (Mt. 4:10; Lk. 4:8; Acts 10:26). If we can honor our mother and father (Ex. 20:12), why can we not honor the saints? Peter, James, and John venerated Jesus, Elijah and Moses in the event of the Transfiguration (Mk: 9:4). Joshua fell

103

prostrate before an angel (Jos. 5:14), Daniel fell prostrate before the angel Gabriel (Dan. 8:17), Tobiah and Tobit fell to the ground before the angel Raphael (Tob. 12:16). If these great ones could venerate angels and saints, why can't we?

- Often, in some English speaking countries (i.e., England), worship and veneration are sometimes used interchangeably. But the Catholic faith has always made a distinction between the honor given to the saints and Mary, and the honor given to God. In the United States we make the distinction between veneration and worship.

What about the communion of the saints?

Let us not forget those who have died in our prayer. Let us not forget the patriarchs, prophets, apostles, and martyrs who bring our petitions to God; let us not forget the holy fathers and bishops who have died as well as all those most close to us who bring our petitions to God.

Cyril of Jerusalem (ca. 350)
Catechetical Lectures, 23 [*Mystagogic* 5], 90

We as Catholics venerate or honor the saints, but we do not worship the saints. Only God is worthy of worship (Mt. 4:10; Lk. 4:8; Acts 10:26). If we can honor our mother and father (Ex. 20:12), why can we not honor the saints? Peter, James, and John venerated Jesus, Elijah and Moses in the event of the Transfiguration (Mk: 9:4). Joshua fell prostrate before an angel (Jos. 5:14), Daniel fell prostrate before the angel Gabriel (Dan. 8:17), Tobiah and Tobit fell to the ground before the angel Raphael (Tob. 12:16). If these great ones could venerate angels and saints, why can't we?

We recognize that there is only one mediator, Jesus Christ (1 Tim. 2:5). We recognize that Christ is the one mediator, but that he has gifted us and the saints with the ability to engage ourselves in that one mediation. As Paul states: "Be imitators of me, as I am of Christ" (1 Cor. 11:1; also 1 Thess. 1:6-7; 2 Thess. 3:7) In other words, do what I do as I do what Christ does. Isn't this serving in Christ's mediation? Likewise, 1 Thessalonians 1:5-8 reminds us that we must become examples to all believers, and Hebrews 13:7 reminds us that we are to remember our leaders, and that we are to consider and imitate their faith and life. By being a Christian, by being an example of Christ, one shares in Christ's mediation.

Paul also reminds us that "we make up what is lacking in the sufferings of Christ" (Col. 1:24). If this is so, then to be a Christian means that we are by nature sharers in Christ's one mediation.

The very nature of being a Christian is to be a mediator, for by growing in the image and likeness of Christ, which is what it means to grow in holiness, is to inevitably share in Christ's suffering, and by sharing in his suffering means that one shares in Jesus' living sacrifice on the cross to the Father. Just as Christ suffered on the cross for our salvation, we by our suffering, and by being in the image and likeness of Christ, are inevitably participators in the redemptive work of Christ. The lives of the faithful are a living sacrifice to God. Likewise, since the head, Jesus, suffers, the body, the people of God, suffer—for head and body are inseparable.

Scripture points out that the saints are first and foremost in heaven with Christ before the general resurrection (2 Macc. 15:11-16; Mk. 12:26-27; Lk. 23: 43; 2 Cor. 5:1, 6-9; Phil. 1:23-25; Rev. 4:4; 6:9; 7:9; 14:1; 19:1, 4-6). God is the God of the living, and not the dead (Mk. 12:26-27). The thief on the cross turns to Jesus, repents, and is reminded that he will be in paradise with him that very day (Lk. 23:43). In Hebrews 12:1 we are reminded that we are surrounded by a cloud of heavenly witnesses. The Old and New Testaments remind us that the martyrs are in the hand of God (Rev. 6:9-11; 20:4; Wis. 3:1-6). The *Didache* affirms: "The Lord will come and all his saints with him."

The Scriptures point to the fact that the faithful on earth are in communion with the saints of heaven (1 Cor. 12:26; Heb. 12:22-24), and that they assist us by their intercessory prayers (Lk. 16:9; 1 Cor. 12:20f; Rev. 5:8). For example, the Scriptures point out that "in his life [Elisha] performed wonders, and after death, marvelous deeds" (Sir. 48:14). Even after death, Elisha was interceding for us and bringing us "marvelous" things. In Tobit 12:12 we see how an angel offers the prayers of the holy ones to God. In Revelation 5:8 we read: "Each of the elders [in heaven] held a harp and gold bowls filled with incense, which are the prayers of the holy ones [being brought to God]."

The communion of saints is one of the most precious gifts that God has given us (cf. 1 Cor. 12:24-27). How sad it is for me as a Catholic priest to hear words like "until we meet again" from people of other denominations. For the Catholic, our relationships never end. The communion we share with each other here on earth (1 Cor. 12:24-27) is one that extends into purgatory and heaven. Our relationships change, but they continue into eternity. How comforting it is to know that we are able to help people by our prayers when they are being purified (2 Macc. 12:45). How comforting it is to know that from heaven they are interceding for us in the presence of God (cf. Rev. 5:8; 1 Cor. 12:20f; Heb. 12:22f).

Let us never be fearful of invoking the saints of heaven, for they are a gift that God has entrusted the world with. How many cancerous tumors have disappeared by the invocations of saints? How many ills have been healed by the invocation of the saints? History attests to the miraculous intercession of the saints and their communion with us.

I encourage you to investigate the historical accounts of the canonized saints and the process of canonization. I also encourage you to investigate the accounts regarding the Marian apparitions with particular attention to Lourdes and Fatima. Our God is not a God of the dead, but the God of the living (Mt. 22:32; Mk. 12:27).

Christ is the One True Mediator, but we and the saints in communion with us have been gifted with sharing in that one mediation.

Furthermore, may we never forget the greatest saint of all, Mary. At the wedding feast of Cana it was Mary who interceded for the wedding couple in order for them to have more wine. Jesus performed his first miracle, the turning of water into wine, for his mother (Jn. 2:1-11).

May we remain in communion with God and all his saints, for to love and venerate the saints is to honor God (cf. Gal. 1:24), for his saints are the beauty of his creation and will.

The communion of saints is a sign of the reality of the Trinity. All of Creation echoes the image of the Trinity. Since the Trinity is a communion of Persons, a communion of love (Gen. 1:26), it only makes sense that what he created in his image and likeness (Gen. 1:27) would engage in a similar communion.

Saints and angels, because of their union with God, are worthy of veneration for they reflect their maker. As 1 John 3:2 explains, "We shall be like him, for we shall see him as he is." If this is so, then saints are worthy of respect and veneration.

Recent Canonizations

The following are a few examples of American saints that have interceded for people. These miracles were associated with their canonizations—their being declared saints or blessed.

Elizabeth Ann Seton

Through the intercession of Elizabeth Ann Seton, Anne Theresa O'Neill was cured in 1959 of acute lymphocytic leukemia. Carl Kalin was cured of fulminating rubeola meningo-encyphalitis in 1963. Sister Gertrude Korzendorfer was cured of inoperable pancreatic cancer in 1935.

John Neumann

Through the intercession of John Neumann, eleven year old Eva Benassi was cured on her deathbed of acute peritonitis. Michael Flannigan was diagnosed at the age of six with cancer and given six months to live. He was cured in 1963.

Frances Xavier Cabrini

Through her intercession, Peter Smith, blinded by an accident, recovered his sight in 1921.

Katherine Drexel

Her intercession is attributed to the healing of Amy Wall and Robert Gutherman in 1974. Both were cured of deafness.

Kateri Tekakwitha
   Jake Finkbonner, an eleven year old Indian boy, was healed in 2006 of a flesh-eating bacteria.

   The saints are in communion with us!

Lourdes
   One of the most famous places to find documented miracles is found in Lourdes, France where it is believed that Mary, the mother of Jesus, appeared to a young girl Bernadette.
   Lourdes has a medical bureau with doctors of various religious persuasions, including atheist doctors. If a cure seems to have no medical reason behind it, the case is sent to the International Medical Committee of Lourdes—a committee of specialists. After examination, a pronouncement is made. The doctors never pronounce "a miracle," rather they make the pronouncement that the "cure" is "unexplainable" according to modern science and the modern scientific literature. Since 1905, with the establishment of the medical bureau, sixty-four inexplicable phenomena have been declared as "unexplainable" by modern science.
   Henri Busque was cured on April 28, 1858 of tuberculosis, purulent adenitis, a septic ulcer, and inflamed lymph glands. Louis Bouriette was cured of blindness in his left eye on July 28, 1858. Justin Bouhort, unable to walk and suffering from *consumption*, was restored to complete health in July of 1858. Madelaine Rizan was cured on October 17, 1858 of a left-sided paralysis that kept her bedridden. Marie Moreau was restored to health on November 9, 1858 after suffering from blindness. Blaisette Cazenave was healed on January 18, 1862 of a chronic infection of the conjunctivae and eyelids. Aline Bruyere received her miracle on September 1, 1889, being cured of pulmonary tuberculosis. Joachime Dehant was cured on October 13, 1878 of a gangrenous ulcer on her right leg. Ameilie Chagnon was restored to health on August 21, 1891 after suffering from a long series of "bone diseases" and tuberculous arthritis. Clementine Trouve was healed of tuberculous osteoperiostitis of the right calcaneum on August 21, 1891. Elisa Lesage was cured of ankylosis of the joint in the right knee on August 21, 1892. Father Cirette was restored to health on August 31, 1893, being cured of a nervous disorder brought about by influenza. Aurelie Huprelle was healed of "cavitating pulmonary tuberculosis" on August 21, 1895. Esther Brachman regained her health on August 21, 1896 after suffering from tuberculosis. Jeanne Tulasne was healed of Pott's disease on September 8, 1897. Clementine Malot came to Lourdes with a case of "tuberculosis with spitting blood" and was cured on August 8, 1898. Rose Francois was restored to health on August 8, 1899 after a year of suffering from the effects of a "chronic infection of the right arm, with numerous fistulae and gross lymphoedema of the upper arm and forearm." The capuchin priest, Father Salvator was healed of tuberculous peritonitis on June 25, 1900. Marie Savoye was healed of rheumatic fever and heart

disease (with signs of a mitral lesion) on September 20, 1901. Sister Hilaire was cured of chronic gastroenteritis on August 20, 1904. Sister Beatrix was cured of tuberculosis and laryngeal-bronchitis on August 31, 1904. Marie-Therese Noblet was healed of Pott's disease "of peculiar appearance, owing to some concomitant nervous phenomena" on August 31, 1905. Cecile Doubille de Franssu was restored to health on September 21, 1905 after being cured of tuberculous peritonitis. Antonia Moulin suffered from an abscess of the right leg with phlebitis and lymphangitis; she was restored to health on August 8, 1907. Marie Borel was healed of abscesses, fistulas, and bowel obstructions on August 21, 1907. Sister Macimilien was restored to health after being cured of a hydatid cyst of the liver with phlebitis of the left leg on February 5, 1908. Virginie Haudebourg suffered from constant urinary infections, cystitis and nephritis. She was cured on May 17, 1908. Johanna Bezenac suffered from progressive cachexia, localized lesions, and a severe pneumonia when she was cured on July 2, 1908. Pierre de Rudder, on July 24, 1908, regained his ability to walk. Marie Mabille was cured of a "longstanding chronic infection in the right iliac fossa, with vesical and colonic fistulae" on August 8, 1908. Sister Marie of the Presentation was saved from starvation on August 15, 1908 after being cured of a case of "chronic gastro-enteritis." Anne Jourdain was healed of "tuberculosis with gross apical lesions" on October 10, 1908. Elisa Seisson was made well on July 12, 1912, being healed of "chronic bronchitis with severe organic heart disease."

The saint, Mary, Mother of Jesus, is in communion with us and intercedes for us, just as she did at Cana! The little saint Bernadette is in communion with us and intercedes for us!

Jesus, the fulfillment of Judaism's hope!
In Matthew 1:1f and Luke 1:32-33; 3:33 we are reminded that the Messiah, the "blessed one," the "anointed one," the "savior of his people" would be a descendent of Abraham, Isaac, and Jacob, that he would be of the throne of David and of the tribe of Judah (cf. Gen. 12:3; 17:19; 18:18; 49:10; Nb. 24:17; Is. 9:7). Micah 5:2 makes mention that the Messiah would be born in Bethlehem (cf. Mt. 2:1; Lk. 2:4-7) the town of David. In Isaiah 7:14 we are reminded that from the "house of David" a savior would be born of a virgin and he would be Emmanuel—God is with us (cf. Mt. 1:18; 23; Lk. 1:26-35). His birth would be followed by the slaughter of innocent children (Jer. 31:15; Mt. 2:16-18). He would be forced to flee to and return from Egypt (Hosea 11:1; Mt. 2:14-15). Born in Bethlehem he would however be known as a Nazarene (Jgs. 13:5; Mt. 2:23).
His ministry would be prepared by John the Baptist, the "voice of one crying in the wilderness" (cf. Is. 40:3; Jn. 1:23). As he grew to maturity, the King of kings, the Lord of lords, would mark the beginning of his "Passion" by a triumphal entry into Jerusalem on a donkey (Zech. 9:9; Jn. 12:13-14). He would be betrayed by his own people (cf. Is. 53:3; Jn. 1:11). He would

be betrayed by a friend for 30 pieces of silver (cf. Zech. 11:12; Ps. 41:9; Mk. 14:10). The 30 pieces of silver would be taken and used to buy a "potter's field" (cf. Zech. 11:13f; Mt. 27:6-7). Judas, his betrayer, would be replaced by another, Matthias (cf. Ps. 109:7-8; Acts 1:18-20). The Messiah would be accused by false witnesses (Ps. 27:12; 35:11; Mt. 26:60-61; Mk. 14:57), hated without reason (Ps. 69:4; 35:19; 109:3-5; Jn. 15:24-25), and yet would remain silent (Is. 53:7; Mt. 26:62-63; Mk. 15:4-5). Soldiers would take off, gamble for, and divide his clothing amongst themselves (Ps. 22:18; Mt. 27:35). He would be crucified, pierced in his hands and feet (cf. Zech. 12:10; Ps. 22:16; Mt. 27:35; Jn. 20:27) given gall and vinegar to quench his thirst (cf. Ps. 69:21; Mt. 27:24,48; Jn. 19:19) and placed among thieves on a cross (cf. Is. 53:12; Mk. 15:27-28; Ex. 6:6). Not a single bone would be broken (cf. Ps. 34:20; Ex. 12:46; Jn. 19:32-36). And before his death, he cried out *"Eli, Eli, lama sabachthani"* to remind the faithful that he was the fulfillment of Psalm 22, the innocent, just man who would be sacrificed for the world. To assure he was dead, they would pierce his side (Zech. 12:10; Jn. 19:34). He was pierced for us and our transgressions, taking upon himself the sins of the world (Is. 53:4-5, 6, 12; Ex. 6:6; Mt. 8:16-17; Rm. 4:25; 5: 6-8; 1 Cor. 15:3). He would be placed in a rich man's tomb (cf. Is. 53:9; Mt. 27:57-60). He would be deserted by his followers (Zech. 13:7; Mk. 14:27). He would rise on the third day (cf. Hos. 6:2; Ps. 16:10; 49:15; Lk. 24:6-7; Mk. 16:6-7). He would ascend into heaven (cf. Ps. 68:18; 24:3; Lk. 24:50-51; Acts 1:11; Mk. 16:19) and would be seated at the right hand of the Father (cf. Ps. 110:1; Hb. 1:2-3).

In one of the most poignant moments in the Scriptures, Solomon ponders: "[W]ill God indeed dwell on the earth" (RSV, 1 Kgs. 8:27)? Easter is that unique recognition that God came to dwell among us on earth in the most precious and valued of ways—to teach us to live life abundantly and to live it eternally! Yes, King Solomon, God did come to dwell among us on earth!

V
MARY

Is Mary the Mother of God?

"Look, the virgin shall conceive and bear a son, and they shall call him Emmanuel, which means "God is with us" (Mt. 1:23).

Mary is the mother of Jesus, the Son of God (Lk. 1:35; Gal. 4:4). The Son of God, Jesus, is God, the second Person of the Trinity? Therefore, Mary is the Mother of God.

The Old Testament prefigures Mary as being the Mother of God. During the time of King Solomon until the end of the kings of Judah, the Queen Mother always sat on the right hand of her son as a confidant and advisor. Jesus, the New Testament Davidic king, has a New Testament Queen Mother, Mary.

Mary is referred to as the "Mother of my Lord" in Luke's Gospel (Lk. 1:43). This is significant for in the Jewish world the title "Lord" was a title usually reserved for God, Yahweh. And in the Greek New Testament the title "Lord," or "Kyrios" refers **only** to God!! It is no coincidence that just two verses later (v. 45), the divine title "Lord" is being used in such a way that one could not confuse it for anything other than the title for "God." Mary is the Mother of the Lord, the Mother of Yahweh, the Mother of God.

Mary is what the ancient Church called the "theotokos," the "God-bearer." In fact, this title for Mary was so common that the anti-Christian emperor Julian the Apostate (361-363 AD) would mock Christians for its "incessant use."

At the Council of Ephesus (431), in seeking to understand more profoundly the mystery of Christ, the Council Fathers could hear the crowds outside the walls chanting "theotokos, theotokos, theotokos!" This was no coincidence. For to truly understand Jesus, the crowds, under the power of the Spirit, knew that one needed to understand Mary. Who knows a son better than a mother?

Thus, it is no happenstance that the identity of Jesus and the identity of Mary would be clarified together. Mary always points to her Son! Who knows a son better than a mother?

The Council Fathers (i.e., bishops) reaffirmed Jesus as being fully human, fully divine, without any confusion, division, or separation between his two natures (cf. Mt. 3:17; 9:6; Mk. 1:1; 8:31; Lk. 1:32; 19:10; Jn. 1:34; 3:13-14; 8:46; Rm. 1:3; 2 Cor. 5:21; Heb. 4:15; 1 Pet. 2:22). Mary therefore could not be the Mother of Jesus "only," or the Mother of God "only." To separate Jesus' divinity from his humanity would be to make Jesus into two distinct persons. Yet Jesus is one Person, the Second Person of the Trinity, the Son of God, with two inseparable natures--a human and a divine nature (cf. Mt. 3:17; 9:6; Mk. 1:1; 8:31; Lk. 1:32; 19:10; Jn. 1:34; 3:13-14; 8:46; Rm. 1:3; 2 Cor. 5:21; Heb. 4:15; 1 Pet. 2:22).

All mainline Christians accept this logic, yet why do they not accept the inevitable philosophical conclusion that Mary is--given the above well-accepted Christology--the Mother of God?

Ignatius of Antioch (110 A.D.), the friend of the apostle John, and the bishop of Antioch through the "laying on of hands" by the apostles Peter and Paul wrote the following:

> *Our God, Jesus Christ, was conceived by Mary in accord with God's plan (Ephesians, 18:2).*

The Catholic Irenaeus (180-199 A.D.), the friend of Polycarp, who in turn was the friend of the apostle John wrote:

> *The Virgin Mary...being obedient to His word, received from an angel the glad tidings that she would bear God (Against Heresies, 5,19).*

But what about the three Protestant founders, the three pillars of Protestantism?

Martin Luther, the founder of Protestantism, recognized the important role of Mary as the Mother of God. As he stated in defense of his strong devotion to Mary:

> *Mary was made the **Mother of God**, giving her so many great things that no one could ever grasp them...* (*The Works of Luther*, Pelikan, Concordia, St. Louis, v. 7, 572).

John Calvin, the second most famous Protestant founder, recognized this reality when he stated:

> *It cannot be denied that God in choosing and destining Mary to be the Mother of his Son, granted her the highest honor.... Elizabeth called Mary the Mother of the Lord because the unity of the person in the two natures of Christ was such that she could have said that the man engendered in the womb of Mary was at the same time the eternal God* (*Calvini Opera, Corpus Reformatorum*, Braunschweig-Berlin, 1863-1900, v. 45, 348, 35).

And the last of the three fathers of mainline Protestantism, Ulrich Zwingli argued:

> *It was given to her what belongs to no creature, that in the flesh she should bring forth the Son of God [who is God](Corpus*

Reformatorum, vol. 6, I).

What ever happened to their Protestant disciples?

Mary is the greatest of God's creatures. She is the greatest creature created by the Son of God.

The greatest cosmic event to ever have occurred, an infinite being, God, becoming, through Mary, a finite being occurred in the Incarnation. How can we deny Mary her special place in Christianity?

Mary is unique for she is the spouse of the Holy Spirit. When we examine the phrase "to overshadow" as used in the annunciation scene in Luke 1:35 we cannot but be made aware of the spousal relationship between Mary and the Holy Spirit. Jewish rabbis knew that the phrase "to overshadow" when used in the context of conception was a euphemism for a spousal relationship (*Midrash Genesis Rabbah* 39:7; *Midrash Ruth Rabbah* 3:9). The Holy Spirit "overshadowed" Mary (cf. Lk. 1:35). Thus, Mary entered a spousal relationship with the Holy Spirit.

No other human being can make the claim of being the "spouse of the Holy Spirit!" And because of this reality, Mary is the Mother of the God who "is with us," (Mt. 1:23). When Mary visited Elizabeth, Elizabeth responded: "And how does this happen to me that the mother of my Lord (Yahweh) should come to me" (Lk. 1:43)? Who is the Lord here in this passage? Jesus. And who is Jesus? God and man, or as Thomas would say, "my Lord (Yahweh) and my God (Elohim)" (Jn. 20:28). (Yahweh was the Yahwistic name for God, and Elohim was the Elohistic term for God. Yahweh is often translated as "Lord" and Elohim as "God"). Mary is the mother of Emmanuel, which means "God with us" (Lk. 1:23). Mary is the Mother of "God with us."

One must study at the "school of Mary," as Pope St. John Paul the Great explained, if one is to truly understand the mystery which is Christ. No one knows Christ better than Mary.

Let us always seek to grasp the mysteries of Mary, for as we do, we will discover the wonders of her Son. As Blessed Mother Teresa would often say, "Let us love Mary as much as Jesus' loved her, nothing more, nothing less." Can we ever love Mary as much as Jesus?

> *Mother of God listen to my petitions; do not disregard us in adversity, but receive us from danger.*
> *Second Century Papyrus, Or. 24, II.*

The fact is this:
1) All mainline Christians affirm that Mary is the mother of Jesus.
2) All mainline Christians affirm that Jesus is God.
3) Therefore, when push comes to shove, all mainline Christians, no matter how uncomfortable, recognize that Mary is the Mother of God. To deny this reality is to distort who we all agree Jesus is and who we all agree is the Triune God.

What is the Immaculate Conception?

In the year 306 AD we read in Ephraeim's *Nisbene Hymn* (27, 8) the following:

> *You alone and your Mother*
> *Are more beautiful than any others;*
> *For there is no blemish in you,*
> *Nor any stains or sins upon your Mother*

Ambrose (340-370) wrote of Mary:

> *Lift me not up from Sara but from Mary, a Virgin not only undefiled but Virgin whom grace has made inviolate, free from every stain of sin (Commentary on Psalm 118, 22, 30).*

The Immaculate Conception is the teaching which affirms that Mary was redeemed by Jesus from the very moment of her conception. She was preserved from "original sin" and personal sin by Jesus, her Redeemer and Savior.

Where do Catholics come up with this teaching? The teaching has always been part of the deposit of faith and can be seen through the logical philosophical implications that flow from Luke 1:28. Mary is *kecharitomene*; that is, she is "full of grace." She is full of grace because of Christ and thus if one is full of grace one cannot have the stain of "original sin" or the stain of any personal sin; otherwise, the angel would have said: "Hail Mary, partially full of grace." But the angel didn't say that as we all know. He said, "Hail Mary, full of grace." Jesus was without sin, and because of Jesus, Mary was without sin.

Mary is the New Eve as Jesus is the New Adam. In the Garden of Eden the devil, a fallen angel, brought the words that would lead to death. At the annunciation, the angel Gabriel would bring the words that lead to life to Mary. Eve disobeyed God and brought about the fall of the human race. Mary obeyed God and helped to bring about the redemption of the human race. Where Eve was a poor disciple and poor mother, Mary, the New Eve, was the perfect disciple and perfect mother. Jesus, the New Adam, was without sin; Mary, the New Eve, by virtue of her son, is likewise without sin! Mary, which means "excellence" or "perfection," truly lived up to her name.

As Jesus is the New Adam (1 Cor. 15:45), Mary is the New Eve. After the fall of Adam and Eve we read in Genesis 3:15: "I will put enmity between you and the woman, and between your offspring and hers; He will strike at you head, while you strike at his heel." The woman's son, Jesus, will crush the head of the serpent. If this is so, then who is the woman? Mary! Just as Adam and Eve brought death to the world, the New Adam and Eve, Jesus and Mary, bring life to the world, bring redemption. The Old

Adam and Eve became sinners and brought sin into the world; the New Adam, Jesus, and the New Eve, Mary, remain sinless and are responsible for bringing redemption into the world.

St. Irenaeus, the friend of Polycarp, who was in turn the friend of John the Apostle wrote:

> *Just as [Eve]...having become disobedient, was made the cause of death for herself and for the whole human race; so also Mary, ...being obedient, was made the cause of salvation for herself and the whole human race.... Thus, the knot of Eve's disobedience was loosed by the obedience of Mary. What the virgin Eve had bound in unbelief, the virgin Mary loosed through faith (Against Heresies, 3, 22, 4).*

The Old Testament Eve was the mother of the human race in the order of nature. Mary, the mother of Jesus, is the New Eve, the new mother of the human race in the order of grace. The Old Eve was the natural mother of the human race; the New Eve, Mary, is the *supernatural* mother of the human race.

Mary is the pure temple in which the Savior came to dwell in. In Luke 1:35 the angel of the Lord states: "The power from the Most High will overshadow (*episkiazein*) you." The phrase "to overshadow" is the same one used to describe how the cloud of God's glory came to overshadow the Ark of the Covenant (Ex. 40:35; Num. 9:18, 22).

This is not accidental. Luke was making allusions to the Ark of the Covenant which contained the very presence of God (cf. Ex. 40). The Ark is the most holy object in all the Old Testament! The Ark was to be made "perfect in every detail" to allow that which is perfect to "fill it" (Ex. 25; 40:5). Not only did the Ark have to be perfect, it had to be kept free from all impurity and profanation (In 2 Samuel 6:6-7 Uzzah was struck dead for simply touching the Ark). For Luke, and thus for us, Mary was the pure Ark, the pure temple, that held the divine presence, the Son of God, Jesus. And what God dwells in is pure and perfect. God does not co-exist with impurity or imperfection.

When comparing the Greek and Hebrew imagery used for the Ark of the Covenant (Ex. 25:20; 40:35; Num. 9:18, 22) and the scene of the annunciation (1 Chr. 28:18; Lk. 1:35f), one cannot but see—when read in their original languages--the powerful and unquestionable parallel. Compare Exodus 40:34-35, Numbers 9:15 with Luke 1:35; compare 2 Samuel 6:11 with Luke 1:26, 40; compare 2 Samuel 6:9 with Luke 1:43; compare 2 Samuel 6:14-16 with Luke 1:44. Can anyone doubt that Mary is the New Ark of the Covenant?

The Ark was to be made perfect for God to dwell within. Mary was created "full of grace," "without sin" so that Emmanuel, the "God who is with us," Jesus, could dwell within her.

The Ark carried the *written* Word of God; Mary carried the *living* Word of God. Ambrose writing around the year 390 said of Mary:

The Ark contained the Ark of the Tables of the Law; Mary contained in her womb the heir of the Testament. The Ark bore the Law; Mary bore the Gospel. The Ark made the voice of God heard; Mary gave us the very Word of God. The Ark shown forth with the purest of gold; Mary shown forth both inwardly and outwardly with the splendor of virginity. The gold which adorned the Ark came from the interior of the earth; the gold with which Mary shone forth came from the mines of heaven.

Mary is spouse of the Holy Spirit. How can the Holy Spirit dwell in that which is sinful? Mary gave Jesus his body and cooperated in her "fiat" with God in giving him his soul. This body and soul could not carry on "original sin" nor concupiscence. Therefore, Mary had to be without "original sin" or personal sin.

Now one may argue by saying: "How can Mary have been saved prior to the crucifixion and how is it that she had no "original sin" or personal sin on her soul?"

Is Abraham in heaven? Is Isaac in heaven? What about Moses, Isaiah, Hosea, Amos, Joel, Micah, Jonah, Nahum, Ezekiel, Elijah, Elisha, Jeremiah, Habakkuk, Obadiah, Zephaniah, Haggai, Zechariah, Malachi, or Daniel? Are they in heaven? Of course they are, yet they lived before the Incarnation of the Son of God and lived before the crucifixion (Lk. 16:22; 1 Pet. 3:18f)?

We must remember that Christ's salvific event, his dying for our sins on the cross, was not limited to one time period. Jesus salvific event engulfed all of history. It engulfed that which is beyond the limits of space and time. Thus Mary being preserved from the stain of "original sin" and personal sin is not so hard to grasp in this context.

Let us not forget, Mary needed a Savior: "My spirit rejoices in God my savior" (Lk. 1:47). The Catholic Church has never denied this.

Now one may argue from Romans 3:23 that since "all have sinned" Mary must have sinned in her lifetime. But this begs the question: How would you apply Romans 3:23 to infants? Infants who are below the age of reason cannot sin, for in order to sin one must have reason and free will. To sin one must know what one is doing and have the freedom to do it. An infant has no idea of what he or she is doing and consequently cannot commit any personal sin. Romans 3:23 is a reference not to one particular individual or individuals but to the mass of humanity. Furthermore, Jesus obviously had no sin (Heb. 4:16). Paul is using "all have sinned" in the collective sense, not the distributive sense.

In Genesis 1:2 and following we are reminded that from the *immaculately* created cosmos God created Adam (Evil and chaos entering the world only after the fall, Gen. 3.). In Romans 5:14 and 1 Corinthians 15:22 we are reminded that Jesus is the second Adam. If the first Adam was created from pristine organic materials, what would the second Adam be created from? Obviously an immaculate, pristine Mother!

Brothers and sisters of the Lord?

> *I will pour out on the house of David and on the inhabitants of Jerusalem a spirit of grace and petition; and they shall look on him whom they have thrust through, and they shall mourn for him as one mourns **for an only son** and they shall grieve over him as one grieves **over a firstborn.** "*
>
> *The Prophet Zechariah (cf. 12:10-11)*

The prophet Zechariah reminds us that the Messiah, the Christ, the Savior, would be an "only child" and that he would have the privileges of the "firstborn." If Jesus had blood brothers and/or sisters then, according to this prophecy of Zechariah regarding the Messiah, the Christ, Jesus could not be the Messiah!

Mary remained a virgin throughout her life. She had no other child than Jesus.

Catholics believe in the perpetual virginity of Mary. The title "ever-virgin" has been a title for Mary from antiquity. If she had given birth to anyone else other than Jesus, that ancient title would have ceased to exist.

Even the pillars of all modern mainline Protestant denominations affirm Mary's perpetual virginity. Martin Luther wrote:

> *It is an article of faith that Mary is Mother of the Lord and still a virgin.... Christ we believe, came forth from a womb left perfectly intact (Works of Luther, 6, 510).*

Ulrich Zwingli wrote:

> *I firmly believe that Mary, according to the words of the gospel, as a pure Virgin brought forth for us the Son of God and in childbirth and after childbirth forever remained a pure, intact Virgin (Zwingli Opera, v. 1, 424).*

What ever happened to their Protestant offspring?

In the Scriptures and in history we never find the appellation "Mary's children." If Mary would have had children, the title "Mary's children" would certainly have been found somewhere in history. When Jesus was found in the temple at the age of twelve by Mary and Joseph, the context of the scene makes it quite clear that Jesus was Mary's only child (Lk. 2:41-51). In Mark 6:3 we are reminded that Jesus is the "son of Mary" and not "a son of Mary."

So how do we respond to quotes such as those found in Matthew 12:46, Mark 3:31-35; 6:3, John 7:5, Acts 1:14, in 1 Corinthians 9:5 and

Galatians 1:19. And how do we respond to the word for brothers as *adelphoi* which means "from the womb."

First, our English word for "brother" comes from "from the same parents." Yet we use the word brother or brothers more broadly (i.e., "brothers in arms").

Secondly, when interpreting the Scriptures we need to understand the term "brother" in the same way the people during Jesus' time understood the term. When we do this, the use of the term "brother" becomes clarified. In the ancient Jewish culture of Jesus' time, there was no word for cousin, uncle, close relative, and so forth. The word "brother" was used for all such appellations. It is for this reason that the word "brother" in the New Testament is used over 105 times and the word "brothers" is used more than 220 times.

In the Old Testament, or what we refer to as the Hebrew Scriptures, brothers and sisters are often meant to refer to close relations. Brothers and sisters in Semitic usage can refer to nephews, nieces, cousins, half-brothers, half-sisters, etc. (cf. Gen. 13:8; 14:14-16; 29:15, Lev. 10:4, etc.). For example, when we look at the original texts and even the better English translations we find the following: Lot is described as Abraham's brother, yet Lot is the son of Aran (cf. Gen. 14:14). Lot was Abraham's nephew. Jacob is called the brother of Laban, yet Laban is his uncle (Gen. 29:15). When we look to Deuteronomy 23:7-8 and Jeremiah 34:9 we notice the appellation brothers is used in terms of a person who shares the same culture or national background. When we look to 2 Samuel 1:26 and 1 Kings 9:13 we notice that brother is used in terms of a friend. When we look at Amos 1:9 we see that brother is used in terms of an ally.

The New Testament makes it quite clear that this is the appropriate understanding of brothers and sisters in reference to Mary. For example, James and Joseph are called "brothers of Jesus," yet in examining the Bible we see that this is impossible, for James and Joseph "are sons of another Mary, a disciple of Christ," whom Matthew significantly calls "the other Mary," Mary the wife of Clopas (Jn. 19:25) (Mt. 13:55; 28:1; cf. Mt. 27:56). In the Acts of the Apostles, Peter in addressing the "one hundred and twenty brothers" [*adelphon*] (Acts 1:15f), was certainly not addressing one hundred and twenty blood-brothers! In Acts 22:7 fellow Christians are called "brothers," "*adelphon*," and the Jewish leaders are called "brothers," "*adelphon*." The Greek word *adelphoi* has a broad meaning like the English understanding of the word. In fact, in the ancient world it had an ever broader meaning!

Once again, nowhere in the New Testament is there the appellation "sons of Mary." Furthermore, when we hear that the "brothers" advised and reprimanded Jesus (i.e., Jn. 7:3-4; Mk. 3:21), the idea of blood brothers of Jesus becomes even more incongruous since younger brothers in the Jewish culture did not admonish older brothers!

It is not an unusual or an odd practice to call people who are not related to us as brothers or sisters. Even today in many Protestant denominations

118

people like to refer to themselves as brothers and sisters in the faith. Yet they are not real brothers or real sisters. They are close friends within the Body of Christ. As Jesus himself mentions we are "all brothers" (Mt. 23:8).

Other examples of the use of brothers in a non-familial sense can be seen in the following: In Romans 14:10, 21, we read, "Why then do you judge your brother?" "It is good not to…do anything that causes your brother to stumble." In 1 Corinthians 5:11 we read, "I now write to you not to associate with anyone named a brother, if he is immoral, greedy…." In 2 Corinthians 8:18 we read, "We have sent to you the brother who is praised in all the churches for his preaching of the gospel." In 1 Thessalonians 4:6, we read, "Do not take advantage or exploit a brother." In 1 John 3:17 we read, "If someone who has worldly means sees a brother in need and refuses him compassion, how can the love of God remain in him?" In 1 John 4:20 we read, "If anyone says, 'I love God,' but hates his brother, he is a liar." And on and on the pattern goes. In fact, Paul makes use of the appellation "brothers" in 97 scriptural verses.

Another issue that needs to be dealt with is the issue of the phrase that we find in Luke 2:7 where Jesus is mentioned as the "firstborn." In the English language firstborn most often implies the birth of other children; however in the time of Jesus "firstborn" had no such implication. For example, in the Old Testament Psalm 89:27 David is referred to as the "firstborn," yet he is the eighth son of Jesse (1 Sam. 16). In the Old Testament book of Genesis (43:33), we read about Joseph as being referred to as the "firstborn." Yet this cannot be understood in the modern sense of firstborn since Joseph was one of the youngest children of the Patriarch Jacob (He was the firstborn of Rebecca but not Leah). In the book of Exodus, Moses reminds the Pharaoh, because of his obstinacy "every firstborn in the land of Egypt shall die" (Ex. 11:5). Obviously, no implication for second-born children can be inferred. (A further point is that in the ancient world the term "firstborn" often had the connotation of only-born). The firstborn son had to be redeemed within forty days (Ex. 34:20). There would be no way of knowing if other children would be born after!

The term "firstborn" is primarily a legal term, a term indicating rights and privileges (i.e., Gn. 27; Ex. 13:2; Nm. 3:12-13;; 18, 15-16; Dt. 21:15-17). For example, the term "firstborn" often referred to a child that was responsible for opening the womb of a woman, without any further implication (Ex. 13:2; Nb. 3:12). Sometimes it referred to someone as being special, as being sanctified (Ex. 34:20). According to the Law of Moses, all Jewish firstborn children were to be presented in the temple and offered to God in thanksgiving (cf. Lk. 2:22f). This very fact did not mean that the parents of this firstborn child, presented in the temple, were going to have a second-born child or any other children! Another account that explains the term "firstborn" comes from within the context of the whole of the infancy narrative (1:5 to 2:52). Firstborn within this context is a reference to Jesus as the "firstborn of God" (cf. Col. 1:15, 18; Heb. 1:6; Rev. 1:5). Jesus is the "firstborn" of all creation (Col. 1:15).

Some like to refer to Matthew 1:25 where the phrase used is "until she bore a son." They imply that the word "until" implies children after the birth of Jesus. Again, we must look at the way this word was understood in the time of Jesus. No implication can be made regarding marital relations by the use of the word. It was a common phrase of the period which had no further implications regarding further births.

"Until" in ancient Greek is a compound word *heos-hou*. This compound word implies no implication of further events. For example, in Luke 1:80 John the Baptist was called by God to remain in the desert "until the day of [the Messiah's] manifestation to Israel." Yet John remained in the desert after the Savior's manifestation to Israel and even after Jesus himself began baptizing in the Jordan—only with John's capture by Herod's men, did he cease to be in the desert. In Acts 25:21 Paul was to remain imprisoned "until" (*heos-hou*) he was sent up to Caesar. Yet the Acts of the Apostles (cf. 28:20) show Paul remaining in custody even after his meeting with Caesar. In the Septuagint version of Isaiah 46:4 God says: "I am until you grow old." Did God cease to exist when Isaiah grew old? NO! When God the Father spoke to his Son saying, "Sit on my right hand until I make your enemies your footstool," he certainly was not implying that the Son would no longer sit on his right hand once his enemies were restrained? In the Septuagint version of Psalm 111:8, the version the early Christians used, we read of a man whose heart is steadfast and who "shall not be afraid until (*hous-hou*) he looks down upon his foes. Obviously this man will not suddenly become afraid after conquering his foes. If anything, he would have been afraid before gaining dominance over his enemies. In 2 Peter 1:19 Peter reminds the faithful to remain dutiful to God until (*hous-hou*) the "day dawns and the morning star rises in your hearts." If "until" had further implications, then Peter would be saying that once the morning star rises we can forget about God's word.

Another word for "until" used in the Scriptures is *heos*. In Mathew 28:20 Jesus reminds the faithful that he will be with them until (*heos*) the end of the world. Does that mean that at the end of the world Jesus, God, will disappear? Obviously not! In 1 Corinthians 15:25 Paul states that Christ will reign as king until (*heos*) he has positioned his enemies under his feet. Will he cease to reign as king once he has triumphed over his foes? In 1 Timothy 4:13 we hear Paul exhort Timothy to preach and teach the faith until (*heos*) Paul's arrival. Does that mean that once Paul arrived Timothy would never again preach the faith? Clearly, Timothy continued to preach the faith even after Paul's arrival.

The word "until" has no further implications in the Greek of Jesus' time. The purpose of verse 25 was to emphasize that Joseph was not in any way responsible for the birth of Jesus.

In some translations of the Bible *heos* or *hous-hou* is translated as "when" as opposed to "until" in order to avoid any confusion (i.e, Jerusalem Bible).

The most powerful argument however for the perpetual virginity of the Blessed Mother is found at the foot of the cross.

> *When Jesus saw his mother and the disciple there whom he loved, he said to his mother, "Woman, behold your son." Then he said to the disciple [John], "Behold, your mother." And from that hour the disciple took her into his home (Jn. 19: 26-27).*

It makes absolutely no sense for Jesus to give his mother over to the apostle John if a brother or brothers or sister or sisters were around. Wouldn't you entrust your mother to a brother or sister? And would a mother abandon her own children so as to become the mother of another? As Athanasius of Alexandria (ca. 295) states:

> *If Mary had had other children, the Savior would not have ignored them and entrusted his Mother to someone else; nor would she have become someone else's mother. She would not have abandoned her own to live with others, knowing well that it ill becomes a woman to abandon her husband and her children. But since she was a virgin, and was his Mother, Jesus gave her as a mother to his disciple, even though she was not really John's mother, because of his great purity of understanding and because of her untouched virginity (De virginitate, in Le Museon 42: 243-44).*

In Matthew 15 Jesus condemns the Pharisees for the "Korban rule," a rule that allowed children to avoid taking care of their parents. Jesus would not have brothers or sisters who would ignore the taking care of Mary.

Hence, Mary is the "ever-virgin" as the Church has from the beginning of time always called her. It is significant that this belief was so universally held that it only began to be questioned in the year 380 when a man by the name of Helvidius saw "brothers and sisters" as being real brothers and sisters. Jerome, who translated the Bible from the original languages into Latin, felt that Helvidius' interpretation was so ridiculous that it was not worthy of a single comment.

> *There is no child of Mary except Jesus...*
> *Origen (ca. 250)*
> *Commentary of John 1:4;*
> *PG 14, 32; GCS 10, 8-9.*

Why was Mary assumed into heaven?

> *Even though your most holy and blessed soul was separated from your happy and immaculate body, according to the usual course of nature, and even though it was carried to a proper burial place, nevertheless it did not remain under the dominion of death, nor was it destroyed by corruption. Indeed, just as her virginity remained intact when she gave birth, so her body, even after death, was preserved from decay and transferred to a better and more divine dwelling place. There it is no longer subject to death but abides for all ages.*
>
> *John Damascene (ca. 645)*
> *Homily 1 on Dormition 10: PG 96, 716 A-B*

Jesus was "full of grace" (Jn. 1:14) and "without sin" (Heb. 4:15). Jesus ascended body and soul into heaven (Lk. 24:50-53). Mary, being the perfect disciple, the perfect imitator of her son, the perfect model of the Church, the one who knew her son more than any other creation of God, would be granted the gift of imitating her Savior, her son, by being "full of grace" and without sin. And at the end of her earthly journey, she would imitate her Savior, her son, by being assumed by Him into heaven body and soul.

The fact that one could be raised without decay should not be troubling to a Christian. In Matthew 27:52 we are reminded that many saints who had fallen asleep were raised--without decay taking place to their bodies—at the Crucifixion. In 1 Thessalonians 4:17 we are reminded that many will be caught up to meet the Lord in the air body and soul.

The fact that Mary was assumed into heaven should not be a shocking idea for the Christian. After all, in Genesis 5:24 and Hebrews 11:5 we read how Enoch was "taken up" to God. And in 2 Kings 2:1, 11, we are told how Elijah was taken up to heaven in a whirlwind. If Enoch and Elijah are taken up to God, why would we have trouble believing that the Mother of Jesus, the Mother of the Savior would not be taken up, assumed, into heaven.

The teaching of Mary's assumption into heaven is the belief that Mary after the course of her earthly life was assumed body and soul into heaven.

In the ancient Byzantine Liturgy of the Catholic Church we hear the following liturgical expression by the Eastern Fathers on the Feast of the Dormition:

> *In giving birth you kept your virginity; in your Dormition you did not leave the world, O Mother of God, but were joined to the source of Life. You conceived the living God and, by your prayers, will deliver our souls from death (CCC 966).*

Original sin and personal sin are what prevent a person from entering into heaven. But because of the merits of Jesus, Mary was "full of grace" and therefore without "original sin" or personal sin. Heaven was open to her, and because of her special place in the life of Jesus, she was assumed into heaven.

Mary is the spouse of the Holy Spirit. How can the Holy Spirit dwell in that which is sinful? Mary gave Jesus his body and cooperated with God in giving Jesus his soul. This body and soul could not carry on "original sin" nor concupiscence. Therefore, Mary had to be without "original sin" or personal sin.

When we look to the historical evidence of those who were close to Jesus we notice that their bones are venerated and held in places of honor in churches throughout the world. Yet no mention has ever been made about the bones of Mary and no mention has ever been made about the veneration of her bones anywhere.

Mary knew no decay, for she was free from original sin and concupiscence. As Psalm 16:10 reminds us: [the beloved will not] know decay." The beloved blessed Mary knew no decay. She was assumed body and soul into heaven.

Just as the Ark of the Covenant was to remain intact, the New Ark of the Covenant, Mary, was to remain intact, Body and Soul!

The Bible, logic, and history point to Mary's assumption.

It is interesting to note that August 15 has always been reserved by Lutherans and Anglicans as a day for Mary. In recent years, Anglicans have allowed their followers to believe in the Assumption; they concluded that this belief was in perfect conformity with the Scriptures. Likewise, some branches of Lutheranism allow for the belief in the Assumption--as a matter for personal devotion.

Mary, the "woman" (cf. Jn. 2:4; 19:26)

Mary is the "woman" of Genesis 3:15, who with her son, will crush the serpent's head; she is the "woman" at Cana that gives birth to Jesus' first miracle, who gives birth to the "new wine," the new age of life and grace, the new covenant; she is the "woman" at the foot of the cross at Calvary, the "skull-place," where the serpent's head is crushed Mary is the "woman" who obeys God as opposed to the "woman" who disobeyed God in the Garden. Mary is the "woman" who wages war against the dragon, the serpent, the devil (cf. Rev. 12).

How much should we love Mary?

Pope Benedict XVI, in his ecumenical discussions, has found that more and more Protestants are turning back to Mary, for they recognize that a Christianity without Mary is a Christianity that is lacking, lacking the feminine dimension of human life.

Blessed Mother Teresa of Calcutta was about to give a talk at a conference when a young woman rushed to her side and mentioned that one of the hot topics at the conference dealt with the issue of Mary and how much we should love her. Some were arguing that we were showing too much love for her, others argued we were not showing enough love for her.

The debate went back and forth with no resolution in sight. Mother Teresa looked at the messenger and said that she need not worry. She would take care of the dilemma. Mother Teresa proceeded to the stage and began to address the impasse in a very simple fashion. She said: "You want to know how much to love Mary? I'll tell you. Love her *no more* or *no less* than Jesus loved her." Wow! How can we poor creatures ever equal the love of Jesus? We can never love Mary too much, for she always leads us to her Son.

Let us not forget that Jesus was obedient to Mary at the wedding feast of Cana and at the temple. God was obedient to Mary.

Let us never forget Mary's special place in history. Remember to honor Mary is to honor her son, Jesus, for it is Jesus who gave Mary all her privileges. To deny Mary's privileges is to deny Jesus' will and work on behalf of Mary! In honoring Mary we are being obedient to God's will of honoring her; Mary's privileges were given by God and not man. Let us be obedient to the Scriptures which remind us that "all generations will call me blessed" (cf. Luke 1:48).

We as Christians are members of the Body of Christ, the Church (1 Cor. 12). Mary is the Mother of the Head of the Body, Jesus. So Mary is our mother too! She is the Mother of the Church, Christ's Body!

VI
END-TIME ISSUES

Hell, a reality

Do not doubt, the evil will depart this world and enter into the unquenchable fires of hell.

Ignatius of Antioch (ca. 107)
Disciple of the apostle John

Many groups refuse to believe in the reality of hell. They argue that an all-loving God would never condemn anyone to hell.

This might seem to be culturally and politically comforting but the reality of hell is something that one cannot run away from.

To argue that because God is all-loving he would never condemn anyone to hell is a misunderstanding of the nature of love. There is no such thing as love without justice, and justice demands that those who accept God's grace are to be rewarded for that acceptance, and those who blatantly reject God's grace are to receive their desire, life without God in hell.

Those who deny the existence of hell deny the preciousness of the gift of grace, of free will, and the reality of authentic love, which cannot be divorced from justice.

God loves us so much that he respects our free will decision to choose, in response to grace, eternal life with him or eternal life without him.

The reality of hell as a place of endless suffering is attested to throughout the Bible (Is. 66:24; Mt. 8:12; 25:41; Lk. 16:25; 13:28; 2 Thess. 1:9; Rev. 14:10; 18:7).

We cannot be, as the late John Cardinal O'Connor argued, "Cafeteria Catholics" or "Cafeteria Christians." We cannot pick and choose what we like or don't like. Catholicism is an all or nothing faith. Either we accept all of its infallible teachings or we might as well join a superficial version of Christianity where one can believe in anything.

The denial of the existence of hell is a sin, the sin of presumption. The sin of presumption distorts the relationship between God's mercy and justice.

Where do you get purgatory from?

Some like to argue that since the word "purgatory" is not in the Bible, it does not exist. The words "Bible," "Incarnation," and "Trinity" are likewise nowhere to be found in the Bible! The word may not be present but the reality certainly is!

The Bible makes reference quite often to a "cleansing fire" (i.e., cf. 1 Pet. 1:7; Wis. 3:1-6). We would call this cleansing fire purgatory, where God's fiery love "burns" away the soul's impurities, where one is "saved, but only through fire" (1 Cor. 3:1-16). The Bible also testifies to the reality of paying debts, as in the case of the Judge who reminds us that we "will not be released until [we] have paid the last penny" (Mt. 5:21-26; also 18:21-35; Lk. 12:58; 16:19-31; 1 Pet. 3:19; 4:6). In other words, we will not be released until every sin, every word, is accounted for (Mt. 12:36).

Gregory the Great (ca. 540-604) while reflecting on Matthew 12:31-32 explains with great insight the following in regards to purgatory:

> *As for certain lesser faults, we must believe that, before the Final Judgment, there is a purifying fire. He who is truth says that whoever utters blasphemy against the Holy Spirit will be pardoned neither in this age nor in the age to come. From this sentence, we understand that certain offenses can be forgiven in this age, and certain others in the age to come (Dial. 4:39: PL 77, 396).*

The Jewish feast of Chanukah is a commemoration of a battle and the cleansing of the temple that followed this event. This is a passage that would have been in the hearts and minds of all the apostles.

> *On the next day [after the battle with Gorgias]...Judas [Maccabee] and his men went to take up the bodies of the fallen and to bring them back to lie with their kindred in the sepulchers of their ancestors. Then under the tunic of each one of the dead they found sacred tokens of the idols of Jamnia, which the law forbids the Jews to wear. And it became clear to all that this was the reason these men had fallen. So they all blessed the ways of the Lord, the righteous judge, who reveals the things that are hidden; and they turned to supplication, praying that the sin that had been committed might be wholly blotted out. The noble Judas exhorted the people to keep themselves free from sin, for they had seen with their own eyes what had happened as a result of the sin of those who had fallen. He also took up a collection, man by man, to the amount of two thousand drachmas of silver, and sent it to Jerusalem to provide for a sin offering. In doing this he acted very well and honorably, taking account of the resurrection. For if he were not expecting that those who had fallen would rise again, it would have been superfluous and foolish to pray for the dead. But if he was looking to the splendid reward that is laid up for those who fall asleep in godliness, it was a holy and pious thought. Therefore, he made atonement for the dead, so that they might be delivered from their sin (2 Macc. 12:39-46, NRSV).*

In this passage we see that Judas Maccabee finds that the dead on the battlefield have sinned by wearing amulets associated with a false god. Now Judas does something critically important: he prays for the forgiveness of their sins; he takes up a collection for an expiatory sacrifice, and seeks atonement for his dead comrades so that those who died in sin might be freed from sin.

This passage is the most powerful proof for purgatory in all of the Scriptures. If one dies, one either goes to heaven, purgatory, or hell. If one goes to heaven, one has no need for one's sins to be blotted out, since one is enjoying eternal paradise. If one is in hell, then all the prayers in the world cannot release one from hell since hell is eternal (Mt. 25:41; 2 Thess. 1:9). Hence, if sin can be blotted out after death, then there needs to be a place for purification; that place is called purgatory.

Historically, prayers for the dead have always been part of Hebrew and Christian tradition. In the Jewish Orthodox culture, prayers for the dead were common. At the time of Jesus, prayers for the dead in the Jewish faith were said in temples and synagogues on feasts such as Passover, Booths, and Weeks. Jews to this very day still utter the "Mourner's Kaddesh" after the death of a person for the purification of his or her soul.

Graffiti in the catacombs of Rome from the first three centuries of Christianity, when the Church was under persecution, attests to this common practice. In the first century catacombs we read: "Sweet Faustina, may you live in God." "Peter and Paul, pray for Victor."

Basil the Great in 370 illustrates that the very nature of the Christian life, as a struggle and battle, makes the reality of purgatory an absolute necessity:

A man who is under sentence of death, knowing that there is One who saves, One who delivers, says: 'In You I have hoped, save me' from my inability 'and deliver me' from captivity. I think that the noble athletes of God, who have wrestled all their lives with the invisible enemies, after they have escaped all of their persecutions and have come to the end of life, are examined by the prince of this world; and if they are found to have any wounds from their wrestling, any stains or effects of sin, they are detained. If, however, they are found unwounded and without stain, they are, as unconquered, brought by Christ into their rest (Ps. 7, n. 2).

Augustine of Hippo in 387 records in his masterpiece *Confessions* the words of his mother, Monica: "All I ask of you is that wherever you may be you will remember me at the altar of the Lord." In other words, prayers were to be said for her, particularly the prayer of the Mass.

In Augustine's *De fide, spe, caritate liber unus* (39, 109) we read:

The time which interposes between the death of a man and the final resurrection holds souls in hidden retreats, accordingly as each is deserving of rest or of hardship, in view of what it merited when it was living in the flesh. Nor can it be denied that the souls of the dead find relief [in purgatory] through the piety of their friends and relatives who are still alive, when the Sacrifice of the Mass is offered for them, or when alms are given in the church. But these things are of profit to those who, when they were alive, merited that they might afterwards be able to be helped by these things. For there is a certain manner of living, neither so good that there is no need of these helps after death, nor yet so wicked that these helps are of no avail after death. There is, indeed, a manner of living so good that these helps are not needed [in heaven], and again a manner so evil that these helps are of no avail [in hell], once a man has passed from this life.

It is not until the Protestant Reformation that prayers for the dead become seriously challenged.

Pure logic attests to the need of a place called purgatory. We are reminded to be "perfect as [the] heavenly Father is perfect" (Mt. 5:48). We are called to "strive for that holiness without which one cannot see God" (Heb. 12:14). In Revelation 21:27 we are told that "nothing unclean shall enter heaven." Heaven is a place of perfection where "nothing impure" can enter (Rv. 21:27). If this is so, then one who dies in sin must be purified. In Hebrews 12:33 we are reminded that the "spirit of the just are made perfect;" made perfect to enter into heaven. If anything impure were to enter into heaven, then heaven would no longer be a place of purity for it would have been tainted with impurity. (Pure water, for example, if it is contaminated with a chemical, is no longer pure water. Likewise, heaven, if it is contaminated with imperfection, is no longer a place of perfection.).

Another interesting clue to purgatory is seen in 1 Corinthian 15:29-30 where people where baptizing themselves for their dead loved ones. This very practice--albeit a wrong practice--by some within the Christian community points to early Christianity's recognition that there had to be something more than just heaven or hell. There had to be a place where the efforts of the living on earth could have an impact on those in the afterlife. We call this place purgatory.

Another fascinating example is that of Jesus preaching to the "dead" after the crucifixion (1 Pet. 3:18-20: 4:6): "For this is why the gospel was preached even to the dead, that, though condemned in the flesh in human estimation, they might live in the spirit in the estimation of God." Clearly Jesus was cleansing, purging them through his preaching to enter into heaven!

Hence from a Scriptural point of view and from a philosophical point of view, derived from the Scriptural understanding of heaven, purgatory is a reality of Christianity.

In purgatory one is assured of heaven, but is purified to enter the realm of perfection. In purgatory a man gains, as Gregory of Nyssa (ca. 379) states, "knowledge of the difference between virtue and vice, and finds that he is not able to partake of divinity until he has been purged of the filthy contagion in his soul by the purifying fire" (*Sermones*, 1).

How sad it must be for those who cannot pray for their deceased loved ones. There is no greater sense of psychological closure than to pray for one that has passed away. That is why Paul asked for mercy on the soul of his dead friend Onesiphorus in 2 Timothy 1:16-18. He knew his prayers would release him from that place of purification that has become known as purgatory. (If Onesiphorus was in heaven he would be in no need of prayer, and if he was in hell no amount of prayer could release him. Therefore, Onesiphorus was in purgatory where Paul's prayers could be effective.).

Is there such a thing as temporal punishment?

Some have made the argument that when God forgives, he forgives, and therefore there is nothing to be made be up, or accounted for, or paid off. They therefore deny the reality of purgatory and the reality of temporal punishments. The above makes it quite clear that there is such a thing as purgatory, but let us address the issue of temporal punishment separately.

Temporal punishment refers to the earthly punishments that flow from sin. A sin may be forgiven, but the punishment due for that sin is either being made up for, or accounted for, or paid off in this life or in the life to come (cf. Mt. 5:26; 12:36; 1 Cor. 3:15; Rev. 21:27). As Catherine of Genoa would say, "We either do our purgatory here on earth or in the afterlife." The Bible is replete with examples of temporal punishment. But let us look at just one.

In 2 Samuel 12:13-18 we see the consequences of David's sin of adultery with Bathsheba and David's subsequent killing of her husband Uriah. The prophet Nathan reprimands David, then David says,

> '*I have sinned against the LORD.*' *Nathan answered David:* '*The LORD on his part has forgiven your sin: you shall not die. But since you have utterly spurned the LORD by this deed, the child born to you must surely die.*' *Then Nathan returned to his house. The LORD struck the child that the wife of Uriah had borne to David, and it became desperately ill. David besought God for the child. He kept a fast, retiring for the night to lie on the ground clothed in sackcloth. The elders of his house stood beside him urging him to rise from the ground; but he would not, nor would he take food with them. On the seventh day, the child died.*

Notice that even though David's sins were completely forgiven, there was still a temporal, earthly, punishment associated with the sin. Though forgiven, he was still punished.

Temporal punishment is an essential part of the Christian life for God is a loving father who does what every loving father does. He calls us to live a good and holy life. And when we are disobedient he chastises us for our own good and the good of our soul. In Wisdom 3:1-6 we see how God allows for chastisements for our very good:

> But the souls of the just are in the hand of God, and no torment shall touch them. They seemed, in the view of the foolish, to be dead; and their passing away was thought an affliction and their going forth from us, utter destruction. But they are in peace. For if before men, indeed, they be punished, yet is their hope full of immortality; Chastised a little, they shall be greatly blessed, because God tried them and found them worthy of himself.

David paid a heavy price for his sin, but he also changed as a person because of the temporal punishment that was inflicted upon him. David would become one of the Bible's greatest saints.

Is hell eternal or are the souls of the evil annihilated?
All orthodox Christians believe in a hell, but some groups such as the Jehovah's Witnesses and the Seventh Day Adventists argue that at death the soul "rests" or is "suspended in existence" until it is resurrected on the last day. Those that are good will enjoy eternity with God in heaven, while the evil will be condemned and their souls annihilated.

For the Catholic or the orthodox Christian the soul lives eternally from the moment of conception, either eternally with God or eternally without God, depending on one's response to grace.

For mainline Christians, the pains of hell are endless and the soul is immortal. In Isaiah 33:11, 14 we are reminded of the everlasting flames of hell; in Matthew 3:12 hell is a place where the damned "burn with unquenchable fire"; in Matthew 25:41 we read, "Depart, you accursed, into the eternal fire." In Matthew 25:46 we are reminded that the evil "will go off to eternal punishment." In Luke 3:16-17 the evil "will burn in unquenchable fire." In 2 Thessalonians 1:6-9 the evil will pay the penalty of eternal ruin." In Revelation 20:10 we read: "The Devil who had led them astray was thrown into the pool of fire and sulfur, where the beast and the false prophets were. There they will be tormented day and night forever and ever." Our souls are immortal and therefore hell is everlasting for the evil.

Furthermore, for mainline Christians there is a distinction between the particular judgment (which occurs immediately with death) and the general or last judgment (which occurs at the second coming of Christ). When we die (death being when the soul and body are separated), we are immediately judged and our soul enters into heaven, purgatory, or hell (cf. Mt. 17; Lk. 16:19-31; Heb. 9:27; 10:31; Wis. 3:1f; Eccl. 8:6-8; 11:9; 12:14; Sir. 11:28f; 16:13-22; 2 Macc. 12:43-46).

The soul is not "suspended" or at "rest" until the end of time. In Luke 23:42f we read: "[The thief hanging next to Jesus] said, 'Remember me when you come into your kingdom.' He replied to him, 'Amen, I say to you, today you will be with me in paradise.' Jesus assured the thief that **today** was his day! The thief's soul would be shortly enjoying the gift of paradise, while his body would begin to decay in the tomb.

At the end of time, at the last or general judgment, our body will be resurrected in a glorified form (Phil. 3:21) and be reunited with our soul in heaven (cf. Rv. 6:14-17; 7; 8:9). The last judgment and the resurrection of the bodies of the dead is well attested to in many Scripture passages such as Acts 24:15: "I have the same hope in God as they themselves have that there will be a resurrection of the righteous and the unrighteous." Judgment will follow. In Philippians 3:20-21 we read about the gift of the glorified body: "Our citizenship is in heaven, and from it we also await a savior, the Lord Jesus Christ. He will change our lowly body to conform with his glorified body by the power that enables him also to bring all things into subjection to himself."

Those who are still living at the time of Jesus' second coming, the *parousia*, will be judged body and soul at that very moment (cf. 25:31f).

Heaven and hell are eternal. A person is born to eternal life, eternal life with God or eternal life in hell, depending on his or her response to grace.

The concept of the annihilation of souls is found in eastern religions and particularly in the heresy of Gnosticism—with its idea of inferior gods. For the Gnostics, the non-elect, the *hylikoi,* would be annihilated.

Jehovah's Witnesses likewise have a similar belief in the annihilation of the soul. For Jehovah's Witnesses a man does not have a soul but is a soul. The death of man is the death of the soul. At the end of the world the good shall be created anew.

What the Jehovah's Witnesses fail to recognize is that there are three ways of understanding the soul in the Bible. It is often referred to as the seat of wisdom and emotions (Ps. 42:2), as a whole person (1 Peter 3:20), and as a life principle (Mt. 10:28; Rev. 6:9-10).

When humans were created they were created in the image and likeness of God (Gen. 1:26f). God is immortal and so are we! In Matthew 17:1-8 we see Jesus, Moses, and Elijah conversing. In Luke 16 we read about the resurrection of Jesus, body and soul. In Revelation 6:9-10 we read: "...I saw underneath the altar the souls of those who had been slaughtered because of the witness they bore to the word of God. They cried in a loud voice, 'How long will it be, holy and true master, before you sit in judgment, and avenge our blood on the inhabitants of the earth." Clearly these people were not in a state of "rest" or "suspension."

For Christians hell is permanent; there is no annihilation of souls or the ceasing of the existence of hell or the ceasing of the existence of the person (Mt. 3:12; 9:43; Rev. 20:10; Mt. 18:8; Mt. 25:46).

These groups are making the same mistake that those who were around Jesus were making. Jesus always reprimanded the Sadducees for their lack of belief in an afterlife; whereas, he affirmed the Pharisees in their belief in the afterlife.

Orthodox, Catholic Christianity (as well as Protestant Christianity) has always viewed the annihilation of souls as heretical and unchristian. Ignatius of Antioch (110), the friend of the apostle John, reminds the evil of the pain of the eternal "unquenchable fire" of hell (Ephesians 16:1). Polycarp, the friend of the apostle John, reminded the faithful to keep their eyes on Christ in order to avoid the "eternal and unquenchable fire" of hell (2:3). The list is unending regarding the eternity of hell!

Premillennialism, Postmillennialism, Amillennialism and the Rapture

Revelation 20 and 1 Thessalonians 4:15-17 are among the most fascinating passages in Scripture in that they have been interpreted in such radically different ways. The primary reason for this is the confusion over the placing of the thousand year reign, the rapture, and over the sense in which these passages were meant to be understood.

Premillennialism

Premillennialism holds that after the period of the Church there will be a time of tribulation that will be followed by Christ's Second Coming, the binding of Satan, and the resurrection of the faithful who have died in Christ. Christ and the risen faithful will reign on earth physically for a thousand years. This will be followed by another period of tribulation, albeit short, the Final Judgment and the rapture of the faithful into heaven. The creation of a new heaven and a new earth will follow.

The Catholic Church has always rejected this view.

Postmillennialism

Postmillennialism holds to the idea that after the period of the Church, Satan will be bound, and a thousand year reign will follow, followed by the rapture into heaven of the living faithful before the period (or during the middle) of the tribulation. The people left on earth will await the Second Coming of Christ, the resurrection of the dead, the Final Judgment, and the creation of a new heaven and a new earth.

The Catholic Church rejects Postmillennialism.

Amillennialism—Catholicism's View

Catholicism rejects both Premillennialism and Postmillennialism—and their variations. It believes in what is called Amillennialsim. It holds that Revelation 20 is a symbolic passage and that the thousand year reign is a symbolic term for the period from Christ's salvific act on the Cross to the time of Christ's Second Coming (the number 1000 is used in the Scriptures to refer to a long, but indeterminate time, a time known only by God). Christ's Second Coming will be preceded by a short tribulation period. Jesus' return will be followed by the resurrection of the dead (Acts 24:15), the Final Judgment (Mt. 25:31; 32; 46; Jn. 5:28-29; 12:49) and the creation of a new heaven and a new earth (Rom. 8:19-23; Eph. 1:10; 2 Pet. 3:13; Rev. 21:1-2; 14-5; 9; 27). How this transformation of a new heaven and a new earth will take place and how it will look like or when the Second Coming will occur is a mystery.

The Second Coming is the end of time as we know it!

The Catholic Understanding of the Rapture

And what is the Catholic understanding of the rapture as found in 1 Thessalonians 4:15-17? At the second coming of Christ, the dead will be resurrected, the Final Judgment will take place, and those faithful who are still alive when Christ returns—and after the Final Judgment--will go with the resurrected faithful to be with Christ forever.

What about the 144,000?

Basing their beliefs on Revelation 7:1-8 and Revelation 14:1-5, Jehovah's Witnesses and other pseudo-Christian groups and fundamentalists argue that only 144,000 people will be saved.

The 144,000, for virtually all mainline Christians, is a symbolic number, for if it were not, Jehovah's Witnesses, fundamentalists, and most Christians would surely not be among the 144,000, for the 144,000 are made up of only male virgins according to Revelation 14:4. And since these religious groups are not made up of entirely male virgins, they will not be counted among the 144,000. Furthermore, in the first 300 years of Christianity alone, more than one million Catholic Christians were martyred for their faith in Jesus Christ. Are they not in heaven? Of course they are! It would be nonsensical to think otherwise!

For Jehovah's Witnesses there are two groups of people: the 144,000 "anointed," and the "other sheep." The "anointed" go to a heavenly paradise and the "other sheep" go to an earthly paradise.

This is contradicted by the Bible. How do the Jehovah's Witnesses explain 2 Kings 2:11 or Hebrews 11:5 or Luke 13:28? According to the Jehovah's Witnesses the Old Testament people could not reach the heavenly paradise—they could only live in the earthly paradise for they are part of the "other sheep." Yet these passages from the Old Testament say that Enoch and Elijah were both taken up to heaven! And in Luke 13:28 Jesus reminds us that Abraham, Isaac and Jacob are in heaven!

Furthermore, if you read a little further on you see that there is a "great multitude which **no one could count**" standing before the throne of the Lamb in heaven (cf. Rev. 7:9). In 1 John 3:2 we read that all the faithful will see God in the beatific vision, "see him as he is." In Philippians 3:20 we are told that our citizenship is in heaven. In Matthew 5:11-12 we are enlightened to the fact that the persecuted will receive a great reward in heaven—just like the one million who died painful, barbaric, and tortuous deaths for the faith in the first 300 years of Christianity!

The real and traditional interpretation is as follows: 144,000 comes from the square root of 144, which is twelve, the number of Israel's tribes, multiplied by a thousand, the symbolic number for the New Israel that embraces all peoples, races, tongues, and nations (cf. Rev. 14:1-5; Gal. 6:16; Jas. 1:1).

The 144,000 is a symbolic number that denotes that those who remain loyal to Christ, even amidst trials and tribulations, even amidst the most severe of persecutions, will be saved (cf. Phil. 3:17-21; Rom. 8:16-17; 2 Pet. 1:1-10; 1 Jn. 3:1-3). Remember, in the first 300 hundred years of Christianity, over one million people were martyred, died for the faith of Christianity! In the twentieth century alone, there were more Christians killed for their faith than in the early Church.

Celestial marriages?

The idea of celestial marriages is an invention of the 19th century founder of Mormonism, Joseph Smith. It was completely unheard of till then. Basing themselves on a faulty interpretation of 1 Corinthians 15:40-42, Mormons believe that there is a *Telestial* kingdom where the non-believers go to, a *Terrestrial* kingdom for non-Mormons or lukewarm Mormons, and a Celestial kingdom for the righteous Mormons. The wicked, after a temporary period in hell, go into the *Telestial* kingdom.

To become part of the Celestial kingdom you must be a baptized Mormon, follow Mormon teaching, and be married in a Mormon temple. Interesting to say the least: This would exclude Jesus and the apostles John and Paul!

Those whose marriages have been "sealed" in a Mormon temple will be part of the Celestial kingdom and have an eternal marriage where they will beget "spiritual children" in the afterlife. They will also become gods of their own worlds.

This belief system is contrary to the Scripture's understanding of the world and the human person. Jesus reminds us that there is no marriage or sex or child-bearing in heaven. As Jesus says in Matthew 22:29: "You are misled because you do not know the Scriptures or the power of God. At the resurrection they neither marry nor are given in marriage but are like the angels in heaven." Furthermore, Jesus praises celibacy in Matthew 19:12 and the apostle Paul recommends celibacy for full-time ministers in 1 Corinthians 7:32-35. And in 1 Timothy 5:9-12 the older widows are encouraged to take a pledge of celibacy and become enrolled in the order of religious or widows.

But what about 1 Corinthians 15:40-42? For Catholics and mainline Christians 1 Corinthians 15:40-42 is interpreted in the following manner: In Jewish tradition the world was understood to have heavenly bodies like the stars, the sun, the moon, and earthly bodies, the things that dwell on the earth (cf. 1 Enoch 18:13-16; 21:3-6; Philo, *De plant.* 12). Paul uses this understanding of the world to explain the qualitative differences of the human body before and after death, after the resurrection. Before death, a body is animated by a lower, natural life principle—*psyche*--and endowed with the properties of corruptibility and weakness. After death, the body is

134

animated by a higher life principle (*pneuma*) and thus endowed with incorruptibility, glory, power, etc.—the qualities of God himself. In other words, after the resurrection of our bodies at the end of time, our bodies will be glorified. As St. Paul explains in his letter to the Philippians (3:20-21): "Our citizenship is in heaven, and from it we also await a savior, the Lord Jesus Christ. *He will change our lowly body to conform with his glorified body...*"

There is no foundation for Mormon beliefs in the Bible or in Christian history!

What are we to think of Bible prophecy?

Bible Prophecy has become the rage among many Pentecostals. Many books have come out in recent years predicting the end-times. Many television programs find popular support regarding end-time issues. This is not new, for every generation has made predictions about the end of the world and the second coming of Christ. Many claim that all we have to do is look at the signs of the times and we will find indications regarding the end. They often quote Mark 13:39 in their favor.

Yet history has shown us what Christ has taught us that only the Father in heaven knows the hour or time, and that the end will come like a thief in the night when we least expect it (Mt. 24:36; 2 Pet. 3:10; Rev. 3:3).

Let us not bother ourselves with predicting the future from Bible quotations. Rather let us be content with living every moment in the present with our Lord and Savior, and let us encourage others to do the same. Instilling fear, which is often the subconscious or conscious motive behind Bible prophecy, is not a proper motive. The great Catholic mystics of the Church have always shown us by their lives that as one grows in holiness, one is less concerned with going to hell as much as with not loving enough. Let us love, according to God's understanding of love, according to authentic love.

135

VII
SALVATION

Do Catholics have a different understanding of the human person than Protestants?

Yes. Catholics and Protestants--at least the original Protestants such as Luther, Calvin and Zwingli--have a different understanding of "original sin," and because of this difference of understanding, we have a differing view of the human person.

Original sin was the sin committed by Adam and Eve in the Garden of Eden. At the heart of "original sin" is disobedience to God and the lack of trust in God: "[S]educed by the devil, [man] wanted to be "like God," but "without God, before God, and not in accordance with God" (cf. Gen. 3:5; CCC 398).

Original sin led to the distortion of all of creation.

Because "original sin" was passed down to all generations (Ps. 51:7), all human nature was affected with the loss of original holiness and justice. The gates of heaven were closed.

By the merits of Christ, his Passion, eternal life was restored to us.

In baptism "original sin" is washed away, although the consequences of "original sin," such as suffering, illness, decay, etc., remain. The human person's nature was not completely destroyed by "original sin"; it was simply wounded (cf. Mk. 1:4; 16:16; Jn. 3:5; 1:33; Acts 2:38; 8:12f; 16:33; Rom. 6:3-6; Gal. 3:27; 1 Cor. 6:11; Eph. 5:26; Col. 2:12-14; Lk. 3:3; Heb. 10:22).

This last point is the crucial difference between Catholic theology and Protestant theology. For the Protestant, "original sin" did not simply wound human nature; they argue that it radically destroyed and perverted human nature. Thus one lost free will and the ability to count on one's reasoning abilities.

This is why Protestantism would resort to a theology that emphasized faith alone, the Bible alone, and the predestination of the elect, or a variation on this theme, the absolute assurance of salvation.

The Catholic position is much more optimistic. Human nature, as was mentioned, was wounded by "original sin," but not destroyed or perverted. It "is wounded in the natural powers proper to it; subject to ignorance, suffering, and the dominion of death: and inclined to sin, an inclination to evil called concupiscence" (CCC 405).

Since human nature is only wounded, one has not lost the gift of free will, despite an inclination to evil, and one has not lost the gift of reasoning, despite its being subject to ignorance. Thus, one can use one's natural reasoning abilities to understand one's faith and the mystery of creation. One can even reason to a knowledge of a divine reality (cf. Rom. 1:19:20; Wis. 13:1-9). One is free to love and respond to God and one is free in seeking to uncover the hidden mysteries of God. This is a much more optimistic understanding of human nature.

The following quotes should be helpful in understanding the Catholic understanding of the human person in reference to the Fall: Genesis 3:5-17, 19; 2:17; 4:3-15; 6:5, 12; 8:21; Job 14:4; 15: 14; Psalm 51:7; Sirach 8:5; Romans 1:18-32; 3:9, 23; 5:12, 17, 18; 6:23; 8:6-8, 11, 13, 17, 21; 1 Corinthians 1-6; Galatians 5:17; Ephesians 2:3; Revelation 2-3.

Predestination or providence?

> *If the human race does not have the power of a freely deliberated choice in fleeing evil and in choosing good, then men are not accountable for their actions, whatever they may be. That they do, however, by a free choice, either walk upright or stumble, we shall now prove. God did not make man like the other beings, the trees and the four-legged beasts, for example, which cannot do anything by free choice. Neither would man deserve reward or praise if he did not of himself choose the good; nor, if he acted wickedly, would he deserve punishment, since he would not be evil by choice, and could not be other than that which he was born. The Holy Prophetic Spirit taught us this when he informed us through Moses that God spoke as follows to the first created man: 'Behold, before your face, the good and the evil. Choose the good.'*
>
> *Justin Martyr (ca. 100)*
> *First Apology, 43*

There are some Christian groups that believe in a strict form of predestination. They believe that God predestined some people to heaven and some people to hell. People consequently have no free will to respond to God's grace. They are either members of the elect or members of the damned.

This extreme view of predestination is rejected by the Catholic Church, for it is a rejection of a human person's ability to love God. How can one truly love if one is predestined to love? That is not love. That is a robot programmed to do what the programmer has asked him or her to do.

True love implies freedom. One loves because one makes a decision to love. A Catholic makes a decision to love God in response to God's showering grace. Strict predestination, therefore, is rejected by the Catholic Church.

The Catholic Church believes in God's providential will. Providence can be seen as a reality somewhere in between extreme predestination and extreme free will. That is, somewhere in between a strict predestination where some are predestined from birth to heaven or hell, and an extreme understanding of free will where God has no say in the world. Providence is the belief that God has a predestined plan for the world and that he knows everything that will take place; he even knows in advance the free will decisions we will make, for these free will decisions are part of God's divine plan.

Free will is affirmed throughout the Scriptures within the scope of God's plan (Gn. 4:7; Dt. 30:19; Sir. 15:14; Prov. 1:24; Is. 5:4; Ez. 18:23; Mt. 23:37; Lk. 13:34; Acts 7:51; Heb. 12:15; 2 Pet. 3:9; Rev. 20:4).

Clement of Rome, the friend of the apostle Peter, in his *Letter to the Corinthians* affirms this Catholic position:

> *Let us look back over the generations, and learn that from generation to generation the Lord has given an opportunity for repentance to all who would return to Him (7).*

Is salvation assured?

"Are you saved?" is the question that is often posed by all kinds of Protestants. As Catholics we can say that at this moment I am saved (cf. Rom. 8:24; Eph. 2:5, 8; 2 Tim. 1:9; Tit. 3:5), but because of the gift of free will, I can in the future deny Christ and lose the salvation that was gifted to me (cf. Phil. 2:12; 1 Pet. 1:9; Mt. 19:22; 24:13; Mk. 8:3-5 Acts 15:11; Rom. 5:9-10; 13:11; 1 Cor. 3:15; 5:5; Heb. 9:28).

For some Christians, all that is required for salvation and its continual assurance is the acknowledgment of Christ as one's personal Lord and Savior (Acts 2:21;19:15, 28; 19:17; Rom. 10:13; 1 Cor. 6:11; 2 Thess. 1:12; 2:19; 1 Jn. 6:11; 5:13). This is what it means, for them, to be "born again" (Jn. 3:3-5). Once this step has been taken the person is saved and can never lose his or her salvation. Guided by God this person will from this moment on live a good life, and if he or she should fail at some moment to live a good life, then the Holy Spirit will come to punish, purify, and to return that person back to wholeness. No matter what, one is saved and can never lose that salvation. It is assured!

Some would point out that if one's life exemplifies great sinfulness, then one really did not accept Jesus Christ as his or her Lord and Savior. On the surface they may have appeared to, but in their soul they did not.

Given the above Scripture quotations, this may appear a convincing explanation for the assurance of one's salvation. Yet the above Scripture quotes do not make any such claim of assured salvation upon the simple proclamation of Jesus as Lord and Savior. These quotes must be taken within the context of the whole of the Bible. When this is done, then the above Scripture quotes can be properly understood.

Basing itself on the correct interpretation of the Scriptures and the constant teaching of the Church, the Church has always affirmed that salvation is conditional. (The belief in the absolute assurance of one's salvation is a novel position that can be traced to the heresies of Gnosticism and 16th century Protestantism). Catholics believe that one's salvation is dependent on one's constant "yes" to God's grace, to God's call. To say that one is assured of salvation by one act, as some Protestants argue, is to essentially say that once one has proclaimed

Jesus as Lord and Savior, one's free will has been lost, since one cannot reject God from that point on.

The question must be asked in such a case: "How can one truly love God if one is assured of salvation?" Love implies a free will. Love is a decision, a free decision. To deny any future decision is to eliminate the capacity to love God. We would be saved robots waiting to die and enter into heaven. Where would the virtue of hope be?

For the Catholic, then, one needs to freely choose to respond to God's grace at every moment. One does not lose his or her free will after what some call being "born again." Although these people may argue that one's free will is not lost, the obvious philosophical consequence of saying that one is assured of faith is to claim that one has no more say in the future of one's eternal destiny.

As Catholics, we argue that our salvation is dependent on the state of our mortal soul at the moment of our death (cf. Mt. 25:31-46). A person that dies in the friendship of God, in a state of grace, is granted the rewards of eternal heaven with God and the saints and angels. The person who dies in mortal sin (1 Jn. 5:16-17) will reap what they have sown, eternal damnation.

For Catholics there is a distinction made between redemption and salvation. Jesus has redeemed the world by his blood; he has restored our friendship with God. But redemption is not the same as salvation.

Salvation presupposes redemption, but is distinguishable from redemption. Christ opened the gates of heaven for us, delivered us from sin, and restored humanity to the life of grace by the redeeming act on the Cross. We in turn must respond to the redemption won for us. We must respond to the engulfing grace he has released upon us (Phil. 1:6; Heb. 13:20-21). The gates are open, but one must choose to enter through those gates (Rom. 2:3-8; 5:9-10; 3:1-13; 3:19-31; 11:22; 13:2; 1 Cor. 1:8; 3: 12-15; 4:3-5; 6: 9-11; 9:27; 10:11-12; 13:1-3; 15:1-2; 2 Cor. 2:15; 5:10; 13:5; Gal. 5:13-21; 6:8-9; Eph. 2:8-10; Phil. 2:12; 3:7-16; Heb. 10:26-29; 1 Tim. 5:3-8; 2 Pet. 1:1-11; 2:20-21; 1 Jn. 1:5-10; 2:1-11; 3:7; 3:10-17; 3:21-24; 4:20-21; 5:1-5; Mt. 7:21; 19:16-21; 25:31-46; Rev. 2:23; 22:12-15).

If salvation is assured why would we have to be careful and pray for strength against temptations (Mt. 26:41; Mk. 14:38; Lk. 22:46; Gal. 6:1)? Why would one have to train oneself like an athlete for fear of losing one's salvation (1 Cor. 9:27)? If salvation is assured, why do we need to "persevere" (Mt. 24:13; 2 Tim. 2:12)? If salvation is assured, why would we need to do penance (Mt. 3:8; Acts 2:38; 8:22; 2 Cor. 7:10)? If salvation is assured why would we need to be judged by the Lord (1 Cor. 4:4-5; 2 Cor. 5:10)? If salvation is assured why would we be concerned about being paid "according to our works" (Rom. 2:6) or being paid according to our "conduct" (Mt. 16:27)? If salvation is assured, why would we need to "remain in his kindness" for fear of being "cut off" (Rom. 11:22)? If salvation is assured, how can one be in the process of "being saved," or "perishing" (2 Cor. 2:15)? If salvation is assured, why are we called to "test ourselves" and fear the failing "of the test" (2 Cor. 13:5)? If salvation is assured, why must we "work out our salvation with fear and trembling" (Phil. 2:12)? If one is assured of salvation, why bother with religious duties and moral obligations (cf. 1 Tim. 3:8)? If salvation is assured, why bother follow in Jesus' footsteps (1 Pet. 2:21)? If salvation is assured, why acknowledge our sinfulness (1 Jn. 5-10). If salvation is assured, why bother to follow the commandments (1 Jn. 2:1-11; Jn. 14:21; Mt. 19:17)? If salvation is assured, why is crying "Lord, Lord" insufficient for entering the kingdom of heaven (Mt. 7:21)? If salvation is assured how do we explain these words from Jesus: "If anyone wishes to come after me, he must deny himself and take up his cross daily and follow me. For whoever wishes to save his life will lose it and whoever loses his life for my sake will save it" (Lk. 9:23-24).

If one was assured of salvation, then faith would not have a future goal? Yet Peter reminds the faithful to persevere during times of trial for they are achieving in this process "faith's goal, salvation" (cf. 1 Pet. 1:6-9). Or as Paul states: "I continue my pursuit toward the goal, the prize of [salvation]" (Phil. 3:14).

One must avoid the sin of presumption, the sin that boasts in a false sense of assured salvation (Jms. 4:13-16). One must remember the words of Paul who reminds us to "work with anxious concern to achieve one's salvation" (Phil. 2:12), and to let no one "think he is standing upright...lest he fall" (1 Cor. 10:12).

The *Didache, The Teaching of the Twelve Apostles*, 16, reminds us that we need to "endure in our faith in order to be saved." And the *Epistle of Barnabas* (ca. 96) reminds us that salvation can be lost at any moment:

> *Let no assumption that we are among the called ever tempt us to relax our efforts or fall asleep in our sins; otherwise the Prince of Evil will obtain control over us, and oust us from the kingdom of the Lord* (*Barnabas*, 4, trans. Walter Mitchell in *Early Christian Prayers*, Chicago: Henry Regnery Co., 1961).

The view that one could be assured of salvation has always been a heretical teaching. The Catholic Church was embroiled for centuries with the heresy of Christian Gnosticism—with its "Great Silence," its aeons, its demiurge, with its elect, with its certainty of salvation (for the *pneumatikoi* or *psychikoi*). Heresies never really go away, they just recycle themselves.

To argue for the assurance of salvation would be to make grace "cheap," as Dietrich Bonhoeffer would say. It would be an insult to the majesty of God.

What about this faith and works?

> *The quality of holiness is shown not by what we say but by what we do in life.*

141

While it is true that we are justified by faith (Acts 13:39; Rom. 1:17; 3:20-30; 4:5; Gal. 3:11); we are not justified by faith alone (Jms. 2:14f). Let us look at what the Bible says:

> *What good is it, my brothers and sisters if you say you have faith but do not have works? Can faith save you? If a brother or sister is naked and lacks daily food, and one of you says to them, 'Go in peace, keep warm and eat your fill,' and yet you do not supply for their bodily needs, what is the good of that? So faith by itself, if it has no works, is dead.*
>
> *But someone will say, 'You have faith and I have works.' Show me your faith apart from your works, and I by my works will show you my faith. You believe that God is one; you do well. Even the demons believe and shudder. Do you want to be shown, you senseless person, that faith apart from works is barren? Was not our ancestor Abraham justified by works when he offered his son Isaac on the altar? You see that faith was active along with his works, and faith was brought to completion by the works. Thus the scripture was fulfilled that says, 'Abraham believed God, and it was reckoned to him as righteousness,' and he was called the friend of God. You see that a person is justified by works and not by faith alone.... For just as the body without the spirit is dead, so faith without works is also dead (Jms. 2:14-24, 26, NRSV).*

This passage has been a stumbling block for Protestants from the very beginning. Martin Luther, the first Protestant, wanted to drop the book of James from the New Testament. He called it a "straw letter." It was only after much opposition that he reluctantly left the book in the Bible. This passage is a clear challenge to Protestant theology.

In Matthew 7:21 we read: "Not everyone who says, 'Lord, Lord,' will enter the kingdom of heaven, but the one who does the will of my heavenly Father."

And in Matthew 25:41-46 we read:

> *[Jesus] will say to [those] on his left, 'Depart from me, you accursed, into the eternal fire prepared for the devil and his angels. For I was hungry and you gave me no food, I was thirsty and you gave me no drink, a stranger and you gave me no welcome, naked and you gave me no clothing, ill and in prison, and you did not care for me. Then they will answer and say, 'Lord, when did we see you hungry or thirsty or a stranger or naked or ill or in prison, and not minister to your needs?' He will answer them, 'Amen, I say to you, what you did not do for one of these least ones, you did not do for*

me. And these will go off to eternal punishment, but the righteous to eternal life.

It is true that we are **not** saved by our works (Eph. 2:8-9). The Church has always believed this. In fact, the heresy of Pelagianism which argued that one could work out one's salvation was condemned in the fifth century.

What Catholics argue is that salvation implies works (Jms. 2:20, 22). That is, one cannot be saved by faith alone. Martin Luther is the one that inserted the word "alone" after faith in his translation of the Scriptures. He did this in Romans 3:28 and Galatians 2:16. Notice that in any scholarly translation "alone" does not appear after the word "faith" in Romans 3:28 and Galatians 2:16.

Salvation for Catholics implies faith and works. Authentic faith always implies the fruits of that faith, works. And authentic holy work always implies a source for that holy work, faith. Faith and works therefore cannot be separated. John Chrysostom's (ca. 344) commentary on the Gospel of John (31, 1) illustrates this point succinctly:

> *He that believes in the Son has everlasting life. Is it enough then to believe in the Son in order to have everlasting life? By no means! Listen to Christ declare this himself when he says, 'Not everyone who says to Me, Lord, Lord! shall enter the kingdom of heaven'; For if a man believe rightly in the Father and in the Son and in the Holy Spirit, but does not live rightly, his faith will avail him nothing toward salvation.*

Maximus the Confessor wrote: ""faith must be joined to an active love of God which is expressed in good works." (Cf. *Centuria, cap.* 1, 30-40: PG 90, 967). "If I have all the faith in the world, but am without love, I gain nothing" (cf. 1 Cor. 13:1-3). It is for this reason that the Scriptures remind us that we will be rewarded according to our works: "None of those who cry out, 'Lord Lord, will enter the kingdom of God but only the one who does the will of my Father in Heaven" (Mt. 7:21). "If you wish to enter into life, keep the commandments" (Mt. 19:17-18). "The one who holds out to the end is the one who will see salvation" (Mt. 24:13). "Work with anxious concern to achieve your salvation" (Phil. 2:12). "The just judgment of God will be revealed when he will repay every man for what he has done" (Rom. 2:6). "He will receive his wages in proportion to his toil" (1 Cor. 3:8). "It is not those who hear the law who are just in the sight of God; it is those who keep it who will be declared just" (Rom. 2:13). "[We are saved' by faith, which expresses itself through love" (Gal. 5:6). "[We are] created in Christ Jesus to lead the life of good deeds" (Eph. 2:10). (also cf. Mt. 25:34-36; Lk. 6:27-36; 46-49; Rom. 8:25; 11:22-23; Col. 3:23f; Heb. 10:24-29; Jms. 1:22-25: 2:14-26; 2 Pet. 2:20-21; 1 Jn. 3:7; 5:3; 2 Jn. 8; Rev. 22:12)

Polycarp, a disciple of John, writing on the importance of good works, declares:

> *When it is in your power to do good, withhold not, because alms deliver from death. All of you be subject to one another, having your behavior blameless among the Gentiles, that by your good works you may receive praise, and the Lord may not be blasphemed in you (10).*

The *Epistle of Barnabas* (ca. 96) likewise affirms that

> *[e]veryone will be recompensed in proportion to what he has done (4). Remember the day of judgment day and night, and seek out every day the faces of God's holy people, either laboring in speech by exhorting others and trying to save souls by what you say, or by working with your hands for the remission of your sins (Epistle of Barnabas, 18:19, trans. Alun Idris Jones in Promise of Good Things: The Apostolic Fathers, New Rochelle: New City Press, 1993).*

Authentic faith implies authentic works, and authentic holy works implies authentic faith.

Blessed Mother Teresa of Calcutta, a saint in our own time, exemplified this inseparable nature between faith and works when she stated:

> *The fruit of silence is prayer.*
> *The fruit of prayer is faith.*
> *The fruit of faith is love.*
> *The fruit of love is service.*

Let us never forget to bear the good fruit that comes from our obedience to faith. Let us keep in mind the words of Paul: "I do not run like a man who loses sight of the finish line. I do not fight as if I were shadowboxing. What I do is discipline my own body and master it, for fear that after having preached to others I myself should be rejected" (1 Cor. 9:27).

Faith operates through love, a work (cf. Gal. 5:6). We will receive our reward from God according to our grace-filled works (Rm. 2:6), for faith operates through love, a work (cf. Gal. 5:6).

Let us never commit the sin of presumption. Let us follow Paul's teaching which reminds us to "work out... [our] salvation with fear and trembling" (Phil. 2:12).

Why do Catholics believe that "non-Christians" can be saved?

Joseph of Arimathea...was a disciple of Jesus, though a secret one... (Jn. 19:38).

144

Joseph of Arimathea was an anonymous follower of Christ. What lesson can we learn from him?

Mohandas Gandhi, the great Indian leader, was killed by gunfire in 1948 by an assassin's bullet. As Gandhi fell to the ground, he placed his hand on his forehead. This was quite significant, for in the Hindu culture, one indicates forgiveness by such a gesture. Gandhi, before his death, had forgiven his assassin. Is this not a holy act? Does this not require grace? Is one not saved who performs such an act?

The Catholic Church affirms that Christ is the way and the truth and the life and that no one goes to the Father except through the Son (Jn. 14:6), and consequently through his Body, his Bride, the Church. All salvation therefore comes from Christ and his Body the Church (1 Cor. 12:12f; 2 Cor. 11:2; Rom. 12:5; Eph. 1:22f; 5:25, 27; Rev. 19:7).

Lumen Gentium 14, in acknowledging Mark 16:16 and John 3:5, affirms the following:

> *Basing itself on Scripture and Tradition, the Council teaches that the Church, a pilgrim now on earth, is necessary for salvation; the one Christ is the mediator and the way of salvation; he is present to us in his body which is the Church. He himself explicitly asserted the necessity of faith and Baptism, and thereby affirmed at the same time the necessity of the Church which men enter through Baptism as through a door. Hence they could not be saved who, knowing that the Catholic Church was founded as necessary by God through Christ, would refuse either to enter it or to remain in it.*

Faith--which implies holy works--baptism, and consequently the Church are necessary for salvation.

The Church, however, makes adamantly clear that there are those who "through no fault of their own" who will be saved.

> *Those who, through no fault of their own, do not know the Gospel of Christ or his Church, but who nevertheless seek God with a sincere heart, and, **moved by grace**, try in their actions to do his will as they know it through the dictates of their conscience those too may achieve eternal salvation (LG 16).*

Given the above teachings we must ask ourselves, "How do we reconcile these two positions of the Church?"

The key is found in the second passage's key phrase "moved by grace." One who is authentically holy is one who has the gift of grace at the core of his or her being. And since Christ is another word for grace, Christ consequently is the source of salvation for a person of authentic holiness, whether that person is explicitly aware of it or not. Such a person is saved by Christ who is the way and the truth and the life and

145

that person is brought to the Father through the Son (Jn. 14:6). The soul of such a person is one in which *implicit* faith is being experienced. Such a soul makes one a member of the Mystical Body of Christ, the Church.

This reality finds its most beautiful expression in Matthew 25:

> *Just as you did it to one of the least of my brethren, you did it to me.... Come, you blessed by my Father inherit the kingdom prepared for you from the foundation of the world; for I was hungry and you gave me something to drink, I was a stranger and you welcomed me, I was naked and you gave me clothing, I was sick and you took care of me, I was in prison and you visited me.*

Or in the words of St. Anselm:

> *When we speak about wisdom, we are speaking of Christ. When we speak about virtue, we are speaking of Christ. When we speak about justice, we are speaking of Christ. When we speak about peace, we are speaking of Christ. When we speak about truth and life..., we are speaking of Christ* (Ps. 36, 65-66: CSEL 64,123-124).

But one may ask about the necessity of baptism. The Church from the earliest of times has recognized three forms of baptism: baptism by water; baptism by desire; and baptism by blood. Since grace, Christ, is in the soul of a person who through no fault of his or her own has not grasped the explicit proclamation of the Gospel, that person, because he or she is moved by grace, has accepted a baptism by virtue of desire at an implicit level. In other words, if such a person was fully aware of the Gospel message in its explicit form, then that person would have gladly been baptized by a baptism of water.

So people from other religions (i.e., Jews, Muslims, Buddhists, Hindus, etc.) can be saved if they are holy; that is, moved by grace to a life that can be viewed as a continual "yes" to God. They are saved by Christ who is the way and the truth and the life and by his Church, his Body, his Bride (1 Cor. 12:12f; 2 Cor. 11:2; Rom. 12:5; Eph. 1:22f; 5:25, 27; Rev. 19:7).

If this is so, some may argue, "What's the point in evangelizing?" Evangelizing is not diminished by recognizing holiness in others. In fact, it is made easier. For the mystery of Christ is already within the person at an implicit level. All we need to do, in evangelizing, is nourish the response to grace in that person until that person comes to an explicit recognition of that which is at the very core of that person's being seeking to be expressed fully.

VIII
MISCELLANEOUS ISSUES

Do Catholics practice idol worship?

In Exodus 20:4-5 we read:

You shall not make for yourself an idol, or any likeness of what is in heaven above or on the earth beneath or in the water under the earth. You shall not worship them or serve them; for, I the Lord your God, am a jealous God...(NASB).

Upon reading such a command from God we would wonder why Catholics would have statues or any art work for that matter.

Again when we interpret the Bible we need to interpret it within the context of the whole Bible. It is in interpreting a passage within the context of the whole Bible that we are able to come to the correct understanding of what is meant by a particular Scripture passage. When taken in the context of the whole, this passage refers to worshiping a "graven image" as a god. In other words, worship which is only due to God is being given to a man-made object. Most Christians today understand this, and virtually all scholars, with the exception of--unfortunately—some ill-informed anti-Catholic writers.

I recently went into a fundamentalist book store and, to my surprise, found statues of angels, rings with images of fishes (a symbol for Christ) and rings with WWJD (the abbreviation for "What Would Jesus Do?"). These are all "graven images." I saw paintings and pictures on the wall for sale and all kinds of cards with all kinds of images on them. And as I approached the counter I saw one of the salespersons showing photographs he had taken of his family on a recent trip. Another person was reading a children's book with pictures in it of Jesus and the apostles. How can they be looking at anything that resembles anything in heaven or on earth? Isn't this forbidden by the entire reading of Exodus 20:4-5?

Obviously this is not what God meant by forbidding the making of images.

Let us look at the Scriptures. In Exodus 25:18-22 we read where God spoke to Moses and instructed him to do the following:

[You] shall make two cherubim of gold; of hammered work shall you make them, on the two ends of the mercy seat. Make one cherub on the one end, and one cherub on the other end. The cherubim shall spread out their wings above, overshadowing the mercy seat with their wings, their faces facing one another. Toward the mercy seat shall the faces of the cherubim be (RSV).

147

Isn't this a graven image? There it is right in the Bible! God had commanded the making of statues. In Numbers 21:8-9 we read how God commanded Moses to "make a bronze serpent and mount it on a pole." In the fabrication of the tent cloth covering the "Dwelling" the artisans were commanded to embroider cherubim on the cloth (Ex. 26:1). In the building and furnishing of the temple (1 Kings 6:23-28; 7:23-45) images and carved figures abound—images of cherubim, trees, flowers, oxen, lions, pomegranates, and so on.

Archaeological evidence of the first centuries demonstrates that Jewish synagogues were adorned with murals depicting all sorts of things found in nature. The burial grounds of the Christians and the Catacombs also illustrated various symbols for Christ as well as various biblical images—the most popular being the woman at the well.

This is no wonder since images, icons, and statues were the books of their time, image-books for those who could not read. The ability to read was primarily the domain of the well-to-do, the clerics, the aristocrats and the scholars. The common classes saw stories (i.e., two story churches; that is, two levels of stain glass windows depicting biblical stories) as opposed to reading stories. Preachers would often point to stained-glass windows, icons, frescoes and all forms of art to help the faithful understand the message of the Gospel. Churches were "visual libraries" for the faithful in a time when people could not read.

What is forbidden by the commandment expressed in Exodus 20:4-5 is the worship of anything which is not God. Only God is due worship.

In many ancient pagan cultures it was thought that after a statue of a god was made, the god would come to dwell within or around the object created. So pagans would worship the object for they believed their god was dwelling in the object.

As Catholics, and as most Christians today recognize, we do not see statues or any object as worthy of worship. Statues and other forms of art are simply reminders of the true God we worship. Statues and art help us to move our hearts to love the true God that is not found in any statue or work of art. It is just like a husband who has not seen his wife for a long period of time; he looks at a picture of his wife and his emotions are stirred and comforted in his love for her. He does not love the picture; he loves the person represented by the picture.

And so images are reminders to our calling, our love. As Cyril of Alexandria (ca. 429) explains:

> *Even if we make images of pious men it is not so that we might adore them as gods but that when we see them we might be prompted to imitate them; and if we make images of Christ, it is so that our minds might wing aloft in yearning for him (On Ps. 113B (115):16).*

For John Damascene (ca. 645), in Jesus Christ, in the Incarnation, the Son of God has ushered in a new "economy" of images. As he stated:

Previously God, who has neither a body nor a face, absolutely could not be represented by an image. But now that he has made himself visible in the flesh and has lived with men, I can make an image of what I have seen of God... and contemplate the glory of the Lord, his face unveiled (De imag. 1,16: PG 96:1245-1248).

Because of the Incarnation, a new era entered into the world. Images representing Christ and therefore the Gospel would take on a new veracity: The words communicated by the Scriptures are illuminated by the image, and the image in turn is illuminated by the words. (Interestingly enough Paul refers to Jesus as the *ikonos*, the icon, of the living God). The second Council of Nicea (787) stated:

We declare that we preserve intact all the written and unwritten traditions of the Church which have been entrusted to us. One of these traditions consists in the production of representational artwork, which accords with the history of the preaching of the Gospel. For it confirms that the incarnation of the Word of God was real and not imaginary, and to our benefit as well, for realities that illustrate each other undoubtedly reflect each other's meaning (Council of Nicea II (787): COD 111).

Artwork which was common among Christians and Jews would now take on a new and more powerful significance. As the *Catechism of the Catholic Church* states: "Christian iconography expresses in images the same Gospel message that the Scriptures communicate by words. Image and word illuminate each other (1160). The word on the written page serves as one means of communication and the image on the canvas serves as another.

Catholics do not worship statues or images. We worship God.

As an aside, the God who was without image took in the Incarnation an image, Jesus. After the Ascension, the glorified body of Christ was assumed into the Trinity. Thus, the image of God in heaven will be the image of the glorified body of Jesus—for the Father and Spirit are image-less.

Why relics?

A relic is that which is from a saint or associated with a saint and is intended for the spiritual enrichment of the faithful. There are three classes of relics. A *first class relic* is one that is part of a saint's body. A *second class relic* is one that is a part of the clothing of the saint or something that was used or belonged to the saint during his or her lifetime. A *third class relic* is one that a saint has touched, such as a piece of cloth or other object.

Relics are placed in shrines, reliquaries of churches, and placed in altar stones during the consecrations of church altars.

Relics are intended to stir a person's devotion to living a Christ-like life. They are reminders that living the Christian life is not impossible. If others have been able to live it, we likewise can be comforted in the fact that we too can become saints.

Relics have also been associated with various miracles.

In the Bible we read in 2 Kings 13:21: "Once some people were burying a man... They cast the dead man into the grave of Elisha, and everyone went off. But when the man came in contact with the bones of Elisha, he came back to life and rose to his feet." In Acts 5:15-16 we read, "[People] carried the sick out into the streets and laid them on cots and mats so that when Peter came his shadow could fall on one or another of them...and they were all cured." In Acts 19:11-12 we read, "So extraordinary were the mighty deeds God accomplished at the hands of Paul that when face cloths or aprons that touched his skin were applied to the sick, their diseases left them and the evil spirits came out of them."

A relic is that which is from a saint or associated with a saint and is intended for the spiritual enrichment of the faithful.

Why do some Catholics believe in the theory of evolution? Are they not contradicting the Scriptures?

There are three competing theories to describe the creation or evolution of man and woman. Some argue for the theory of *Creationism* which maintains that God created man and woman, Adam and Eve, without the necessity of an evolutionary process. There is the theory of *atheistic evolution* which maintains that human life evolved from lower forms to higher forms by a random process. Finally, there is the theory of *theistic [God-guided] evolution*, the belief that God created the world out of nothing and that he guided an evolutionary process from a lower form of life to a higher form of life, until he finally placed an immortal soul into the first human beings.

One, as a Catholic, can believe in a form of *Creationism* or one can believe in *theistic [or God-guided] evolution* as understood here. One cannot however believe in atheistic evolution, for it denies God's creative power and his providential will.

One may wonder how the belief in *theistic [God-guided] evolution* can be believed in terms of the account of creation in the book of Genesis. First and foremost, Genesis is not a historical account of the way the world began, nor the way human life began. All one needs to do is to compare Genesis 1 with Genesis 2:4f. Here, within the first two chapters of Genesis, you find two different accounts of Creation. It is obvious that Genesis was not meant to be a literal historical account of how human beings came into being.

The Book of Genesis is a theological account teaching us that God is the ultimate source of being. He created the world and people out of nothing. He created them good. It is an account of freedom and the cost of using freedom in a negative manner. It is an account of two people, Adam and

Eve, who chose to rebel against God and sought to live without God. By their sin they forever distorted the nature of the world. Christ would have to come to save the world from the damage that was caused by the Fall, the "original sin" of Adam and Eve.

Genesis is the Word of God told to a people thousands of years ago about the eternal truths of God, a God of mercy and love, a God of second chances.

Consequently, one, as a Catholic, can believe in a form of *Creationism* or one can believe in *theistic [God-guided] evolution* as understood by the Church.

Our evangelical brothers tend to favor a form of Creationism. Catholics tend to favor *theistic [God-guided]* evolution.

As an aside, it is worth noting that the "father of genetics," the man who gave evolution its laws of inheritance, was the Catholic monk Gregor Mendel. And the man who developed the theory of the "Big Bang," which started the whole process, was the Belgian priest, astronomer, and professor of physics, Fr. Georges Henri Joseph Edouard Lemaitre.

Are Catholic doctrines invented?

Many evangelicals like to point to a council and say: "You see, this belief only began in such a time." For example, they would argue that the title "Mother of God" was invented at the Council of Ephesus (ca. 431) or that Papal infallibility was invented at Vatican I (ca. 1869-1870). This of course is an absurdity to any historian or any well-informed Catholic or Protestant. Just because a doctrine is defined specifically at a certain period of time does not mean it was not always held to be true. The inscription "theotokos," "God-bearer" is found on the walls of the Catacombs hundreds of years before the Council of Ephesus ever took place.

In terms of Papal Infallibility, Augustine of Hippo (ca. 400) would say in issues of faith and morals the famous phrase: "Rome has spoken; it is settled."

The popes always had primacy of power: Pope Clement of Rome's *Letter to the Corinthians* (ca. 88) was so respected by the community of Corinth that the letter was almost put into the canon of the New Testament. Anacletus (76-88) was consulted regarding the proper consecration of bishops. Alexander I (105-115) issued the decree that unleavened bread was to be used for consecration; Sixtus I (115-125) decreed the praying of the *Sanctus* and Telesphorus (125-136) the praying of the *Gloria*. Pius I (140-155) issued the decree regarding the proper date for the celebration of Easter. Hyginus (136-140) was asked to squash the heresy of Gnosticism, Anicetus (155-166) the heresy of Manichaeism, Soter (166-175) the heresy of Montanism, and Victor I (189-199) the heresy of Adoptionism, and on and on.

When you study all 266 popes, all 265 successors of Peter, you find without a question that the faith held by the popes became the faith of the Church!

151

Councils help to clarify a teaching when confusion seems to be harming the belief of the faithful. The Church usually defines a doctrine in a council when there is either hostility to a teaching or confusion over a teaching.

The Church can only teach infallibly what has always been present in the deposit of the faith. It can grow in its understanding of that deposit of the faith and therefore bring about clarification, but that deposit of faith always remains the same.

A final point: If we were to take the arguments of anti-Catholics seriously, then we would have to argue that Christ's divinity was invented at the First Council of Nicea (ca. 325), that the divinity of the Holy Spirit and the reality of the Trinity was only invented at the Council of Constantinople (ca. 381), and that the Bible was invented at the Councils of Hippo (ca. 393), Carthage III (397) and Carthage IV (419). How absurd! But if such anti-Catholics are to be consistent in their argumentation, then they must believe the absurd.

What is a heretic?

A heretic is one who chooses to deviate from the true and authentic teachings of Jesus Christ and his Body, the Church. One may ask the question, "How is it that some of the earliest saints believed in something different than Catholics believe today?"

When we look at some of the early Fathers of the Catholic Church we see a slow process of understanding with regards to the nature of the Trinity (i.e., the relation of the Three Persons, the relationship between Jesus' human nature and divine nature, etc.). These Fathers were pioneers. They were not denying something that was already defined as infallible. They were doing theology.

These Fathers of the Church were not heretics? They were pioneers! Once the Church defined infallibly a dogma of the Church, these Fathers obeyed and accepted these teachings.

A heretic is one that after an infallible teaching has been proclaimed, denies that infallible teaching. That person is not a pioneer, but a heretic-- that is, one who deviates from the truth. Martin Luther, Ulrich Zwingli and John Calvin are considered heretics, for they denied what was "infallible teaching."

Today the term is rarely used since it has a malevolent connotation. The reality remains, but the term has been abandoned for the most part.

The Crusades and their necessity

In the year 610 Mohammed, a wealthy merchant of Mecca in Arabia had what he argued was a vision of what he was to become—the prophet foretold by Moses.

Thus arose the beginnings of Islam. Mohammed, in his attempt to convert his home, Mecca, would be driven out to Medina. He would conquer Medina and impose Islam upon the inhabitants. In 630 he would return to capture Mecca.   By the time of his death in 632 much of Arabia had been conquered.

Under the Caliphs, his successors, Islam would conquer Syria, Armenia, Palestine, Cyprus, Egypt, and North Africa by the year 711.

In 732, an attempt to conquer Gaul (France) was thwarted by Charles Martel at the Battle of Poitiers.   Eighth century France would experience Muslim incursions into Aquitaine, Burgundy, Bordeaux, Autun, and Toulouse.   In 734 Avignon was captured, Lyons sacked in 743, and Marseilles plundered in 838.   In 889 Tolon would fall to Islamic forces. In 1020 Narbonne was sacked.

By the year 800 Italy would come under attack.   In 800 Ponza and Ischia were plundered.   Civitavecchia, the port of Rome, was sacked in 813. In 827 Syracuse was invaded. In 831 Palermo was conquered.   In 837 Naples was attacked. Messina was captured in 842.   In 846 Taranto and Bari fell.   In 846 Muslims sacked Rome and St. Peter's Basilica, forcing Pope Sergius II to flee the Vatican. In 849 Enna was conquered. Malta and Anzio fell in 871, Capua and Calabria in 872.   In 879 Pope John VIII was forced to pay tribute or a tax of 25,000 *mancuses* a year to Aghlabid Muslims. In 900 Catania was captured.   In 934 Genoa was attacked. By 965 all of Sicily was in Muslim control.   In 1005 Pisa was sacked.   In 1010 Cosenza was attacked.   And in 1015 Sardinia fell.

Muslims made incursions into Spain and Portugal between 711 and 718.   Spain, save for small areas in the Northwest, came under Islamic control.   A Muslim presence would remain till 1492.

In Greece, Crete would be invaded in 820.   In 902 Demetrias was sacked and destroyed.   In 904 Thessalonica would fall.

In 1009 the Church of the Holy Sepulcher, the site where Jesus was crucified, was destroyed and pilgrims were massacred.

In 1067, a group of approximately 6000 German pilgrims were attacked, leaving two-thirds of their number dead.

The eleventh century saw the Seljuk Turks or Tartars establish the caliphate of Bagdad and conquer most of Asia Minor.   In 1071, the Seljuk Turks made safe pilgrimages to Jerusalem impossible.

It is under these conditions that Pope Urban II called for the First Crusade in 1095 to free the Holy Land from the hands of Islamic forces. Englishmen, Frenchmen, Italians and Germans became the first crusaders.   The crusaders would take possession of Jerusalem in 1099.

The Second Crusade, headed by Conrad III of Germany and Louis VII of France, took place in 1147.   Lack of discipline, and the lack of unity among the leaders, led to its failure.   The Islamic threat to the West would be renewed after this failure.

The Third Crusade took place in 1190 and was led by Frederick Barbarossa of Germany, Philip Augustus of France and Richard the Lionhearted of England.   The Crusade was plagued by difficulties and abuses.   Frederick Barbarossa drowned; 100,000 disillusioned Germans returned home to Germany.   Philip of France found it impossible to campaign with Richard the Lionhearted of England, and thus returned to France. Despite this, Richard was able to gain control of the city of Jaffa and to win entry into Jerusalem for Christian pilgrims.

The Fourth Crusade began in 1212 and ended in an ignoble and moral disaster. The original intention of protecting the Christians in Constantinople from Islamic conquest, resulted in the siege of Constantinople, its plundering, and the dividing of the spoils between the leaders of the Crusade and Venetian merchants.

The Fifth Crusade from 1217-1221 was led by King Andrew II of Hungary and John of Brienne. The crusaders captured Damietta at the mouth of the Nile, only to lose it again. The Crusade was a failure.

The Sixth Crusade in 1248 was led by St. Louis IX, the King of France. St. Louis captured Damietta but was himself taken captive. He was released for a ransom and the return of Damietta to the Muslims.

The Seventh Crusade was led by St. Louis IX, King Edward I and Charles of Anjou in 1270. Saint Louis died of fever at Tunis. Charles of Anjou negotiated a treaty, and Edward returned to England after a few minor victories.

And finally, at the Battle of Lepanto, the Ottoman Empire's attempt to conquer Europe and extinguish Christianity and Western civilization was thwarted in 1571 by a Holy League of maritime nations of southern Europe led by Pope Pius V.

The word "crusade" would eventually be used for every Christian-Muslim conflict (i.e., Vienna, Hungary, the Balkans, etc.).

The Crusades were a response to unprovoked Muslim aggressions against Christian states.

The Crusades, as with any human endeavor, came with abuses. Competing commanders, different agendas, disorganization, and the desire for revenge caused many to lose sight of the purpose of the Crusades. Looting, the killing of innocent Jews and Muslims took place, but never under the sanction of the popes or the Catholic Church, and in no way to the extent that anti-Catholic extremists would like people to believe.

Modern scholarship is correcting many of the embellishments regarding the atrocities associated with the Crusades.

The Crusades were not colonialist or commercial endeavors, nor were they intended to force Christianity upon Muslims and Jews. The goal was the defense of Europe, the protection of Christians in the East, and the recovery of the Holy Land for Christendom. Did abuses take place? There has never been a war in the history of the world where abuses did not take place!

It is estimated that anywhere from 300,000 to 1 million people were killed during the approximately six centuries of Crusades, most of which were combatants. In the modern era, the six years of World War II (1939-1945) killed approximately 30 million civilians and 30 million combatants.

It can be argued that Western civilization, despite all its problems, flaws, and over-secularization, would not exist as the shining light of the world if it were not for the Crusades.

The Inquisitions

The Inquisitions were instituted by the Church and civil authorities to protect the Church and the State from beliefs detrimental to the common good. They were law courts that sought to balance the good of the individual with the good of society in general. As with every human endeavor, abuses took place, but overall, the process was just—contrary to modern myths.

The Medieval Inquisition operated from 1184-1500 and executed 2000 individuals. The Spanish Inquisition operated from 1481-1834 and had 3,230 executions. The Portuguese Inquisition operated from 1540-1794 and executed 1,175 criminals.

The total number of death sentences handed down by the inquisitions, over a 700 year period of time, is 6,405—this averages to 9 people a year being executed for crimes against the Church and the State. To put this statistic in perspective, the United States executed 25 criminals in 2014.

As with many things, people often seek to misrepresent the truth for an agenda, and sadly this becomes popularized in the culture. As with the Crusades, modern scholarship has brought and continues to bring a new perspective into our understanding of the Inquisitions.

Did abuses take place? Yes. When humans are involved, abuses will always take place.

IX
MORAL DOCTRINES UNDER ATTACK

The Ten Commandments and their implications for Catholics (cf. Exodus 20:2-17)

The first commandment forbids acts of voluntary doubt (the disregarding or refusing to believe as true what God has revealed), incredulity (the refusal to assent to truth), heresy (the denial of truth), apostasy (the rejection of the Christian faith), schism (refusal to submit to the Catholic Church), despair (ceasing to hope in salvation), presumption (the counting on one's own capacities for salvation), indifference (the failure to appreciate or care in God's goodness), ingratitude (the refusal to return love for love), lukewarmness (a hesitation in responding to God's love), spiritual sloth (refusing the joy that comes from God), hatred of God (denying God's goodness), idolatry (divinizing worldly "things" such as power, pleasure, race, country, etc.), sacrilege (profaning things and persons of God), atheism (the denial of God's existence), and agnosticism (a refusal to affirm or deny the existence of God). Occult beliefs and practices such as superstition, divination, magic and sorcery are also forbidden.

The second commandment demands a respect for the sacredness of the Lord's name. Acts of blasphemy (asserting words or thoughts of hatred, reproach, or defiance against God), the taking of oaths (the superficial misuse or lack of respect for God's name), false oaths (swearing to take God as a witness to something that is not true), and perjury (making a promise under oath with no intention of keeping it) are sinful.

The third commandment is a summons to keep the Lord's Day a holy day. It demands the faithful attendance at Sunday Mass, and an attitude of profound worship. It is a time to spend with God and to abstain from any work that distracts from authentically consecrating Sunday as a precious day of love of God and love of neighbor. One seeks comfort, but one also seeks to be challenged to grow.

The fourth commandment demands the authentic honoring of father and mother. Children owe just obedience, respect, gratitude, assistance, and the repaying of love for love to their parents. Parents have the responsibility of caring for their children's physical and spiritual needs, fostering a vocation, and teaching them to serve and follow God above all. The family forms the foundation for societal and ecclesiastical life.

The fifth commandment is an affirmation of the dignity of life. Being created in the image and likeness of God, the human person is sacred from conception to natural death. Murder is a violation of the dignity of the person and the creator.

The sixth commandment is a command that demands fidelity. Any act which is contrary to the dignity of chastity, such as fornication, adultery, polygamy, divorce and remarriage (without an annulment), open or free marriages, same-sex marriages or unions, homosexual and bisexual acts, masturbation, contraceptive use, pornography, prostitution, incest and rape are forbidden. Artificial insemination and the use of a surrogate uterus are forbidden. The sixth commandment is a call to authentic sexual integration, authentic life and love.

The seventh commandment is a prohibition against stealing. Stealing is characteristic of a lack of charity and injustice. Often stealing is done in subtle ways: For example, on the part of employers in a business a violation of the seventh commandment is often exemplified by business fraud, ignorance of contracts, and the mistreatment of workers through unfair wages and lack of health and retirement benefits. On the part of the employee this injustice and lack of charity is often seen in acts of laziness and all forms of lack of effort in the work environment. The seventh commandment forbids social relationships based solely on economic factors, as opposed to the nature of the human person. It acknowledges that the goods of creation are for the entire human family. The "author, center, and goal of all economic and social life is the human person." The seventh commandment demands the tithing of one's talent and treasure to God.

The eighth commandment is a prohibition against bearing false witness against one's neighbor. Lying, duplicity, hypocrisy, boasting, dissimulation (hiding under a false appearance), rash judgment (assuming without reason the moral fault of another), detraction (disclosing another's faults to someone who did not know them), betrayal of confidences, calumny (character assassination), and slander (a false statement that damages a person's reputation) are all acts contrary to the dignity of persons.

The ninth commandment is a prohibition against coveting one's neighbor's wife. It prohibits moral permissiveness, and seeks the purification of the social moral climate. This commandment calls one to live a life of decency, chastity and modesty. It is a call for purity of heart, intention, and vision.

The tenth commandment is a call to avoid coveting another's goods. It is a call to avoid greed, envy, and all immoderate desires. It is a call to desire a detachment from all that is contrary to the glory and honor of God. One is called to desire God above all.

[A lawyer asked Jesus:] "Teacher, which is the greatest commandment in the law?" And he said to him, "You shall love the Lord your God with all your heart, with all your soul, and with all your mind. This is the great and first commandment. And a second is like it. You shall love your neighbor as yourself. On these two commandments depend all the law and the prophets" (Matthew 22:37-40, RSV).

To authentically love is to fulfill and grasp the true intentions of the commandments. The "culture of life" and the roadmap to light, peace, and happiness are based on the fulfillment of these commandments.

The natural and moral law, essential dimensions to moral theology
The Bible alone approach can often lead individuals to miss another important aspect of revelation, *natural revelation*. Natural revelation is based on the natural law and the laws of nature that God created. By being aware of that inner principle called conscience one can know right from wrong. By observing the order and structure of God's creation one can know the right from the wrong in terms of our interactions with all of creation and God. When natural revelation is corrected by divine revelation- -Scripture and Tradition--then one can come to a knowledge of God by human reason and have a greater understanding of the world. Faith seeks understanding and the more we understand the more our faith is nourished.

Thus, a sin is not only that which is condemned in the Bible or Sacred Tradition but it is also condemned by the natural or moral law. What is contrary to the natural and moral law is a sin. In Genesis 1:1-2:4 a perfectly ordered, harmonious world is created. This is followed by the Fall, the 'original sin" (Genesis 3) where this harmony and order are destroyed. As we will see in the case of homosexual acts and the other moral sins, they are sins that are condemned by God in the Scriptures, Tradition, and by the very nature of God's creation.

The Ten Commandments above are not arbitrary laws or rules of conduct; rather, they are the expression of that God-given reality which is at the core of every human being guiding him or her into the ways of righteousness or depravity.

Why is homosexual activity (and same-sex marriages) contrary to the Word of God?
The Church makes it clear that a person's *orientation* is not sinful. As the *Catechism* states: Homosexuals "must be accepted with respect, compassion, and sensitivity. Every sign of unjust discrimination in their regard should be avoided. These persons are called to fulfill God's will in

their lives and, if they are Christians, to unite to the sacrifice of the Lord's Cross the difficulties they may encounter from their condition" (CCC 2358). The *Catechism* goes on to say: "Homosexual persons are called to chastity. By virtue of self-mastery that teach them inner freedom, at times by the support of disinterested friendship, by prayer and sacramental grace, they can and should gradually and resolutely approach Christian perfection" (2359).

The Catholic Church, however, basing "itself on Sacred Scripture... [argues that homosexual acts] are contrary to the natural law. They close the sexual act to the gift of life. They do not proceed from genuine affective and sexual complementarity. Under no circumstances can they be approved" (CCC 2357).

Scripture is clear. The story of Sodom and Gomorrah in Genesis 19:1-14, while often argued as an account of inhospitality, is an account of the evil of homosexual activity (the Bible's Letter of James affirms this interpretation); If this were not so, we would be left with at least two puzzling questions: Why have generations of people called those who perform homosexual acts sodomites? And why would God destroy an entire city over the sin of inhospitality?

Leviticus 18:22 states: "You shall not lie with a man as with a woman..." Leviticus 20:13 states: "If a man lies with a male as with a woman, both of them.... [will be held accountable]."

Now some like to argue that there are many things forbidden by the Hebrew Scriptures which are no longer held by Christians. This is true. There are those laws which Jesus specifically addressed--as in the case of the woman caught in adultery (Jn. 8:3f) or in the case of those suffering from leprosy (Lk. 5:13). Also, there is the example of the apostles eliminating the law of circumcision (Acts 15). And there is the making of what was once "unclean" clean, according to God's revelation to Peter (Acts 10:9-33).

Having said this, it is important to remember that unless Jesus and his Church specifically clarified or overturned certain Hebraic laws, the laws were to remain. Leviticus forbids sex with your mother (18:7), sister (18:9), or aunt (18:14). It forbids bestiality (18:23) and orgies (18:23). I don't think that those who favor the overturning of the Hebraic laws are in favor of practicing these evils?

But let us look at the New Testament writings written after the death and resurrection of Christ, when the Spirit of truth (Jn. 15:26; 16:13) was sent to the Christian community. Furthermore, let us never forget the promises of Christ, the promise that the gates of hell would not prevail against his Church (Mt. 16:18f; Jn. 16:13; 28:20; 1 Tim. 3:15) and the promise that he would be with his Church till the end of time (Jn. 20:29).

Let us remember that the letters to Timothy, to the Romans, and to the Corinthians in the Bible were written by Christ's greatest theologian. Paul, who lived after the resurrection of Jesus! If it wasn't for Paul, we would know very little about Christ, his Church, and Christianity in general!

160

In 1 Corinthians 6:9-10 we read: "Do not be deceived; neither fornicators nor idolaters nor adulterers nor boy prostitutes nor sodomites…will inherit the kingdom of God."

In Romans 1:26-27 the Scriptures declare: Their females exchanged natural relations for unnatural, and the males likewise gave up natural relations with females…. Males did shameful things with males…."

In 1 Timothy 1:10-11 we read: The "law is meant not for a righteous person but for the lawless and unruly, the godless and sinful, the unholy and profane, those who killed their fathers and mothers, murderers, the unchaste, sodomites, kidnappers, liars, perjurers, and whatever else is opposed to sound teaching, according to the glorious gospel of the blessed God, with which I have been entrusted."

But it is not simply individual quotes that condemn homosexual acts, the very theology of the Old and New Testaments condemn it.   The underlying theology of God's love for his people in the Old and New Testament is based on the complementarity of the sexes and on the natural law which underlies this complementarity (Genesis 1 illustrates how the complementarity of the sexes reflects God's inner unity).   Men and women are physically and psychologically different, and it is in this distinction that the complementarity between a man and a woman make the possibility of two becoming one through total self-donation possible (cf. Gen. 2; Mt. 19:3-6; Mk. 10:6-9). The theology of Genesis and the entire Pentateuch as well as the theology of the Wisdom and Prophetic books of the Bible are all based on the underlying theology of the love of God for his people in the form of the love of a man for a woman in their distinct natures. In fact, there is *no way* of understanding the Scriptures without understanding the relationship between the sexes!

Tradition is clear.   Some sixteen centuries before the birth of most Protestant denominations, Christians believed that homosexual acts were contrary to the will of God.

In the *Didache, The Teaching of the Twelve Apostles*, written anywhere from 65 AD to 120 AD, we are told to "not be sexually wayward by committing sodomy" (cf. 4).   In Polycarp's *Letter to the Philippians*, the disciple of the apostle John, Polycarp states: "Sodomites shall not inherit the Kingdom of God."   And in Barnabas, often attributed to the same Barnabas who was the companion of Paul, we read: "Thou shall not commit sodomy" (n. 19).

Never, ever has the approval of homosexual acts been accepted in Church history prior to the twentieth century!

Philosophy likewise is clear.   To put it bluntly, a male's genitals were not created for another male, and a male's sexual organ certainly has no place in any male body!   The male and female organs are complementary, just as the psychological distinctions between males and females are complementary.   The homosexual act is a sex act which is contrary to the act's purpose: It is an act completely closed off to physical and spiritual life.

Because of the nature of males and females, the sexual act is unitive and procreative. Homosexual acts are neither unitive nor procreative, and thus are a direct attack on the dignity and the sanctity of the sexual act.

In pagan societies homosexual activity was common and even practiced as part of many cults. It was so common that students that take college courses in Greek and Latin Classics are often shocked by the open discussion of homosexual activity in these cultures.

During the period of the early Church, the distinction between homosexual activity and homosexual orientation was not made, being that it was so closely associated with paganism. It is only with the Church's correct interpretation, guided by the Holy Spirit, that the distinction between orientation and activity was made.

Again, let me re-emphasize the Church's teaching regarding our interaction with homosexual individuals: The Church makes it clear that a person's *orientation* is not sinful. As the *Catechism* states: Homosexuals "must be accepted with respect, compassion, and sensitivity. Every sign of unjust discrimination in their regard should be avoided. These persons are called to fulfill God's will in their lives and, if they are Christians, to unite to the sacrifice of the Lord's Cross the difficulties they may encounter from their condition" (CCC 2358). The *Catechism* goes on to say: "Homosexual persons are called to chastity. By virtue of self-mastery that teach them inner freedom, at times by the support of disinterested friendship, by prayer and sacramental grace, they can and should gradually and resolutely approach Christian perfection" (2359).

No such thing as pro-choice Catholics!

One cannot be a Catholic in good standing by maintaining a pro-abortion stance, and one cannot vote for a pro-abortion politician in good conscience! Induced abortion is intrinsically evil!

The Scriptures

The Scriptures are clear regarding the sanctity of life from conception to natural death: In Genesis 25: 22-24 we read: "The children in Rebekah's womb jostled each other so much that she exclaimed, 'If this is to be so, what good will it do me!' She went to consult the Lord, and he answered her: 'Two nations are in your womb....'" In Jeremiah 1:5 we read: "Before I formed you in the womb I knew you, before you were born I dedicated you, a prophet to the nations I appointed you." In Isaiah we read: "Thus says the Lord who made you, who formed you from the womb: Fear not, O Jacob, my servant whom I have chosen" (v. 2 and v. 24). In Isaiah 49:2 we read: "The Lord called me from birth, from my mother's womb he gave me my name." In Job 10:8, 11 we read: "Your hands have formed me and fashioned me; with skin and flesh you clothed me, with bones and sinews you knit me together." And in Job 31:15 we read: "Did not he who made me in the womb make him? Did not the same One fashion us before our birth." In Psalm 139:13-16 we read: "You formed my inmost being; you knit me in my mother's womb. I praise you, so wonderfully you made me, wonderful are

162

your works! My very self you knew; my bones were not hidden from you, when I was being made in secret, fashioned as in the depths of the earth. Your eyes foresaw my actions; in your book all are written down; my days were shaped, before one came to be." In Ecclesiastes 11:5 we read: "Just as you know not how the breath of life fashions the human frame in the mother's womb, so you know not the work of God which he is accomplishing in the universe." In Luke 1:41-44 we read, "When Elizabeth heard Mary's greeting, the infant leaped in her womb, and Elizabeth, filled with the Holy Spirit, cried out in a loud voice and said, 'Most blessed are you among women, and blessed is the fruit of your womb. And how does this happen to me that the mother of my Lord should come to me? For at the moment the sound of your greeting reached my ears, the infant in my womb leaped for joy." And in Luke 1:36 we read: "Behold, Elizabeth, has conceived a son in her old age, and this is the sixth month for her…"

Finally, in Revelation 9:21f we read: "Nor did they repent of their murders, their magic potions, their unchastity…" The phrase "magic potions" is from the Greek word *pharmakeia*, which means, in this context, an abortion causing agent.

Other quotes worth reviewing: Genesis 16:2-4; 19:36-38; 21:1-18; 38; 50: 20; Exodus 21:22-25; Leviticus 19:14; Numbers 35:22-34; Deuteronomy 27:25; Jeremiah 7:6; 22:17; Isaiah 45:9-12; Psalm 94:9; 106:37-38; Proverbs 6:16-19; Ruth 4:18-22; Matthew 1:3; 18:10-14; Luke 3:33; 17:2; John 9:1-3; Acts 17:25-29; Romans 8:28.

How can anyone understanding the Scriptures ever ponder the possibility of abortion!

Early Church Writings
In the *Didache* (ca. 65) the *Teaching of the Twelve Apostles*, we read: "You shall not kill an unborn child or murder a newborn infant" (II, 2). In Barnabas' *Epistle II* (ca. 70) we read: "You shall love your neighbor more than your own life. You shall not slay the child by abortion." In Tertullian's *Apologetics* (ca. 177) we read: "For us murder is once and for all forbidden; so even the child in the womb, while the mother's blood is still being drawn on to form the human being, it is not lawful for us to destroy. To forbid birth is only quicker murder. He is a man, who is to be a man; the fruit is always present in the seed" (197). In Athenagoras' *Legatio pro Christianis*, (ca. 177) we read: "Those who use drugs to bring about an abortion commit murder and will have to give an account to God for their abortion." In Minucius Felix's *Octavius* (ca. 200) we read: "There are women, who, by the use of medicinal potions, destroy the unborn life in their wombs, and murder the child before they bring it forth. These practices undoubtedly are derived from a custom established by your gods; Saturn, though he did not expose his sons, certainly devoured them." In Clement of Alexandria's *Christ the Educator II* (ca. 150) we read: "If we would not kill off the human race born and developing according to God's plan, then our whole lives would be lived according to nature. Women who make use of some sort of

deadly abortion drug kill not only the seed of life but, together with it, all human kindness." In Augustine's *De Nuptius et Concupiscus* (354-430) we read: "Sometimes this lustful cruelty or cruel lust goes so far as to seek to procure baneful sterility, and if this fails the fetus conceived in the womb is in one way or another smothered or evacuated, in the desire to destroy the offspring before it has life, or if it already lives in the womb, to kill it before it is born." In Jerome's *Letter to Eustochium* (ca. 340-420) we read: "Some unmarried women, when they are with child through sin, practice abortion by the use of drugs. Frequently they kill themselves and are brought before the ruler of the lower world guilty of three crimes; suicide, adultery against Christ, and murder of an unborn child." In Basil the Great's *First Canonical Letter* (ca. 329-379) we read: "The hairsplitting difference between formed and unformed makes no difference to us. Whoever deliberately commits abortion is subject to the penalty for homicide." We could go on and on.

To call oneself a Catholic and pro-abortion or pro-choice is to promote an outrageous lie. To be indifferent or to vote for pro-choice or pro-abortion candidates is to betray one's Catholic faith.

Let us never forget the words of Caiaphas: "It is better for one man to die than for a whole nation to perish" (Jn 11:50). That one person was Jesus.

We were created in the "image and likeness" of God" (Gen. 1:27). We are the "body of Christ" (1 Cor. 12:12f; Rom. 12:5; Eph. 1:22f) and the "Temple of God" (1 Cor. 3:9-10, 15-16). Anyone who aborts a child is aborting the "image and likeness" of God, the "body of Christ," the "temple of God." They are aborting God.

They are committing an act of sacrilege, for we are "not our own" (cf. 1 Cor. 6:19-20)--our bodies belong to God.

Abortion procedure facts
A woman seeking an abortion before the fourteenth week of pregnancy will likely undergo one of the following procedures:

Suction Curettage
1. The cervix is dilated.
2. A suction curette (a hollow tube with a knife-like edged tip) is inserted into the womb.
3. Suction tears apart the fetus (the human person) and sucks the body parts into a container.
4. The container is checked to assure that all the body parts have been removed in order to prevent any infections—infections which can at times lead to the death of the mother.

Dilation and Curettage (D&C)
1. The cervix is dilated.
2. The insertion of a loop-shaped knife (curette) is inserted.
3. The curette scrapes the wall of the uterus and cuts the placenta and fetus into smaller parts.

4. The parts are pulled out of the uterus through the cervix.
5. Body parts must be counted so as to prevent infection.

RU 486 (taken before the ninth week)
1. A steroid drug (taken in the form of a pill or injection) is given to the woman to destroy the placenta or prevent it from being formed.
2. Prostaglandin is injected or orally given to induce the uterus to contract and push the fetus out of the body.

During the first fourteen weeks brain waves (week six) are recorded and the heart is beating (week three). The child can hear, can hiccup, can close and open his eyelids and can respond to touch or pain. The child has permanent fingerprints and an identifiable sex. By week eight the skeletal, nervous, digestive, circulatory, and respiratory system are functioning. By week twelve the child looks like a tiny doll sucking its thumb. The following weeks entail simple refinements of what has already begun.

Pagans routinely aborted their children and abandoned them to die outside city walls. We have outdone the pagans in our cruelty. The revival of paganism is more vicious than its original incarnation.

A woman seeking an abortion after fourteen weeks but before sixteen weeks of pregnancy will likely undergo the following procedure:

Dilation and Evacuation (D&E)
1. The cervix is dilated.
2. A curette (resembling pliers) is used to dismember and crush the large and strong bones of the fetus (such as the skull or head).
3. The dismembered and crushed parts are now small enough for removal through the cervix.
4. Body parts are counted.

A woman seeking an abortion after sixteen weeks of pregnancy will likely undergo one of the following procedures:

Saline Solution Evacuation
1. A concentrated salt solution is injected through the abdomen and into the amniotic fluid, which surrounds the fetus (the child) in the uterus.
2. The child inhales and swallows the solution and dies within two hours either by salt poisoning, dehydration, hemorrhaging, or convulsions.
3. The mother goes into labor twenty-four to forty-eight hours later and gives birth to a dead child.

Prostaglandin Abortion
1. Prostaglandin is injected through the abdomen into the amniotic fluid, which surrounds the child in the uterus.
2. Prostaglandin causes the muscle tissue of the mother to push the fetus, the child, out of the uterus.
3. The child is born dead or alive (when born alive it is left to die).

A woman seeking an abortion during the latter periods of her pregnancy will likely undergo the following procedure:

Partial-Birth Abortion or Dilation and Extraction
1. Laminara is used to dilate the cervix over a two-day period.
2. The abortionist uses large forceps to grasp the leg of the child (the fetus) and pull it down into the vagina and out of the body. The head, being too big, remains lodged in the cervical opening.
3. An incision is made at the base of the fetal skull to spread open the skull in order to insert a suction catheter.
4. The skull contents are evacuated through the suction catheter and the entire body is now capable of being removed.

At approximately seven weeks of pregnancy, when the heart, brain, stomach, liver, and kidney are functioning, approximately 800,000 infants are aborted each year. At sixteen weeks when the child's organs are complete and functioning and the child is breathing (fluid), swallowing, digesting, sleeping, dreaming, and experiencing pleasure and pain, approximately 71,000 American babies are aborted each year (Clowes, *Facts of Life*, 15).

Post-Abortion Trauma
Trauma, if not dealt with, will manifest itself in the most negative of ways. Hence, the trauma of abortion, if not dealt with, will wreak havoc on a woman and consequently on much of society.

Women who have had abortions often seek to deal with the pain in essentially four manners: through suppression, repression, rationalization, and/or compensation (cf. Theresa Burke, Ph.D., *Forbidden Grief*, 2002).

Suppression
Women who seek to suppress the trauma of abortion consciously push away or push down any negative feelings. They do everything possible not to think about the abortion or its trauma. These are women who often turn to alcohol or drugs to numb their pain, or become workaholics to keep busy and distracted, or avoid prayer, church, and God. It is not unusual to notice a person get up and walk out of church when the very word abortion is

mentioned. They are not being disrespectful. They are simply avoiding a reminder of their trauma.

In the most extreme cases, women who suppress their pain will often have more than one abortion (three to ten is not unusual) with the hope that each abortion will lessen the trauma (forty-five percent of women who have had an abortion, will have more than one). The mentality is: "The more I have, the less it will hurt."

Repression

Women who repress the trauma of abortion do so without any conscious awareness. Repression is a subconscious defense mechanism where the mind blocks out any negativity. These repressed feelings manifest themselves through an inability to bond with their husbands or children and an inability to form deep relationships.

Repression also manifests itself in certain disorders and unexplained actions. A woman went in for counseling because of a lingering depression. The woman was astonishingly beautiful with the exception of her hair. It was so short that a comb could not pass through it. After months of therapy, the mystery was uncovered. The woman's hair was so short because she could not bear to hear the sound of a hair dryer. It reminded her of the suction catheter used during her abortion. Likewise, through therapy, another woman was able to recognize that the only reason she had replaced all her carpets in her home with wood flooring, was that the sound of the vacuum cleaner reminded her of the suction catheter used in her abortion. These women were doing things they could not explain because they were subconsciously trying to deal with the trauma of abortion. It was through therapy that what was being repressed came to light.

Rationalization

At a local abortion facility, while a group of pro-life individuals were gently and lovingly praying the Rosary, a woman volunteer from the clinic drove into the parking lot, jumped out of her car, and ran over to confront a woman praying. She was so filled with anger and malice that her body shook as she screamed.

This is a classic example of the coping mechanism of rationalization. Rationalization is an argument that one makes to justify one's action as acceptable. It is marked with intolerance, anger, and hatred. If I were a betting man, I would bet that this volunteer had had an abortion at some time in her life.

The rationalization of many women who have had an abortion is that "if it is legal, it must be okay." Therefore, any threat to the legal status of abortion is a threat to their coping with the trauma.

This is the same rationalization that is behind the efforts to eliminate the "Choose Life" plates in many states. These plates are a threat to the legal status of abortion.

Compensation

Compensation is a coping mechanism that seeks to "make up" for past mistakes. Often women feel they must be punished in order to compensate for the evil of their abortion. This manifests itself in self-mutilation, attempted suicides, anorexia, bulimia, and a wide range of self-punishing behaviors.

This compensation mechanism is often seen in what is known as the "perfect mother syndrome." Mothers often try to make up for what they did to their first child by trying to be the perfect mother for their subsequent children.

They can often become doting and controlling parents in their efforts to make everything perfect.

The reality of post-abortion trauma and its manifestation can in no way be completely described in such a short essay. Book after book has been written about this subject. But my hope is simply to illustrate one small portion of the damage that is done to women in the name of abortion and so-called women's rights.

The Pill vs. Natural Family Planning

If we were to ask most couples about the negative side effects associated with the use of the pill, most couples would have a general idea regarding these effects, either through information obtained from their doctors or from pharmacists. They may not be aware of the fifty-two side effects associated with the use of the pill, but they more than likely would be aware of the most talked about side effects such as strokes, heart attacks, and blood clots.

If, however, we were to ask most couples about the method in which the pill works in preventing the birth of children, there would be a tremendous amount of ignorance.

There are two major types of pills that are being used in preventing the birth of children: those that contain a combination of estrogen and progestogen and those that contain only progestogen. Both of these types of pills prevent the birth of children either through preventing ovulation or preventing the effective migration of sperm in the uterus, or by preventing implantation. In the *Physicians' Desk Reference* the combination pills are described as operating in the following manner: "Combination oral contraceptives act by suppression of gonadotropins. Although the primary mechanism of this action is the inhibition of ovulation, other alterations include changes in the cervical mucus (which increase the difficulty of sperm entry into the uterus) and the endometrium (which reduce the likelihood of implantation)."

In terms of the progestogen-only pill, the *Physicians' Desk Reference* states: "[Progestogen-only pills] alter cervical mucus, exert a progestational effect on the endometrium, interfering with implantation, and in some patients, suppress ovulation."

Therefore, the pill (whether the combination pill or the progestogen-only pill) has the potential for being an abortifacient—an abortion-causing agent. When conception takes place, a human being is present. The pill at this point, because it weakens the lining of the uterus, prevents this human being from being implanted in the womb of the mother.

This is a silent abortion. As the Church teaches in its documents, as in the 1994 American document *Ethical and Religious Directives for Catholic Health Care Services* (n. 45): "Every procedure whose sole immediate effect is the termination of pregnancy before viability is an abortion, which, in its moral context, includes the interval between conception and implantation of the embryo."

What is said of the "pill" can be said, with slight variations, on all the other hormonal methods of contraception, including Norplant, Depo-Provera, RU-486 and Ovral.

Similar abortifacient effects are also apparent in the use of intrauterine devices such as Lippes Loop and the Copper-T 380A.

How many silent victims are being lost because of the unknowing actions of couples? Who is at fault for their ignorance?

Europe is experiencing a decline in its native population through a contraceptive mentality and an attachment to the "culture of death." In many European countries the death rate is overwhelming the birth rate. It is conceivable that within a few centuries the European race will cease to exist!

Natural Family Planning, a Holy Alternative

The old fashion "calendar-rhythm" method, which was highly inaccurate and inadequate, is no longer the means used for natural family planning. Today the methods of determining a woman's fertile period has become more sophisticated and accurate. Some prefer the use of the Ovulation-Billings method, others prefer the Symtpo-Thermal method.

The following is a description of the Billings method for discovering the time of ovulation:

1.   *"The menstrual period at the start of each cycle is considered to be fertile. The reason for viewing the time of menstruation as fertile is that if a woman should have an unusually or unexpectedly short cycle such that the ovulation process were to begin toward the end of menstruation, she would have no warning of this fact, since the presence of the menstrual flow would make it difficult for her to examine her vaginal mucus. Thus, as a precaution, women are advised to regard the menstrual period as fertile.*

2.   *After menstruation there is a noticeable absence of any vaginal discharge or mucus, and a woman experiences a definite sensation of dryness. During these days of dryness, the woman is infertile.*

3.   *At the conclusion of this period of dryness, cervical mucus begins to be discharged from the vagina. At first, this mucus is a kind of cloudy, sticky discharge, but it gradually becomes a clear, egg-*

white, stretchy, and lubricative substance. The "peak" or main sign of ovulation is the last day on which this clear and stretchy mucus is present. The woman's period of fertility, however, is defined as starting with the first day on which the cloudy mucus appears and it continues until three days past the peak symptom of ovulation.

4. *Finally, from the fourth day after the peak symptom until the start of the next menstrual cycle, a period of infertility occurs" (Genovesi, Catholic Morality and Human Sexuality, 229)."*

The Sympto-Thermal method combines, in the words of Dr. Brian Clowes, *"observations of basal body temperature and cervical mucus, and, as an optional cross-check, adds an examination of the cervical os (mouth of the cervix) as well. During fertile periods, the os opens, the cervix rises, and its tip becomes softer... During infertile times, the os closes, the cervix descends, and the tip becomes firmer... The end of pre-ovulation infertility is determined in several different ways. As a general rule, couples may resume intercourse on the fourth day following the peak day of mucus and the third day of upward thermal shift... Every time that a fertile type of mucus appears before ovulation, they must abstain for three days. Once ovulation occurs, the couple is sterile until menstruation and usually sterile during the first two days of menstruation"* (*Facts of Life*, 95).

Obviously the above are fragmentary summaries of the methods used for natural family planning. But the hope is that the above descriptions give couples an idea of the methods for natural family planning, and that they may seek their local parish ministry office and sign up for a course on natural family planning.

Those who practice one of these methods of natural family planning have a less than one in eight chance of divorcing as opposed to those who use contraceptives. Contraceptive users have over a fifty percent divorce rate. The reasons are simple.

1. NFP methods are natural. That is, they do not hinder the natural functioning of the body but observe and respect the natural cycle of fertility and infertility.

2. These methods respect the bodies of the spouses, encourage tenderness, and foster the necessary freedom that is at the base of authentic self-giving love.

3. In the practice of living out the natural methods one is engaging in a love which is expressed by the husband in saying, "I give you everything I am without doubt, without reservation, fully and completely," and the wife in turn says to her husband, "I give you my very self, completely, fully, without doubt, and without reservation." It is only in this grace-filled experience that the Gospel call of two becoming one can be fulfilled (cf. Mark 10:6-9).

4. Human life and the duty of transmitting it in cooperation with God is a spiritual gift that is not limited to this life's horizons, but has its true evaluation and full significance in reference to one's eternal destiny.

Those who practice natural family planning, as opposed to artificial contraception, make the sex act a spiritual act, a unitive, bonding, and creative act.

Genetic engineering, assisted reproduction, scientific research...

Scientific and medical experiments on human individuals can have great benefits for the healing of the sick. However, any forms of experimentation or science which conflicts with the dignity of the human person and the moral law are to be prohibited.

As the *Catechism of the Catholic Church* states:

"Basic scientific research, as well as applied research, is a significant expression of man's dominion over creation. Science and technology are precious resources when placed at the service of man and promote his integral development for the benefit of all. By themselves however they cannot disclose the meaning of existence and of human progress. Science and technology are ordered to man, from whom they take their origin and development; hence they find in the person and in his moral values both evidence of their purpose and awareness of their limits (2293)."

"It is an illusion to claim moral neutrality in scientific research and its applications. On the other hand, guiding principles cannot be inferred from simple technical efficiency, or from the usefulness accruing to some at the expense of others or, even worse, from prevailing ideologies. Science and technology by their very nature require unconditional respect for fundamental moral criteria. They must be at the service of the human person, of his inalienable rights, of his true and integral good, in conformity with the plan and the will of God (CCC 2294)."

Organ Transplants and Donations

Organ transplants are accepted as long as they conform to the moral law; that is, as long as "the physical and psychological dangers and risks to the donor are proportionate to the good that is sought for the recipient" CCC 2296).

Organ donation after death is a holy, noble, and meritorious act of love and solidarity with one's fellow human being, and is in no way contrary to the moral law.

One cannot resort, however, to the disabling mutilation of the body or the death of a human person in order to obtain an organ or organs.

At the heart of organ transplants and donations is the requirement of consent. If the donor's organ or organs are removed without his or her

171

consent, or the consent of a legitimate proxy, then the removal of any organ or organs is an infringement on the dignity of the human body.

Autopsies

Autopsies are permitted for legal inquests and the good of scientific research as long as the body is treated with respect and charity.

Artificial Insemination

Scientific research that aims at eliminating or overcoming sterility is of great merit as long as it seeks to maintain the unitive and procreative dimensions of the sexual act.

It is gravely immoral to separate a husband from his wife (and vice versa) by introducing a third person into the reproductive process.

Donum Vitae II, 1, 5, 4 states:

"Techniques that entail the dissociation of husband and wife, by the intrusion of a person other than the couple (donation of sperm, or ovum, surrogate uterus), are gravely immoral. These techniques (heterologous artificial insemination and fertilization) infringe the child's right to be born of a father and mother known to him and bound to each other by marriage. They betray the spouses' right to become a father and a mother only through each other."

"Techniques involving only the married couple (homologous artificial insemination and fertilization) are perhaps less reprehensible, yet remain morally unacceptable. They dissociate the sexual act from the procreative act. The act which brings the child into existence is no longer an act by which two persons give themselves to one another, but one that 'entrusts the life and identity of the embryo into the power of doctors and biologists and establishes the domination of technology over the origin and destiny of the human person. Such a relationship of domination is in itself contrary to the dignity and equality that must be common to parents and children.' Under the moral aspect procreation is deprived of its proper perfection when it is not willed as the fruit of the conjugal act, that is to say, of the specific act of the spouses' union... Only respect for the link between the meanings of the conjugal act and respect for the unity of the human being make possible procreation in conformity with the dignity of the person."

At the heart of Catholic sexuality is the inseparable bond between the unitive and procreative dimensions of the conjugal act.

These teachings can be a tremendous cross upon a couple that so much desires the gift of children. It must be remembered that children are gifts from God; they are not property that is owed to a couple. No one has a "right to a child." The child is the one that has rights in this situation, the right "to be the fruit of the specific act of the conjugal love of his parents," and "the right to be respected as a person from the moment of conception" (cf. CCC 2378; CDF, *Donum Vitae* II, 8).

For those who are unable to have children by moral means, they are encouraged to unite themselves to the sufferings of Christ, to become generative by their works of charity, and to seek the alternative of adoption, the giving a loving home for parentless children, children hungering for the love of parents.

Designer Babies

When one is able to clone or to select what sex, hair or eye color, intellect, body structure, and so forth by genetic engineering and the manipulation and choice of embryos one is going down a dangerous path. Huge distortions in the gene pool—which is essential for a healthy population—and huge distortions in the balance of the sexes in the population are bound to occur—cultures that prefer male children (often poor countries) will be overpopulated with males and cultures that favor female children will lead to an overpopulation in females. Designer babies will lead to distorted populations susceptible to grave illnesses, because of the diminished gene pool and the imbalance of the sexes.

The striking, unique and unrepeatable qualities that make each of us special and distinctively beautiful are at stake when a culture seeks to play God. A culture that flirts with manipulating the origins of life is a culture flirting with extinction.

"Certain attempts to influence chromosomic or genetic inheritance are not therapeutic but are aimed at producing human beings selected according to sex or other predetermined qualities. Such manipulations are contrary to the personal dignity of the human being and his integrity and identity which are unique and unrepeatable" (Donum Vitae I, 6).

Hybridization

Hybridization is the combining of two species artificially or naturally so as to form a new species. Hybridization is common in agriculture and even in animals. For example, the hybrid of a horse and a donkey is a mule. The hybrid of a lion and a tiger is called a liger.

In a culture without limits, where God is the self, it is just a matter of time before scientists attempt to hybridize higher forms of life. Rumors have existed regarding attempts, in the former Soviet Union, at hybridizing chimpanzees with humans.

It is quite possible that the future will be inhabited with hybridized humanoids-- half human, half something else! The making of all forms of distorted human-like species will wreak havoc on our culture and lead to its genetic disintegration.

This may seem far-fetched, but it is just around the corner!

Prenatal Diagnosis

Prenatal diagnosis can be used as a tool for protecting the integrity of an unborn child. It provides physicians with the ability to take care for and heal unborn children, even by means of performing surgical procedures within a mother's womb. As *Donum Vitae* I, 2 indicates:

Prenatal diagnosis is morally licit, "if it respects the life and integrity of the embryo and the human fetus and is directed toward its safeguarding or healing as an individual.... It is gravely opposed to the moral law when this is done with the thought of possibly inducing an abortion, depending upon the results: a diagnosis must not be the equivalent of a death sentence."

Prenatal Surgery

Prenatal surgery is a powerful gift as long as the surgery is directed toward the healing and care of the child and does not involve disproportionate risks.

"One must hold as licit procedures carried out on the human embryo which respect the life and integrity of the embryo and do not involve disproportionate risks for it, but are directed toward its healing, the improvement of its condition of health, or its individual survival" (Donum Vitae, I, 3).

Stem cells, a Catholic understanding

Stem cells are cells that have not undergone maturation and theoretically can become any of the 220 cell types and any of the 210 specialized tissue types that make up the human body.

Because stem cells are like "blank slates," they theoretically can morph into any kind of human tissue—ideally becoming replacement parts for unhealthy cells and tissues.

The benefits from stem cell research provides the future with great possibilities for the cure and treatment of illnesses such as Parkinson's, Alzheimer's, heart disease, and diabetes.

Stem cells can be obtained through the destruction of human embryos or aborted fetal tissues or they can be obtained from adults in a safe manner--from muscles, bone marrow, blood vessels, skin, teeth, the heart, the liver, etc. In other words, they can be obtained from a wide variety of other adult tissues.

Adult (or Somatic) stems cells, which ethicists fully approve of, are currently being used in the successful treatment of multiple sclerosis, lupus, rheumatoid arthritis, stroke, anemia, Epstein-Barr virus infection, cornea damage, blood and liver diseases, brain tumors, retinoblastoma, ovarian cancer, solid tumors, testicular cancer, leukemia, breast cancer, neuroblastoma, non-Hodgkins' lymphoma, renal cell carcinoma, diabetes, heart damage, as well as cartilage, bone, muscle, and spinal-cord damage.

Seventy diverse therapies have been developed over the years through the use of these adult stem cells.

Where then is the controversy? The controversy is over the obtaining of stem cells through the destruction of human embryos or through the use of aborted fetal tissues, particularly since there is no need to acquire them through such means.

Why do some scientists want to use the human embryo to obtain stem cells? The human embryo in its first divisions is *totipotential*, but as development occurs within the embryo the cells become *pluripotential*, which simply means that they become able to differentiate or morph into many types of cells. Adult stem cells are mostly, albeit not necessarily, *multipotent*, which simply means that the power to morph or differentiate becomes limited—hypothetically less capable of differentiating. The argument is that if we can obtain *pluripotential* cells from embryos or aborted fetal tissues--and since they have the potential to morph or differentiate better--then we should engage in such a practice.

The problem: There is absolutely no need to destroy embryos and experiment on aborted fetal tissues. *Pluripotential* cells can be obtained from the umbilical cord or the placenta, without destroying the human embryo—life at its earliest stage.

As of today, the hoped for beneficial use of stem cells from embryos have as yet not materialized. All significant progress has been through the universally acceptable use of adult stem cells. If we need *pluripotential* stem cells, they are obtainable through the umbilical cord or the placenta. There is absolutely no need today for the use of embryonic stem cells that destroy human embryos or for the use of aborted fetal tissues.

The reason for the continued use of human embryos and aborted fetal tissues is simply based on ease of access.

Euthanasia vs. palliative care

"I have had lots of patients who wanted to commit suicide, but you don't help them do it. You learn why patients don't want to live anymore. If they're in pain, you give them more or better medication. If they have trouble with their families, you help them get the problem solved."

Elizabeth Kubler-Ross

Elizabeth Kubler-Ross was a world-renowned medical doctor and psychiatrist. She did much research and wrote several books and articles in the area of death and dying. In her research, she found that people who face death often experience episodes of denial, anger, bargaining with God, and depression. Most importantly, she pointed out that if a patient was lovingly cared for, the patient's last moments would be ones filled with acceptance and even hope.

Direct euthanasia consists in the murdering of the handicapped, the ill, and the dying—with or without their consent and knowledge—and is thus

175

morally unacceptable (CCC 2277). In the definition used by the Congregation for the Doctrine of the Faith in its *Declaration on Euthanasia* we read: "By euthanasia is understood an action or omission of an action which of itself or by intention causes death in order that all suffering may be eliminated" (CDF, 1980a). And in *Evangelium Vitae* we read from the Holy Father that "Euthanasia is a violation of the law of God, since it is the deliberate and morally unacceptable killing of a person" (n. 65).

Today, too many terminally ill patients are being euthanized before they have come to a stage of acceptance and peace. Too many people are being put to death in times of anger, loneliness, and depression. A great injustice is being done to such people, all in the name of compassion.

The Church in its respect for the dignity of human life, and in its respect for God as the living Creator, promotes a holy death, a holy "letting go" which is filled with acceptance, peace, and hope on the part of the person entering into eternity.

The Church supports palliative care; that is, a form of care which seeks to eliminate pain and understands the redemptive value of unavoidable suffering (CCC 2279; cf. Col. 1:24). The Church therefore strongly encourages the use of painkillers in alleviating suffering, for at no stage is the "ordinary care owed to a sick person…[to be] interrupted" (CCC 2279). And for whatever pain remains, the Church encourages the person to unite his or her suffering to Christ's for the good of one's soul and the souls of those in purgatory.

My uncle died at the young age of fifty-eight from terminal cancer. He received the best of palliative care. He died a peaceful, joyous and holy death in the arms of his loving family. Let no one deprive us of this!

Discontinuing medical procedures
Prolonging life at all cost has never been part of the Catholic tradition (NCCB, 1986). There are times when one must let go and allow oneself or a loved one to enter into eternity.

In the Congregation for the Doctrine of the Faith's document *Donum Vitae* we read: "Discontinuing medical procedures that are burdensome, dangerous, extraordinary, or disproportionate to the expected outcome can be legitimate; it is the refusal of "over-zealous" treatment. Here one does not will to cause death (as in the case of euthanasia); one's inability to impede it is merely accepted."

Pope John Paul II in *Evangelium Vitae* writes: "When death is clearly imminent and inevitable, one can in conscience refuse forms of treatment that would only secure a precarious and burdensome prolongation of life, so long as the normal care of the sick person in similar cases is not interrupted" (CCC 2278).

The normal care of the person consists of prolonging life by ordinary means as opposed to extraordinary means. To put it more succinctly, the ordinary and obligatory means of prolonging life involve "all medicines, treatments, and operations which offer a reasonable hope of benefit for the patient and which can be obtained or used without excessive expense, pain, or burden" (Pius XII, *Discourse on Doctors*, 1957).

This is often understood to mean that proper nutrition (including intravenous feeding) and hydration are not to be withheld. In the U.S. National Conference of Bishops' *Ethical and Religious Directives*, directive 58 explains: "There should be a presumption in favor of providing nutrition and hydration to all patients, including patients who require medically assisted nutrition and hydration, as long as this is of sufficient benefit to outweigh the burdens involved to the patient."

In terms of those means of treatment which can be discontinued, Pius XII argues: "All medicines, treatments, and operations, which cannot be used or obtained without excessive expense, pain, or other burden [can be refused]." In other terms, when therapy will not benefit the person, "letting go" is ethically justifiable. To disconnect a respirator when a person has reached the point of no return is ethically acceptable and appropriate—as in the case of those who are "brain dead."

The decision to let go is ideally made in an environment where the doctor, the priest, and the family come together to pray and say, "We are here for you." It is a time where one prepares the person for eternity through the sacrament of the sick and if possible viaticum, the Eucharist for the journey. It is a time when one is aware that life never truly ends, but only changes. It is the recognition that just as a person loved you and prayed for you on his or her earthly journey, he or she will be loving you and praying for you in the presence of almighty God. "Letting go" is not the end, but the beginning of a new phase of eternal life.

Why do Catholics believe in legitimate wars?

There is such a thing as legitimate war. The Old Testament is filled with stories of God's people fighting to do God's will: Moses against Egypt (Ex. 14), Joshua against Jericho (Jos. 6), the family of Mattathias against the Greeks (1&2 Maccabees).

The Lord asked Cain, 'Where is your brother Abel?' He answered, 'I do not know. Am I my brother's keeper?'

Genesis 4:9

It is true that as Christians we are called to "turn the other cheek" (Mt. 5:39); But as the quote from Genesis above points out, we are also "our brother's keeper" (Gen. 4:9). It is when we are called to be our brother's keeper that we can legitimately--as a last resort--turn to war. It is for this reason that Jesus overturned the tables of the "money changers" and chased them out of the temple with a whip (cf. Jn. 2:13-16).

Therefore, in a spirit of prudence, the Church affirms the legitimate right to self-defense and war: "The legitimate defense of persons and societies is not an exception to the prohibition against the murder of the innocent that constitutes intentional killing" (CCC 2263).

"Legitimate defense can be not only a right but a grave duty for someone responsible for another's life, the common good of the family or the state" (CCC 2265). "Governments cannot be denied the right of lawful self-defense, once all peace efforts have failed" (GS 79,4). In fact, governments are often called to war for the betterment and the good of the world.

Recourse to war is permissible when the following conditions are met (2309; 2313-2314; ST II-II, 64, 7).

1. The cause must be just.
2. All means of avoiding war or ending aggression must be seen to be "impractical and ineffective."
3. The "damage inflicted by an aggressor on the nation or community of nations must be lasting, grave, and certain."
4. There must be an adequate prospect for success in putting an end to the aggression or evil.
5. The use of weaponry must be used with prudence. They must not "produce evils and disorders graver than the evil to be eliminated."
6. Every act of self-defense or war that is aimed at the indiscriminate destruction of whole cities is prohibited. Non-combatants must never be targeted.

Acts of terrorism remind us of the challenge of peace that we as Catholics are faced with. Hostilities, excessive economic inequalities, contempt and distrust for persons, and unbending ideologies are all part of the injustices that ferment war (cf. Ex. 20:2-7). What is needed is a spiritual renewal throughout the world, a renewal that fosters solidarity and a sense of universal cooperation among nations. All nations are called to a spirit of brotherhood and a desire for a universal common good. Social structures, attitudes, and hearts must change (GS 83-90). Unless we take up this challenge for peace, the world will inevitably enter a new dark age. Recent events have pointed to this sad reality.

When the Commandments are ignored (cf. Ex. 20:2-17), when the love of neighbor and the love of God is ignored (cf. Mt. 22:37-40), when the golden rule of do unto others as you would like done unto you is ignored (cf. 25:31f), then wars become inevitable.

God created a harmonious, orderly world (cf. Genesis 1&2). Sin distorts this order and harmony.

The death penalty revisited

The logic behind legitimate wars is very important to understanding the theology regarding the death penalty.

Punishment for criminal offenses has traditionally emphasized the importance of justice, retribution, deterrence and the protection of the moral and structural fiber of society. It is in this way that the death penalty was used in the Old Testament (cf. Gn. 9:6; Ex. 21:16, 22f, 22:18; Lv. 20:10-15, 27; 24:16-17; Dt. 17:12; 21:9, etc.). The key principle in regard to the death penalty has always been the protection of society—either the physical or moral protection of society.

As Christian we are called to turn the other cheek (Mt. 5:39) when we can, but we are called to be our "brother's keeper" (Gen. 4:9) when turning the cheek is ineffective. It is for this reason that Jesus overturned the tables of the "money changers" and chased them out of the temple with a whip (cf. Jn. 2:13-16).

In describing the Church's position on the death penalty, the *Catechism of the Catholic Church* explains: "If nonlethal means are sufficient to defend and protect people's safety from the aggressor, authority will limit itself to such means, as these are more in keeping with the concrete conditions of the common good and more in conformity with the dignity of the human person" (CCC 2267). In other words, if the key principles behind the Old Testament understanding of justice are met without the need to resort to the death penalty, then the death penalty should be avoided.

Many people who read the Catechism passage on the death penalty often scratch their heads while saying: "How can this be? Isn't this the Church that has affirmed and often promoted the death penalty for centuries? What is going on?"

At first glance there may appear to be an inconsistency in the Church's current teaching on the death penalty, but in reality the Church's teaching has remained absolutely consistent.

The change in the Church's position is not due to a change in its theology as much as to developments in the ways of protecting and defending the common good of society. Once again, if the key principles behind the Old Testament understanding of justice are met without the need to resort to the death penalty, then those means of justice should be used.

Prior to the nineteenth century, violently dangerous criminals were dealt with by means of execution or exile (which was essentially another form of capital punishment due to the atrociously harsh conditions associated with it).

The infrastructures of societies prior to the nineteenth century were incapable of dealing with long-term incarcerations; hence, those who posed a serious threat to a society, such as the criminally insane, needed to be taken out of society for the protection of the common good, and the only means available, for all practical purposes, during this period in history, was the death penalty. It is for this reason that the Bible is replete with examples of the death penalty.

By the late nineteenth and early twentieth century, however, developments in the structures and organizations of societies as well as enlightened thought has led to the possibility of incarcerating individuals for life, thereby eliminating the moral justification for the death penalty. As Pope John Paul II explained in *Evangelium Vitae*: "Today...as a result of steady improvements in the organization of the penal system [the justification for the death penalty in a modern society is] practically non-existent."

Justice without mercy is cruelty. Christian justice demands that we be protected from violent criminals, and Christian mercy demands that we forgive the unforgivable and hope for the hopeless. As long as there is life, there is the possibility for repentance and conversion (Lk. 23:39-43). There is always hope. Death extinguishes hope and any possibility of conversion. If Jesus would not pull the switch or inject a person with heart stopping chemicals, why should we? Let society imprison the dangerously uncontrollable for the remainder of their lives, and let people of faith pray for their conversion. Let us remember that "whoever brings back a sinner from the error of his way will save his soul from death and will cover a multitude of sins," and let us also remember that there is "more joy in heaven over one sinner who repents than over ninety-nine righteous persons who need no repentance" (Jms. 5:20; 5:7). And finally let us remember the thief on the cross next to Jesus who obtained eternal salvation at the very end of his life (Lk. 23:43).

In ancient times the death penalty was perfectly acceptable for the protection of the good of society—hence its use in the Old and New Testament period. In a modern, civilized society, the death penalty has no place.

X
SECULARISM

The intolerance of secularism

The Church has always been persecuted for it has always been a source of contradiction in a world that is always tempted to abandon, deny, or manipulate God.

The French Revolution—with its atheist "cult of reason"--forced 20,000 priests to resign under the threat of death or imprisonment. Thirty thousand priests were forced to leave France and those who refused were executed by guillotine or deportation to French Guiana. France's 40,000 churches were either closed, sold, destroyed, or converted for secular uses.

Under Germany's Secular-Atheist Liberal Movement of 1871-1878, half of the Prussian bishops were imprisoned or exiled, a quarter of the parishes lost their priests, half of the monks and nuns were exiled or fled persecution, a third of the monasteries and convents were closed, and 1800 parish priests were imprisoned or exiled.

Hitler, an admirer of the atheists Nietzsche and Schopenhauer, abolished religious services in schools, confiscated Church property, circulated anti-religious and anti-Christian material to his soldiers, and closed theological institutions. Church schools were closed, crucifixes and crosses were removed from schools, Christian presses were shut down, and Christian welfare organizations were banned. Thousands of Christian lay persons and clergymen and nuns were arrested and sent to Nazi concentration camps. Over 300 monasteries and institutions were confiscated by the SS. More than 2,600 priests were killed in Nazi concentration camps. The Dachau Concentration Camp had one barrack dedicated solely for priests.

The militant atheistic Soviet Union confiscated churches and persecuted Christians. Leon Trotsky's regime killed twenty-eight bishops and 1,200 priests. Lenin killed at least 40,000 priests. Between 1917 and 1969 the Soviets destroyed 41,000 of 48,000 churches. Before the communist revolution there were 66,140 priests. On the eve of WWII there were only 6,376.

Mao's atheist China equals in terms of carnage that of the Soviet Union.

The Spanish (atheist) Red Terror of 1936 killed 6,832 priests, 2,265 members of Catholic religious institutes, and 283 nuns. Between 1930 and 1936 the Jesuit religious order was dissolved, Church property was confiscated, religion was prohibited from being taught, and 58 churches were burned to the ground.

Mexico's atheist reign of terror led by the "Red Shirts" and the Radical Socialist Party led between 1926 and 1934 to the expulsion and assassination of over 4,000 priests. In 1926 there were approximately 4,500 priests in Mexico; in 1934 there were only 334.

From 1917 to 2007 approximately 148 million people were killed by atheist run countries. In fact, atheistic states have a 58 percent greater chance of mass murdering their populations than any other group.

The Nobel Prize winner Aleksandr Solzhenitsyn wrote of atheistic communism: *"If I were asked today to formulate as concisely as possible the main cause of the ruinous revolution that swallowed up some 60 million of our people, I could not put it more accurately than to repeat: 'Men have forgotten God; that's why all this has happened.'"*

When one examines the *Encyclopedia of Wars* by Charles Philips one sees that of all the wars in recorded history, only 123 of them can be attributed to religion. That is seven percent of all the wars in history. If we eliminated Islam from the mix, war in the name of religion would account for only three percent of all wars.

God exists

> *Ever since the creation of the world, [God's] invisible attributes of eternal power and divinity have been able to be understood and perceived in what he has made (Romans 1:20).*

Natural revelation is that knowledge about God which can be acquired through the natural gift of reason. By examining the world one can see signs of God's handprint in creation.

The following are examples of "convincing and converging" arguments in favor of belief in God:

Argument from Change and Causes

> *The first and most obvious way [to prove the existence of God] is based on change [and causes]. We see things changing. Anything that changes is being changed by something else.... This something else, if itself changing, is being changed by yet another thing; and this last change by another. Now we must stop somewhere, otherwise there will be no first cause of the change, and, as a result, no subsequent causes.... We arrive then at some first cause of change not itself being changed by anything, and this is what everybody understands by God.*

There must be a beginning to change, and we call this beginning to change, this being not brought about by change, God.

Argument regarding Existence Itself

> *The [argument from existence] is based on what need not be and on what must be.... Some of the things we come across can be but need not be, for we find them springing up and dying away, thus sometimes in being sometimes not. Now everything cannot*

*be like this, for a thing that need not be, once was not; and if
everything need not be, once upon a time there was nothing. But
if that were true there would be nothing even now, because
something that does not exist can only be brought into being by
something already existing. If nothing was in being nothing
could be brought into being, and nothing would be in being now,
which contradicts observation. Not everything therefore is the
sort of thing that needs not be; some things must be, and these
may or may not owe this necessity to something else. But just as
a series of causes must have a stop, so also a series of things
which must be. One is forced to suppose something which must
be, and owes this to nothing outside itself; indeed it itself is the
cause that other things must be. This is God.*

Something cannot come from nothing. Something can only come
from something. Since we live in a world that exists, something had to
make it exist. Since everything that exists in our world has a source for
its existence, then the world must have a source for its existence. We
call this source, without a prior source for existence, God. God put the
world into existence.

Argument from the Natural Law

*[Another argument for the existence of God] is based on the
guidedness of nature. Goal-directed behavior is observed in all
bodies obeying natural laws, even when they lack awareness.
Their behavior hardly ever varies and practically always turns
out well, showing that they truly tend to goals and do not merely
hit them by accident. But nothing lacking awareness can tend to
a goal except it be directed by someone with awareness and
understanding.... Everything in nature, therefore, is directed to
its goal by someone with understanding, and this we call God.*

An arrow cannot hit its target without a bow propelling it. A bow
needs an archer to pull the chord that propels the bow. An archer has
awareness of what his goal is—hitting the target. If he did not have an
awareness of what he was doing or an awareness of his goal, he would
not be able to hit the target.

The sciences like math, physics, astronomy, chemistry, biology etc.
are directed by laws and by goals. These laws of nature are meant to
understand why things do the things they do. The whole scientific
method presupposes laws, goals, and/or ends. Without these laws we
would be blind to nature. Nature would be unpredictable and chaotic.

God is the intelligent being, the archer that pulls the bow that
propels the arrow to its goal, its target. God is the intelligent being of
the intelligent design of creation.

Design implies a designer. God is the designer of creation.

Argument from Gradation

> [A way to prove the existence of God] is based on the gradation observed in things. Some things are better, truer, more excellent than others. Such comparative terms describe varying degrees of approximation to a superlative.... Something therefore is the truest and best and most excellent of things, and hence the most fully in being.... Now when many things possess some property in common, the one most fully possessing it causes it in the others.... Something therefore causes in all other things their being, their goodness, and whatever other perfection they have. And this is what we call God.

How do we know what is better, truer or more excellent unless we can distinguish between levels or gradations of goodness, truth, excellence, etc.? Anything that has gradations must have a perfection, a superlative, from which all lesser gradations can be observed.

What is this superlative?

What is best described as the fullness of goodness, truth, beauty, excellence or any other superlative?

Everything of human origin is flawed. God is by definition perfect, the Superlative! The gradation of observed things points to the existence of God.

Other proofs for the existence of God (The following arguments are more fully developed in Fr. John's book *God Exists: Convincing Arguments*).

Origin of Life Proof

What are some of the theories on the origin of life?

Life is believed to have begun approximately 3.7 billion years ago in a primordial soup—a water based sea of simple organic molecules.

The problem: Science has not been able to prove that a primordial soup existed, and if it did, the conditions of the earth's early atmosphere would not have made life possible in such a soup.

Geochemists argue that the early earth's atmosphere was likely highly volcanic and largely composed of carbon dioxide rather than a mixture of reducing gases like methane, ammonia and hydrogen, and thus not conducive to life.

The *origin of life* theorist, David Deamer (echoing the work of his colleagues), argues that the early earth's atmosphere did not support the necessary array of "synthetic pathways leading to possible monomers." (A monomer is a molecule that reacts chemically to another molecule of the same type to form a larger molecule.)

Without the building blocks to life, life cannot exist!

184

In 2010 the biochemist Nick Lane argued for life arising from undersea hydrothermal vents. The difficulty with this theory—as in the case of the primordial soup theory--is that it fails to adequately explain how amino acids or other molecules link up to form polymers in a non-conducive, soupy, wet environment. A primordial soup or undersea hydrothermal vent would seem to break down protein chains rather than build them up.

Without the building blocks of life, life cannot exist!

If we assume that complex organic molecules could somehow have been formed, then they would have had to somehow develop the ability to replicate. Those complex molecules best suited to replicate would then have needed to be naturally selected for survival. These molecules would eventually have needed to have evolved complex machinery to insure survival and reproduction. What are the chances?

Life on earth is estimated to have begun approximately 3.7 billion years ago. The probabilities of life occurring by chance, without divine assistance, is essentially impossible from a statistical point of view—given the 3.7 billion years. The odds of a *single cell* evolving, never mind a human being, in 3.7 billion years has been estimated by statisticians at 1.6 followed by 59 zeros to one. A statistical miracle!

In summary, non-living materials cannot produce living materials. A universe of mindless, non-living materials cannot produce living beings with intrinsic ends, self-replicating capabilities, and a coded chemistry. Life is brought about by life, by preexisting life structures.

Human experience demonstrates to us that when we find design we can find a designer, when we find order we can find an orderer, and when we find a beginning we can find an originator.

Consciousness Proof

Nature consists of a finite number of elements. Our human bodies consist of those elements. The elements themselves which we consist of, and nature itself consists of, have no consciousness—for elements do not have consciousness. If the elements of the universe do not have consciousness, and we are made up of such elements, why do we have consciousness? How does non-living matter become alive, become living matter?

Many attempts have been made to explain consciousness. Some scientists and neurologists have speculated about consciousness in terms of patterns of electromagnetic activation, brain wave sequences, brain wave collapses, synaptic tunnels, synaptic passages, neural networks, neural excitations, neurotransmitters, quantum waves, quantum discontinuities, and quantum cytoskeletal states. Others have promoted the belief that consciousness comes from the interaction of bosons and fermions, biological oscillators and bioplasma charged particles. Still others have tried to explain consciousness by the trajectory of particles, subtle energies, the excitation of condensates, and the working in unison of molecules. All forms of electro-chemical processes have been postulated. All have failed. No scientific explanation has been able to explain consciousness.

At the heart of the problem is the nature of matter: I am matter. I am conscious. How can matter, which has no consciousness, be put together to produce consciousness?

Another problem deals with evolution. Random, chance evolution cannot explain the complexity of consciousness. The brain contains approximately 100 billion cells. Each cell is allied by synapses to as many as 100,000 other cells. If the brain could not have evolved without divine assistance within 3.7 billion years, if a *single cell* could not have evolved without divine assistance within 3.7 billion years, consciousness certainly could not have evolved without divine assistance within 3.7 billion years.

Another issue is whether consciousness is limited to the confines of the brain, and therefore completely naturalistic.

Is consciousness only within the brain, or does it transcend the limits of the brain. Are there experiences of consciousness that cannot be self-produced, that cannot be explained by a brain-alone, materialistic, atheistic theory? How do we explain the following human experiences?

- *Out of Body*—the ability to acquire new knowledge while being clinically dead.
- *Déjà vu*—the sensation or feeling that one has already experienced something that appears to be happening for the first time.
- *Eureka Experience*—a sudden understanding of what was previously incomprehensible.
- *Precognition*--the procurement of future information that could not be deduced from presently available, acquired sense-based data.
- *Retrocognition*--knowledge of the past which could not have been learned or inferred by normal means.
- *Premonition*—a strong feeling that something is about to occur.
- *Intuition*—an ability to know something without evidence.
- *Telepathy*--the transmission of information from one person to another through the use of the mind only.
- *Psychokinesis*—the ability to move objects with the mind.
- *Remote Viewing*—the ability to acquire knowledge of something that is hidden from view and separated by distance.
- *Bilocation*—when a person appears to be located in two distinct places at the same instance in time.
- *Providence*—the sense that things are not coincidental or chance occurrences.
- *Prophetic Utterances*—insights and predictions into future events.
- *Free Will*—to choose a course of action that is not pre-determined.

If any one of these above experiences are possible, then what are the implications that follow? The fact that these experiences are reported as happening throughout the world and throughout history makes one wonder.

If any one of the listed experiences of consciousness has a transcendental dimension, then we have entered into the realm of the divine?

It can be argued that consciousness is a participation in *existence itself*. If consciousness is a participation in *existence itself, subsistent existence*, then consciousness is not bound by the limits of space and time. Only participation in *existence itself* can make the above list—or part of the list-- of supernatural phenomena possible.

The Cell

The cell is that which reads DNA and translates it into the structures necessary for life. But why does it read this DNA and why does it translate it into structures? What gives it its dynamism? Why must it be anything other than a pile of chemicals and forces just sitting there or moving around aimlessly? What gives it its drive, its purpose, its end? What makes a cell, building material, ordered by a blueprint, DNA, build?

The odds of a cell developing by chance, the odds of DNA developing by chance, the odds of a cell cooperating with DNA by chance is statistically impossible according to scientists and statisticians (1.6 followed by 59 zeros to one).

There is no scientifically solid explanation for the existence of the cell. And when we add the dilemma regarding the origin of life, we are even more perplexed.

Alternative explanations are needed. The Nobel Prize winning scientist Francis Crick, the atheist co-discoverer of the structure of DNA, had trouble dealing with the statistics involved with the birth of the cell. It is for this reason that he proposed what has become known as the *panspermia thesis* which argues that intelligent aliens, in a spaceship, seeded the earth with life. Even the atheist Crick had to concede to an intelligent cause or being for life on earth. But this begs the question: "Who created these aliens?"

Others have been less extreme and have argued that meteors or fragments of astral collisions impregnated with the seeds of life brought life to earth. But who "impregnated" these meteors and fragments with the seeds of life?

Francis Crick rejects these and similar views because, according to his thinking, the seeds of life would have been too fragile to survive on a flying asteroid or meteor. A spaceship, according to Crick, would have been needed to protect the seeds.

Carl Sagan believed that one day extraterrestrials would come to earth and explain the origin of the human cell and human life to us.

Many scientists hold by faith—since there is not a single shred of evidence for its support—that there are billions upon billions of worlds and universes. By proposing *multi-world* or *multi-universe* theories, the statistical probabilities associated with the birth of the cell becomes more palatable, albeit still statistically improbable.

187

The *panspermia, seeded asteroids, seeded meteor,* and *multi-world-universe* theories, or more appropriately unfounded beliefs, are purely theoretical and contrary to cosmological observation.

Ironically, to the dismay of atheists, these theories, if they turned out to be true, would argue more for an intelligent designer than an atheistic worldview!

The earth is a privileged planet, a planet where life, and complex life at that, exists. One would expect that in a universe as expansive as ours that life would be abundant, yet even a single cell cannot be found anywhere except on this privileged planet. What are the odds?

All that we experience is either a product of chance or of design. The evidence, common sense, and logic favors design. Human experience teaches us that order is formed by an orderer and design is formed by a designer. Why would the orderly, finely tuned laws of nature necessary for life be the only "things" that would have no orderer, no designer behind them?

In Conclusion

There are many arguments for the existence of God. The above arguments were simplified for our purposes. The point being made is that Catholics believe that God can be known by the natural light of human reason.

XI
CONCLUDING REMARKS

There are no new questions!

The Catholic Church is 2000 years old. It has heard every question and has dealt with them all. There are no new questions. Therefore, as a Catholic, never feel fearful about your faith. If someone should ever come to you with what appears to be an absolutely perfect argument, do not get discouraged. It has been asked before, and it has been answered before. When such situations come up, all you need to do is to go to a good Catholic reference book and you will find the answer. In fact, you can even go to a good non-religious encyclopedia and find most of the answers you need to find.

Furthermore, let us never forget what Ignatius of Antioch (a disciple of the apostle John, and a bishop by the authority of Peter and Paul) said in his letter to the *Smyrnaeans*: "[Wherever] Jesus Christ is, there is the Catholic Church" (8).

And for those who seek to persecute the Catholic Church let them be reminded of what awaits them by the words of Lactantius (ca. 316) in his treatise on the *Deaths of the Persecutors*:

> *When Nero was already reigning Peter came to Rome, where, in virtue of the performance of certain miracles which he worked by the power of God which had been given him, he converted many to righteousness and established a firm and steadfast temple to God. When this fact was reported to Nero, he noticed that not only at Rome but everywhere great multitudes were daily abandoning the worship of idols, and, condemning their old ways, they were going over to the new religion. Being that Nero was a detestable and pernicious tyrant, he sprang to the task of tearing down the heavenly temple and of destroying righteousness. It was he that first persecuted the servants of God. Peter, he fixed to a cross upside down; and Paul he beheaded (2, 5). [For his persecution of the Church, Nero would pay with his life].*

Those who persecute the Church will always fail as they have always failed!

The ship continues moving!

The Church is like a ship moving towards heaven. One can get on board, stay on board, or get off. But the ship will keep moving forward, with you or without you, with me, or without me. The Church has been sailing for 2000 years. Some have abandoned the ship and some have embarked. The ship will always go on. The gates of hell will never prevail against it (Mt. 16:18; 28:20). Are you on board?

Appendix: From Peter to Francis

The term "pope" finds its origins in the Greek "pappas," "father." Priest continue to be referred to as "Father" to this day. The Latin version of "pappas," "papa," would eventually be rendered "pope" in the English speaking world. Today, "pope" is exclusively used for the bishop of Rome, the successor of St. Peter.

1.	St. Peter (32-67)	49.	St. Gelasius I (492-96)
2.	St. Linus (67-76)	50.	Anastasius II (496-98)
3.	St. Anacletus (Cletus) (76-88)	51.	St. Symmachus (498-514)
4.	St. Clement I (88-97)	52.	St. Hormisdas (514-23)
5.	St. Evaristus (97-105)	53.	St. John I (523-26)
6.	St. Alexander I (105-115)	54.	St. Felix IV (III) (526-30)
7.	St. Sixtus I (115-125)	55.	Boniface II (530-32)
8.	St. Telesphorus (125-136)	56.	John II (533-35)
9.	St. Hyginus (136-140)	57.	St. Agapetus I (535-36)
10.	St. Pius I (140-155)	58.	St. Silverius (536-37)
11.	St. Anicetus (155-166)	59.	Vigilius (537-55)
12.	St. Soter (166-175)	60.	Pelagius I (556-61)
13.	St. Eleutherius (175-189)	61.	John III (561-74)
14.	St. Victor I (189-199)	62.	Benedict I (575-79)
15.	St. Zephyrinus (199-217)	63.	Pelagius II (579-90)
16.	St. Callistus I (217-22)	64.	St. Gregory I (the Great) (590-604)
17.	St. Urban I (222-30)		
18.	St. Pontain (230-35)	65.	Sabinian (604-606)
19.	St. Anterus (235-36)	66.	Boniface III (607)
20.	St. Fabian (236-50)	67.	St. Boniface IV (608-15)
21.	St. Cornelius (251-53)	68.	St. Deusdedit (Adeodatus I) (615-18)
22.	St. Lucius I (253-54)		
23.	St. Stephen I (254-257)	69.	Boniface V (619-25)
24.	St. Sixtus II (257-258)	70.	Honorius I (625-38)
25.	St. Dionysius (260-268)	71.	Severinus (640)
26.	St. Felix I (269-274)	72.	John IV (640-42)
27.	St. Eutychian (275-283)	73.	Theodore I (642-49)
28.	St. Caius (283-296)	74.	St. Martin I (649-55)
29.	St. Marcellinus (296-304)	75.	St. Eugene I (655-57)
30.	St. Marcellus I (308-309)	76.	St. Vitalian (657-72)
31.	St. Eusebius (309 or 310)	77.	Adeodatus (II) (672-76)
32.	St. Miltiades (311-14)	78.	Donus (676-78)
33.	St. Sylvester I (314-35)	79.	St. Agatho (678-81)
34.	St. Marcus (336)	80.	St. Leo II (682-83)
35.	St. Julius I (337-52)	81.	St. Benedict II (684-85)
36.	Liberius (352-66)	82.	John V (685-86)
37.	St. Damasus I (366-84)	83.	Conon (686-87)
38.	St. Siricius (384-99)	84.	St. Sergius I (687-701)
39.	St. Anastasius I (399-401)	85.	John VI (701-05)
40.	St. Innocent I (401-17)	86.	John VII (705-07)
41.	St. Zosimus (417-18)	87.	Sisinnius (708)
42.	St. Boniface I (418-22)	88.	Constantine (708-15)
43.	St. Celestine I (422-32)	89.	St. Gregory II (715-31)
44.	St. Sixtus III (432-40)	90.	St. Gregory III (731-41)
45.	St. Leo I (the Great) (440-61)	91.	St. Zachary (741-52)
46.	St. Hilarius (461-68)	92.	Stephen II (III) (752-57)
47.	St. Simplicius (468-83)	93.	St. Paul I (757-67)
48.	St. Felix III (II) (483-92)	94.	Stephen III (IV) (767-72)

95. Adrian I (772-95)
96. St. Leo III (795-816)
97. Stephen IV (V) (816-17)
98. St. Paschal I (817-24)
99. Eugene II (824-27)
100. Valentine (827)
101. Gregory IV (827-44)
102. Sergius II (844-47)
103. St. Leo IV (847-55)
104. Benedict III (855-58)
105. St. Nicholas I (858-67)
106. Adrian II (867-72)
107. John VIII (872-82)
108. Marinus I (882-84)
109. St. Adrian III (884-85)
110. Stephen V (VI) (885-91)
111. Formosus (891-96)
112. Boniface VI (896)
113. Stephen VI (VII) (896-97)
114. Romanus (897)
115. Theodore II (897)
116. John IX (898-900)
117. Benedict IV (900-03)
118. Leo V (903)
119. Sergius III (904-11)
120. Anastasius III (911-13)
121. Lando (913-14)
122. John X (914-28)
123. Leo VI (928)
124. Stephen VIII (929-31)
125. John XI (931-35)
126. Leo VII (936-39)
127. Stephen IX (939-42)
128. Marinus II (942-46)
129. Agapetus II (946-55)
130. John XII (955-63)
131. Leo VIII (963-64)
132. Benedict V (964)
133. John XIII (965-72)
134. Benedict VI (973-74)
135. Benedict VII (974-83)
136. John XIV (983-84)
137. John XV (985-96)
138. Gregory V (996-99)
139. Sylvester II (999-1003)
140. John XVII (1003)
141. John XVIII (1003-09)
142. Sergius IV (1009-12)
143. Benedict VIII (1012-24)
144. John XIX (1024-32)
145. Benedict IX (1032-45)
146. Sylvester III (1045)
147. Benedict IX (1045)
148. Gregory VI (1045-46)
149. Clement II (1046-47)
150. Benedict IX (1047-48)
151. Damasus II (1048)
152. St. Leo IX (1049-54)

153. Victor II (1055-57)
154. Stephen X (1057-58)
155. Nicholas II (1058-61)
156. Alexander II (1061-73)
157. St. Gregory VII (1073-85)
158. Blessed Victor III (1086-87)
159. Blessed Urban II (1088-99)
160. Paschal II (1099-1118)
161. Gelasius II (1118-19)
162. Callistus II (1119-24)
163. Honorius II (1124-30)
164. Innocent II (1130-43)
165. Celestine II (1143-44)
166. Lucius II (1144-45)
167. Blessed Eugene III (1145-53)
168. Anastasius IV (1153-54)
169. Adrian IV (1154-59)
170. Alexander III (1159-81)
171. Lucius III (1181-85)
172. Urban III (1185-87)
173. Gregory VIII (1187)
174. Clement III (1187-91)
175. Celestine III (1191-98)
176. Innocent III (1198-1216)
177. Honorius III (1216-27)
178. Gregory IX (1227-41)
179. Celestine IV (1241)
180. Innocent IV (1243-54)
181. Alexander IV (1254-61)
182. Urban IV (1261-64)
183. Clement IV (1265-68)
184. Blessed Gregory X (1271-76)
185. Blessed Innocent V (1276)
186. Adrian V (1276)
187. John XXI (1276-77)
188. Nicholas III (1277-80)
189. Martin IV (1281-85)
190. Honorius IV (1285-87)
191. Nicholas IV (1288-92)
192. St. Celestine V (1294)
193. Boniface VIII (1294-1303)
194. Blessed Benedict XI (1303-04)
195. Clement V (1305-14)
196. John XXII (1316-34)
197. Benedict XII (1334-42)
198. Clement VI (1342-52)
199. Innocent VI (1352-62)
200. Blessed Urban V (1362-70)
201. Gregory XI (1370-78)
202. Urban VI (1378-89)
203. Boniface IX (1389-1404)
204. Innocent VII (1404-06)
205. Gregory XII (1406-15)
206. Martin V (1417-31)
207. Eugene IV (1431-47)
208. Nicholas V (1447-55)
209. Callistus III (1455-58)
210. Pius II (1458-64)

211. Paul II (1464-71)
212. Sixtus IV (1471-84)
213. Innocent VIII (1484-92)
214. Alexander VI (1492-1503)
215. Pius III (1503)
216. Julius II (1503-13)
217. Leo X (1513-21)
218. Adrian VI (1522-23)
219. Clement VII (1523-34)
220. Paul III (1534-49)
221. Julius III (1550-55)
222. Marcellus II (1555)
223. Paul IV (1555-59)
224. Pius IV (1559-65)
225. St. Pius V (1566-72)
226. Gregory XIII (1572-85)
227. Sixtus V (1585-90)
228. Urban VII (1590)
229. Gregory XIV (1590-91)
230. Innocent IX (1591)
231. Clement VIII (1592-1605)
232. Leo XI (1605)
233. Paul V (1605-21)
234. Gregory XV (1621-23)
235. Urban VIII (1623-44)
236. Innocent X (1644-55)
237. Alexander VII (1655-67)
238. Clement IX (1667-69)

239. Clement X (1670-76)
240. Blessed Innocent XI (1676-89)
241. Alexander VIII (1689-91)
242. Innocent XII (1691-1700)
243. Clement XI (1700-21)
244. Innocent XIII (1721-24)
245. Benedict XIII (1724-30)
246. Clement XII (1730-40)
247. Benedict XIV (1740-58)
248. Clement XIII (1758-69)
249. Clement XIV (1769-74)
250. Pius VI (1775-99)
251. Pius VII (1800-23)
252. Leo XII (1823-29)
253. Pius VIII (1829-30)
254. Gregory XVI (1831-46)
255. Blessed Pius IX (1846-78)
256. Leo XIII (1878-1903)
257. St. Pius X (1903-14)
258. Benedict XV (1914-22)
259. Pius XI (1922-39)
260. Pius XII (1939-58)
261. St. John XXIII (1958-63)
262. Paul VI (1963-78)
263. John Paul I (1978)
264. St. John Paul II (1978-2005)
265. Benedict XVI (2005-2013)
266. Francis (2013—)

Made in the USA
Las Vegas, NV
29 January 2023

66462728R00114